SCM STUDYGUIDE TO CHRISTIAN ETHICS

SCM STUDYGUIDE TO CHRISTIAN ETHICS

Neil Messer

scm press

British Library Cataloguing in Publication data

A catalogue record for this book is available
from the British Library

978 0 334 02995 3

First published in 2006 by SCM Press
13–17 Long Lane
London EC1A 9PN

www.scm-canterburypress.co.uk

SCM Press is a division of
SCM-Canterbury Press Ltd

Reprint with corrections 2008

Printed and bound in Great Britain by
Biddles Ltd, King's Lynn, Norfolk

Contents

CONTENTS

CONTENTS

List of Ethical Theory Topics

List of Practical Ethics Topics

Preface

This book has grown out of the introductory courses in Christian ethics that I have taught over a number of years to different student groups in different contexts. It could be likened to a map of the territory known as 'Christian ethics' – an analogy that comes naturally to me as, for almost as long as I can remember, I have been fascinated by maps and can get almost as absorbed in a map as in a good book. If this book is a kind of map of the territory called 'Christian ethics', it is the sort of map you would open to give yourself a general overview of an area that was new and unfamiliar. It is intended to cover as much of the ground as possible, though, inevitably, I have had to be selective about what is included: some topics have been either omitted or dealt with more briefly than I would have wished. Also, I have included one or two topics (such as the relationship between the natural sciences and Christian ethics) that are quite often omitted from introductory treatments, but seem to me to be both important and interesting aspects of the subject. Because it is an introductory treatment, designed for those with little or no prior knowledge of the field, the amount of detail that can be included is limited, but each chapter has suggestions for further reading that will offer more detailed treatments of the areas covered.

As I have taught Christian ethics in recent years, I have become increasingly convinced that, in this subject, a sharp separation between 'theory' and 'practice' is both artificial and unhelpful. Accordingly, in this book I have tried to avoid such a separation: most chapters integrate a 'theoretical' topic with one or more issues in 'practical' ethics. I shall say more in Chapter 1 about how this is done. The attempt to integrate 'theory' with 'practice' could make the book slightly harder to navigate around than some, so, as well as the general list of contents, I have given alphabetical lists of both 'theoretical' and 'practical' topics covered in the book, showing where each can be found.

How might this book be used? Individual readers wishing to gain an initial overview of Christian ethics could simply read it from beginning to end. They might also find the case studies, questions and exercises included in each chapter helpful opportunities to reflect on particular issues and review what they have learned. The book could also be used as an introductory reference for investigating particular topics and the contents pages should facilitate this. The topics covered in each chapter are sufficiently self-contained to allow the book to be used in this way, though some of the later chapters do build to some extent on the earlier ones and so may be slightly harder going for readers who have not worked through the earlier ones.

The book could also be used in a variety of ways as a teaching resource for introductory courses in Christian ethics. It could be used as the basis of a course by working through it from beginning to end or selecting chapters and topics according to the needs of the class and the time available. The case studies, questions and exercises may be found useful as class discussion starters or small group exercises – indeed, many of them began life as group exercises on my own courses. The book is primarily designed for students at level 1 – that is to say, those in the first year or at the first stage of an under-graduate degree course.

In writing this book, I have incurred many debts of gratitude. The first is to the students to whom I have taught Christian ethics over the past ten years at Mansfield College, Oxford, the Queen's Foundation, Birmingham, and the University of Wales, Lampeter. Whatever they may, or may not, have learned from me, I have learned a tremendous amount from them and, had it not been for the commitment, interest and critical engagement that many of them have brought to our discussions of the subject, this would not be the book it is. A particular word of thanks is due to my first-year Christian Ethics class at Lampeter in 2004–5, who were generous enough to allow me to road-test several of the draft chapters on them and give me valuable feedback. I have also learned much from colleagues in the institutions in which I have taught. In particular, the section on Christian ethics and pastoral care in

Chapter 9 has its origins in some joint teaching that I did with my former colleagues Rod Burton and Chris Worsley in the Queen's Foundation.

I am enormously grateful to friends and colleagues at Lampeter and elsewhere who read parts of the book in draft: Catherine Cowley and Simon Oliver read and commented on almost the entire book, while Malcolm Brown, Bill Campbell, Mark Cartledge and Dave Leal commented on individual chapters. I have also benefited from stimulating conversations with colleagues, particularly Simon Oliver, about the book and more generally about matters theological and ethical. All of these friends have helped me make the book better than it would otherwise be. It goes without saying that I am entirely responsible for what I have failed, or refused, to learn from any of them. My thanks, too, to Barbara Laing at SCM Press for commissioning the book and to her and her colleagues for all their help and support in seeing it through to publication. I am grateful to Darton, Longman & Todd for permission to include an adapted version of Chapter 10 of Neil Messer (ed.), *Theological Issues in Bioethics: An Introduction with Readings* (London: Darton, Longman & Todd, 2002) as part of Chapter 9 of the present book.

My children Fiona and Rebecca have been very tolerant of the hours I have spent shut away in my study (perhaps they were glad to have me out of the way), but I am also grateful to them for distracting me from time to time when it was good for me to be distracted. My final, and most heartfelt, thanks go to my wife Janet for her unfailing love, support and encouragement, without which the business of writing books would be far lonelier and less enjoyable than it is.

Neil Messer
July 2005

1

Introduction: Deciding How to Decide[1]

1 What is Christian Ethics?

It would be tempting, at the beginning of an introduction to Christian ethics, to try and come up with a brilliant, elegant and informative definition that expressed in a sentence or two what the subject is all about. I am not convinced, however, that it would be time well spent. In the Preface, I said that this book is meant to be a map of the territory known as 'Christian ethics' and the best way to find out what is on a map is to open it up and look at it. In the same way, the best way to find out what Christian ethics is about is not to try and describe it in abstract terms, but to get to grips with it. (It is also true, of course, that if you really want to get to know a region, staying at home and looking at a map is no substitute for actually travelling there. We shall return to this point in the final chapter.) So, in this opening section and the rest of this chapter, I shall only try to say enough to give an idea of the kind of terrain you will find yourself surveying when you open the map.

Words such as 'ethics' and 'morality', fairly obviously, have something to do with right and wrong, good and bad, obligation and value. Moral questions might be about what we ought (or ought not) to do, the way we ought to live our lives, the kinds of people – and communities – we ought to be. In everyday speech, 'ethics' and 'ethical' are often used to mean pretty much the same as 'morality' and 'moral'. When a doctor is found guilty of professional misconduct or a company director fiddles the company pension fund, people often say, 'She/he behaved quite unethically.' They might just as well say, 'She/he behaved quite immorally', though this might create some confusion in the minds of people who believe (wrongly) that 'morals' are only about sex.

Many academic writers, though, distinguish between 'ethics' and 'morality'. Often, they use 'morality' to mean something like a phenomenon: the rules and principles we obey, our convictions about right and wrong, the ultimate values and goals by which we live our lives and so on. By 'ethics' they mean the academic *study* of that phenomenon: critically analysing our moral rules and principles, working out criteria for making judgements about right and wrong and the like. Not everyone makes this kind of distinction and different authors use the words in somewhat different ways, which can be confusing, but it is as well to be aware that the distinction exists.

If we talk about '*Christian* ethics', this suggests that in some way we are locating our talk of right and wrong, good and bad, obligation and value and so on in a context of Christian faith, practice and theology. Perhaps the map entitled 'Christian ethics' covers part of the territory found on the larger map entitled 'Christian theology'. Later in this chapter I shall say a little more about what we might mean by calling it *Christian* ethics. Another piece of terminology that you are quite likely to encounter in this context is 'moral theology'. Like 'Christian ethics', this refers to the study of morality in the context of Christian life and theology. In Western Christianity, largely for historical reasons, you are more likely to find Roman Catholics talking about 'moral theology' and Protestants about 'Christian ethics', but the two terms mean roughly the same.

2 What to Decide

So, what kind of territory will you find when you open the map entitled 'Christian ethics'? I said earlier that, contrary to some people's belief, it is not only about sex (though it does have things to say about sex). So what *is* it about?

It seems fairly obvious that ethics has something to do with making decisions about the right thing to do. If we ask what Christian ethics is about, the first answer that is likely to occur to us is that it concerns *what* we decide: the content of our decisions and our moral lives. What should I do in this situation? What (if anything) should I advise, encourage or tell others to do? What ought we, as a society, to permit or prohibit? The following exercise should give you some idea of the range of issues that could be included under the heading 'What to decide'.

Exercise

Look through one issue of a daily newspaper and identify all the stories you can that raise moral issues of this sort: issues about *what we or others ought to do*. Write down, as clearly and briefly as you can, what the questions are – for example, 'Should patients be entitled to have help from their doctors in committing suicide and, if so, under what circumstances?'

When you do this kind of exercise, you can discover a huge number of questions with 'ought' or 'should' in them referring to every aspect of our private and public lives. There are questions about sex and relationships, the care, discipline and education of children and young people, how society should treat criminal offenders, medical care, particularly at the beginning and end of life, economics, international trade and development, the use of military power and much more besides. Questions of this sort are often labelled 'practical', 'applied' or 'substantive' ethics, though these terms have their problems. Many of these questions appear in this book. However, the 'What to decide' questions are not the only ones that Christian ethics is concerned with.

3 How to Decide

When we are faced with moral decisions – particularly difficult dilemmas in which the right choice is not obvious – a second sort of question arises: '*How should we decide?*' What criteria should we use to tell right from wrong? Where should we look for moral insight, guidance or authority? What influences should shape our moral judgements?

This is not to say, of course, that the first thing we do when faced with a difficult dilemma is work out answers to these 'How' questions, then apply our answers to the problem at hand. Such a procedure would almost certainly be too laborious and time-consuming for our countless everyday moral decisions, and even the more difficult problems that confront us from time to time often demand answers too urgently to allow us the luxury of starting from first principles on each occasion. However, when we are trying to work out the right thing to do in a difficult and confusing situation, we will find ourselves assuming some answers to the 'How' questions, whether we realize it or not. In other words, we will have some idea of *what counts as a good reason* for doing A or not doing B.

Suppose I discover that an old friend of mine is being sexually unfaithful to his partner and she does not know. Should I tell her? All kinds of arguments for and against might occur to me: she has a right to know the truth; he has a right to my loyalty; infidelity is wrong; it might cause them both pain if the truth comes out; it might cause *more* pain in the long run if it doesn't; I hate conflict and find emotional scenes embarrassing; he has been annoying me lately and this will be a good way to get back at him; and so on.

Some of these reasons will weigh more heavily than others, and I will probably dismiss some of them as trivial, irrelevant or plain bad reasons for a decision about what I *ought* to do. The point is that, whether I am aware of it or not, my decision about what to do presupposes a whole set of decisions about *how to decide* what to do.

These decisions about how to decide may only be partly conscious and will have been shaped by many factors: my upbringing, faith commitment, past experience and reflection and so on. Also, in the future, I might look back on the decision I am making now and be critical of the way that I made it. Perhaps I should have paid more attention to the teaching of the Bible or the Church; perhaps I should have taken less notice of what I had been taught by my parents; perhaps I should have been more sensitive to the consequences of my actions. The next exercise invites you to reflect in this way on some of your own past moral experience.

Exercise

Write a brief description (one or two paragraphs) of a moral dilemma or situation from your personal experience. (It might, for example, be about a difficult decision that you or someone close to you has had to make.) Try to state as clearly as possible what the issue or dilemma was. Also state, as clearly as you can, how you (or the person in the situation) decided what to do: what were the reasons for and against; what factors influenced the decision; where did you, or they, look for guidance?

Keep your answer to this exercise – you will be invited to return to it in the final chapter.

Questions of this second sort – the 'How' questions – often go by descriptions such as 'moral theory', 'ethical method' – or even 'methodology', a favourite word of academics.

One way to ask the 'How' questions in Christian ethics is to ask what are its *sources* – in other words, where Christians should look for moral insight, guidance or authority – how those sources should be used and how they should be related to one another. One common way to classify the sources (used, for example, by the New Testament scholar Richard Hays, whom we shall meet again in the next chapter) is as *Scripture, tradition, reason* and *experience*.[2]

By *Scripture*, Christians mean the writings collected together in the Hebrew Bible (Old Testament) and the New Testament – the rich mixture of writings of various kinds, written over many centuries in many different settings, that you will find between the covers of something entitled 'Holy Bible' in your local bookshop. By calling this particular collection of writings 'Scripture', we are marking it off from other writings that come from the same places and times and claiming that it has some kind of special status and authority within the community of Christian faith. (It must be said, of course, that Christians disagree hotly about exactly what kind of status or authority it has and even about which writings count as 'Scripture'.) If we are to regard Scripture as a source of moral authority, we shall need to understand these writings in their own contexts. What kinds of literature are they – history, saga, poetry, law, biography, instruction, warning? What moral content do they have? How do they communicate it – by issuing commands, telling stories with a message, giving examples to follow? We shall also need to tackle the question how (if at all) these texts, written in very different times and places to ours, can speak to our lives, situations and dilemmas.

Tradition has a bad press in modern (or postmodern) society. It is often taken to mean something fusty, backward looking and static – the kind of thing that is appealed to by people who write letters to the newspapers and sign themselves 'Disgusted of Tunbridge Wells'. The phrase 'the dead hand of tradition' sums up nicely how we often understand the word, but it could not be further from what is meant by tradition as a source of Christian ethics.

Richard Hays defines tradition, in the sense I mean, as 'the Church's time-honoured practices of worship, service and critical reflection'.[3] In other words, it is a shared understanding within the Christian community about the kind of community it is, where it has come from, what it exists for and, in the light of that, how it and its members ought to live their lives. That shared self-understanding is both formed and expressed in a variety of ways: by the community's worship and prayer, its preaching and teaching, the lives, relationships and understanding of its members, the thinking and writing of its scholars and so on. This is anything but static. Philosopher Alasdair MacIntyre writes that a healthy tradition is characterized by vigorous conflict and argument, including argument about the fundamental goods or goals that the tradition itself ought to be pursuing.[4] Part of the ongoing argument within the medical community, for instance, should be about what counts as 'good medicine' and how we know it when we see it. Similarly, part of the ongoing argument in a Christian community will be about what that community exists for – and, therefore, what counts as a good life in the context of that community. Those who argue for the importance of tradition point out that it provides a store of collective experience and shared memory on which Christians and Christian communities can draw in their living and acting. In this way, it saves the Christian community from having to 'reinvent the wheel', beginning its moral deliberation from scratch, in each new generation.

In some forms of Christianity, tradition becomes crystallized into official

Church teaching. The idea is that the authorized leaders and teachers of the Church have the responsibility of expressing the community's shared self-understanding. The teachings produced by the Church's leadership are authoritative expressions of its tradition, which are intended to guide the faith and practice of the community and shape the future development of the tradition. This is roughly what is meant in Roman Catholicism by the 'Magisterium', or teaching authority, of the Church.

Our third source is *reason*. Obviously, anyone who makes any kind of moral decision cannot avoid using his or her reason in at least a minimal sense. However, I mean more than this by describing reason as a possible source of moral authority.

To count reason as a source of authority is to say that human powers of thought, understanding and argument can give us insight into what is good and right. Some traditions of Christian thought emphasize this claim. Humans, they argue, have been created by God with minds that are able to grasp something of the moral structure of the created world. This view is found, for example, in the natural law tradition, which we encounter in Chapter 3. Other Christian traditions, as we shall also see, are more pessimistic about the ability of our reason, unaided by divine revelation, to tell us what we need to know about right and wrong.

In a different way, some kinds of philosophical thought also stress the power of human reason as a source (possibly the only proper source) of moral authority. This view is characteristic of what Alasdair MacIntyre has called the 'Enlightenment project' in ethics.[5] By this he means the attempt, from the eighteenth century onwards, to justify moral judgements and provide criteria for moral decision making based solely on reasoned argument, without appealing to tradition, received wisdom or external sources of authority, such as the Bible or God's law. In Chapter 4 we encounter two classes of ethical theory that originated in the Enlightenment project. The eighteenth-century Enlightenment was, in part, a response to the rise of modern science, and in Chapter 5 we explore some of the questions that the natural sciences raise for Christian ethics. In Chapter 6, we examine MacIntyre's critique of the Enlightenment project and his proposed solution to its problems.

Our fourth source is *experience*. As with reason, it is hard to imagine any kind of moral deliberation that does not make at least minimal use of our own and others' experience, but to describe experience specifically as a source of moral authority can mean a variety of different things. It can refer to the role of the individual's conscience in moral decision-making and action. It can mean an inner conviction in the hearts and minds of believers and Christian communities about God's will and guidance. It can also mean an approach to Christian ethics that takes as its starting point the concrete experiences of people's lives – particularly those of people who are oppressed or marginalized in some way. This starting point is characteristic of the various 'theologies of liberation', some of which we meet in Chapters 7 and 8, which often draw on experience in order to critique biblical texts or aspects of the Church's traditional teaching.

These sources can be used in many different ways and combinations.[6] Some Christians have held that Scripture alone has authority in relation to Christian faith and morality and other sources must be treated with the utmost suspicion (this is the so-called *sola Scriptura* position). Alister McGrath gives the example of the sixteenth-century radical Protestant reformer Sebastian Franck, who dismissed Church tradition as a source of authority: 'Foolish Ambrose, Augustine, Jerome, Gregory – of whom not one even knew the Lord, so help me God, nor was sent by God to teach. Rather, they were all apostles of Antichrist.' The more mainstream Protestant reformers, including Luther, Calvin and their followers, regarded tradition more positively, but refused to see it as an independent source of authority that could be weighed against Scripture. Rather, its role was to help us understand and interpret Scripture, which remained the ultimate source of authority. Richard Hays says the same about reason and experience: they are not independent sources of authority, but stand in a 'hermeneutical relation' to Scripture. In other words, they help us to read and interpret Scripture rightly and bring its guidance to bear on new and unfamiliar situations.

For other Christians, two or more of the sources have roughly equal status. For example, a strong strand of Roman Catholic thought regards both Scripture and the traditions of the Church, handed down from the apostles, as vehicles of God's revelation in roughly equal ways. Some Anglican thinkers, taking their cue from the seventeenth-century theologian Richard Hooker, regard Scripture, tradition and reason as working in a kind of creative tension with one another.

4 The Person Who Decides, and What a Good Life Looks Like

The discussion so far might make it seem as though Christian ethical theory is all about how to make moral decisions and resolve dilemmas, but that is only one sort of question that Christian ethics asks. According to some writers, one of the problems with the 'Enlightenment project' is that it has overemphasized these 'How' questions and neglected others that are at least as important – what we might call the 'Who' questions. As we shall see in Chapter 6, philosophers such as MacIntyre and theologians such as Stanley Hauerwas have argued that we need to refocus our attention on questions of *virtue* and *character* in ethics.[7] In other words, we need to think about not only what we should do and what rules or principles we should follow but also *what sort of people, and communities, we ought to be.*

Our characters – the kinds of people we are – are formed by the choices we make, habits we develop and examples we follow as we grow and develop through life. Our individual moral decisions and actions will flow from our character: if we have a virtuous character, we will find it easier both to know what is right in a particular situation and to do the right thing. Hauerwas and other theologians have emphasized the importance of the Church as a 'community of character' in which our characters are formed and we develop the skills for living a good life. If this is so, then the shared life of Christian communities and the practice of their ministers – those who lead Christian communities and give pastoral care to their members – will be crucially important for Christian ethics. In the first part of Chapter 9, we return to this issue by exploring the relationship between Christian ethics and pastoral care.

So far, I have distinguished between 'ethical theory' and 'practical' or 'applied' Christian ethics. Some courses in Christian ethics (including some that I have taught in the past) make a sharp divide between the two. Some deal mostly with one or the other: either they concentrate on theory (the 'How' and 'Who' questions) and only refer briefly to practical issues by way of illustration or they focus on practical issues and offer only the bare minimum of theory as a kind of ethical toolkit. Others cover both theory and practical issues, but keep the two apart in separate sections.

I think these approaches are unsatisfactory, because the separation between theory and practice in ethics is artificial and potentially unhelpful. Obviously ethical theory ought to inform our thinking about practical issues; if it does not, we run the risk of basing our conclusions on unexamined assumptions and prejudices. However, practice informs theory as well: by reflecting on the decisions we make and the real lives of Christian people and communities, we gain greater insight into the 'How' and 'Who' questions of ethics.

For that reason, I shall try to keep theory and practice together in this book and enable each to inform the other. The book's structure is based on ethical theory, with each chapter introducing one major theoretical topic, but each chapter will begin with one or more case studies in sexual, medical, social and environmental ethics. The case studies will both introduce practical issues in these areas of 'applied' ethics and open up the theoretical questions that are introduced in the chapter. The chapter will then conclude with a discussion of the practical issue, which will draw on the theory discussed in that chapter as well as referring to other areas of theory when necessary. This may be a less tidy approach and possibly a slightly more confusing one than others, but I think it is also truer to the way Christian ethics actually works in the lives of people and communities of faith. I shall try to provide enough signposts through the book to help you find your way around without too much difficulty.

5 What Makes It *Christian* Ethics?

So far, I have been somewhat vague about the significance of the adjective 'Christian' in 'Christian ethics'. For example, is Christian ethics only concerned with the moral standards by which Christian people and communities should live their lives or do Christian moral conclusions apply to everyone, believer or not? Take the claim 'Christian ethics prohibits adultery', for example. Does that mean 'Christians should not commit adultery' or 'Christians believe that no one, Christian or not, should commit adultery'? Also, how, if at all, does 'Christian ethics' differ from 'ethics', plain and simple?

The Catholic moral theologian Vincent MacNamara helpfully breaks this issue down into questions about the *distinctiveness* and *specificity* of Christian ethics.[8] The 'distinctiveness' question is about 'how Christian faith bears on moral life', as he puts it. You can, of course, be morally sensitive and concerned without having a faith commitment, but, if you are a Christian believer, your faith commitment is bound to have some implications for your moral vision and life. To the extent that it does, your ethics will be *distinctively* Christian. This distinctiveness might be evident both in the content and in what MacNamara calls the 'context' of Christian ethics. 'Context' here means our understanding of God, the world and our place in it, as that understanding is shaped by the Christian story, centred on the life, death and resurrection of Jesus Christ. The story gives us a worldview that shapes our moral vision and priorities and supplies a distinctive motivation for our moral judgements and conclusions. For example, it might lead us to value and respect all human life because we believe that every human person is created and loved by God and each one is a person for whom Christ died.

The *content* of Christian morality, too, can be said to be distinctive insofar as it follows from some aspect of Christian faith. For example, many Christians (though not all) hold that abortion and euthanasia are always wrong because they contravene the principle of respect for life that I have just stated.

The question of 'specificity' is about whether or not Christian ethics leads to any conclusions that would not be shared by non-Christians and might even be objectionable to them. For example, some Christians and churches hold positions on issues such as abortion, birth control, homosexuality and war that are radically at odds with the prevailing views on those questions in Western liberal democracies.

The debate about the specificity of Christian ethics has been conducted particularly within Roman Catholic theology during the past half-century or so. On one side has been the 'Autonomy' school of thought associated with theologians such as Hans Küng and Josef Fuchs. This school of thought holds that Christian faith teaches nothing about the *content* of moral obligation that could not, in principle, be known by any person of good will, regardless of his or her religious commitments. In other words, ethics is autonomous. Christian faith does, however, offer a distinctive context and motivation for moral obligations and teaches specific religious obligations, such as love of God and vocation to religious life.

This view has been opposed by the 'Faith-ethic' school of thought associated with Joseph Ratzinger (Pope Benedict XVI), Hans Urs von Balthasar and others. This holds that Christian faith *does* teach specific moral obligations that could not be known by human reason in the absence of a faith commitment.

There are rough parallels to this debate within Protestant ethics.[9] For example, referring particularly to medical ethics, James Gustafson wrote in 1975 that 'For most persons involved in medical care and practice, the contribution of theology is likely to be of minimal importance, for the moral principles and values can be justified without reference to God, and the attitudes that religious belief grounds can be grounded in other ways . . .'. This kind of view has been opposed by other Protestant thinkers, such as Stanley Hauerwas, who has conducted a powerful campaign over many years to keep Christian ethics theological. Two years after Gustafson wrote the words just quoted, Hauerwas replied: 'To be sure, Christians may have common moral convictions with non-Christians, but it seems unwise to separate a moral conviction from the story that forms its context of interpretation . . .'.

To some extent, this debate reflects a more basic disagreement in theology about the possibility of 'natural theology' – that is, whether or not it is possible for us to have any reliable understanding of God and the good simply on the basis of our reason and our knowledge of the world without the help of special revelation from God. In twentieth-century Protestant theology, this question was most famously debated in the disagreement between Karl Barth and Emil Brunner in the 1930s.[10] Questions about the relationship between 'ethics' and 'Christian ethics' are revisited in the second part of Chapter 9, where we explore the relationship between Christian ethics and wider public ethical debates.

6 Concluding Remarks

In this chapter I have tried to give an initial idea of what might be meant by 'Christian ethics' and what you will find as you explore it further in the rest of the book. One thing that will have become clear already is that Christians, and Christian communities, vary widely in many aspects of their moral thinking and living. Another is that our moral understanding and living is shaped in complicated ways by where we come from. Our moral judgements and actions are guided by deeply held convictions, considered views, unexamined assumptions, semiconscious beliefs, emotional dispositions, character traits and experiences of life and faith. These things, in their turn, have been shaped by the communities that have formed us, relationships that have been most significant to us, environments we have lived in and so on, as well as things we have read, discussed and thought about.

All theology, and all ethics, comes from somewhere: there is no 'view from nowhere', no completely neutral stance. This book is no exception. It is an attempt to give as good and undistorted a map as possible of the territory called 'Christian ethics', but it is inevitably a map drawn from a particular perspective. I am a relatively privileged white male, a husband and the father of children, uncomfortably aware that I shall soon have to start describing myself as middle-aged. My Christian faith has been formed by the Evangelical tradition of Protestantism and membership of a so-called 'non-conformist' church in the Reformed Christian tradition,[11] but has also been influenced over the years by many of the other traditions described in this book. I am an ordained minister of my church, which has given me a certain amount of status and power and a particular experience of caring pastorally for Christian people and communities. Before I studied theology and was ordained, I was trained as a research scientist. All these things, and many more, have shaped my human and Christian identity and my perspective on Christian ethics.

One of the lessons to be learned from the 'theologies of liberation' introduced in Chapters 7 and 8 is that we need to become critically aware of our own perspectives and biases. As we note the many influences that shape our moral vision, we may find that we gladly own some of them, that others must be modified and perhaps that some are better left behind. I hope that this book will help you to develop this critical self-awareness of your own moral vision, whether you count yourself a member of any faith community or none.

One thing that this book does not do to any significant extent is engage with the moral visions of faith communities other than Christian ones. In part this reflects limitations in my own knowledge and experience and also the limits of what can be done well in one book. I take the view that the encounter between different religious traditions, if it is not to be superficial and simplistic, must be informed and supported by a thoroughgoing engagement with the traditions concerned. I hope that this book will at least be useful in supporting the Christian end of such dialogues about moral questions, even if it does not offer much help with the actual processes of encounter.

Suggestions for Further Reading

There are many general books on Christian ethics from a wide variety of perspectives, some better than others. One very useful volume that goes further into many of the topics covered in this book is by Robin Gill (ed.), *The Cambridge Companion to Christian Ethics*, Cambridge: Cambridge University Press, 2001.

It is worth beginning to read the writings of leading theologians of the past and present on ethical subjects. Wayne G. Boulton, Thomas D. Kennedy and Allen Verhey (eds), *From Christ to the World: Introductory Readings in Christian Ethics*, Grand Rapids, MI: Eerdmans, 1994, is a valuable collection of sources.

For quick reference on a variety of topics in Christian ethics, the following dictionaries may be found useful:

David J. Atkinson and David H. Field (eds), *New Dictionary of Christian Ethics and Pastoral Theology*, Leicester: IVP, 1995.

John Macquarrie and James F. Childress (eds), *A New Dictionary of Christian Ethics*, London: SCM Press, 1986.

2

The Bible in Christian Ethics

1 Case Studies

Read the two case studies below, and make brief notes in answer to the questions that follow. You may wish to keep your notes as you will be invited to revisit them at the end of the chapter.

Divorce and Remarriage: Jim and Helen

Jim and Helen come to see David, the minister of their local church, to ask if he would consider marrying them in the church. They do not go to church regularly, though Helen is an assistant leader of the Cub pack that meets in the church hall. They have been living together for about a year. Both have had previous marriages that ended in divorce. Helen tells the minister that she left her husband because, as she put it, 'he used to beat me up' and Jim says that he and his first wife 'just couldn't seem to get on with each other any more'. Helen has a six-year-old son from her first marriage who lives with her and Jim. Jim has a nine-year-old daughter and a six-year-old son who live with their mother, but have regular contact with him.

Questions

- What biblical commands, principles, stories or themes might be relevant to Jim and Helen's situation? What can David learn from this biblical material and how should he be guided by it in deciding whether or not he should marry Jim and Helen?
- What insights from tradition, reason and experience might also be relevant to David? How should these insights be related to what he has learned from the Bible?
- Imagine David is a friend of yours who asks your advice because he knows that you are studying Christian ethics. How would you advise him: should he agree to marry Jim and Helen or not and why?

Human Cloning and Stem Cell Research1

Early in 2004, it was reported that a team of South Korean and American scientists had succeeded in cloning a number of human embryos and extracting stem cells from one of them.

Cloning – producing a genetically identical copy of an already existing individual – was pioneered in mammals by Ian Wilmut and his colleagues, who produced Dolly the cloned sheep in 1997.

Human reproductive cloning (the use of the cloning technique to produce a live human being) is against the law in Britain and many other countries. However, so-called 'therapeutic cloning' is permitted in Britain. This means using the cloning technique to produce embryos for use in medical research or the treatment of disease and injury. Many of these medical uses would take advantage of the fact that the cells of the early embryo are so-called 'totipotent stem cells' – that is, they have the capacity to develop into any of the specialized forms of cell found in the human body. Researchers believe that cloned stem cells could one day be used to replace dead or damaged cells in patients suffering from diseases such as Parkinson's, Alzheimer's or diabetes.

Embryonic stem cells could be obtained from other sources, such as 'spare' embryos from IVF. However, the advantage of obtaining stem cells from embryos cloned from the patient him or herself is that they would then be identical with the patient's own cells. This would make them less likely to be rejected by the patient's immune system.

Late in 2005, the South Korean team withdrew their claim to have cloned human stem cells after it emerged that some of their data had been fabricated. However, other research groups have continued to pursue this goal. Biomedical researchers and patient support groups usually support such research enthusiastically, but pro-life groups tend to be more sceptical. Some have expressed fears that this research will bring reproductive cloning (the making of cloned babies) a step closer.

Questions

- Can you think of any biblical commands, principles, stories or themes that might be relevant to this issue?
- What insights from tradition, reason and experience might also be relevant? How should these insights be related to any relevant insights from the Bible?
- Should Christians oppose or support human reproductive cloning and why?
- Should Christians oppose or support human embryonic stem cell research for therapeutic purposes and why?

These two case studies illustrate the kinds of difficulty Christians might face if they look to Scripture as a source of moral authority. In the first, there is no shortage of biblical texts that speak in various ways about marriage and divorce. Perhaps the most obvious is the so-called 'hard saying' of Jesus, prohibiting divorce and remarriage under any, or almost any, circumstances. However, as we shall see, even such an apparently clear and unequivocal command has more to it than meets the eye. More fundamentally, some ethicists argue that marriage in the twenty-first century West is so different from marriage in first-century Palestine and other parts of the Roman Empire that the relevance of biblical texts and commands to our situation is not at all clear.

In the second case, it is obvious that the Bible never mentions cloning, stem cell research, or the whole host of scientific, technological, political, social and cultural developments that modern Western readers take for granted but could never even have been dreamt of by the Bible's authors. If the Bible is a source of authority for Christian ethics, does it have anything to say about such things and how can we learn what that might be?

These two problems require us to explore a little further what the Bible is and what might be involved in treating it as a source of authority for Christian ethics.

2 What Is the Bible and Why Is It Important?

I said in Chapter 1 that if we call this particular collection of writings 'Scripture', we are setting it apart from other ancient texts. We are claiming that it is in some sense authoritative for the community of faith that calls it 'Scripture'. To put it like this makes it clear that 'Scripture' and 'Church' belong together. As ethicist Allen Verhey puts it (following theologian David Kelsey), they are 'correlative concepts'.[2] Each is defined with reference to the other: Scripture is the collection of writings that shapes the Church's identity; the Church is the community whose identity is shaped by these writings and the story they tell.

Why *these* writings and why not others? This is a question about the so-called *canon* of Scripture. 'Canon' comes from the Greek word for 'rule' or 'measuring rod' and, in relation to the Bible, it means the list of books that are regarded as Scripture. It was, obviously, the Church that fixed the canon, deciding in the few centuries after Christ which writings were to be included. (Christians, of course, included in their canon an earlier collection: the books of the Law, the Prophets and the Writings, already regarded as Scripture by Jews, that Christians now refer to as the Old Testament or the Hebrew Bible.)

One view is that, the fact that the Church fixed the canon means that the Church has some kind of authority over Scripture – it is the Church that determines which writings are to have this status. Another, more suspicious, view regards it as an exercise in power – that those who had influence in the early Church approved those texts that accorded with their understanding of the Christian faith and excluded dissenting voices. From this viewpoint, the canon of Scripture is history – and theology – written by the winning side. A third view, widely held by Protestant ethicists, regards the canon neither as the creation of the Church nor as imposed by those in power. Rather, the selection of the canonical writings was an act of discernment of those writings that truly *had* authority for Christian faith and life. As Allen Verhey puts it, 'The Church did not so much create Scripture as acknowledge it as the texts within which the Spirit moved to give life and to guide.'[3]

It must also be remembered that Christians do not all agree on the extent of the canon. While the Catholic, Protestant and Orthodox Churches agree about most of the books to be included, each Church's selection is different in some respects to those of the other two. This is essentially because the Catholic and Orthodox Churches base their Old Testament canons on the Septuagint (the Greek translation of the Hebrew Scriptures that was used by the early Church), whereas, at the Reformation, the Protestants based their Old Testament canon on the Masoretic Text (the definitive collection of the Hebrew Scriptures that had been compiled within Judaism in the tenth century CE). The result is that there are books, and parts of books, recognized as Scripture by Catholics and Orthodox but not most Protestants, and some texts only recognized by the Orthodox. These differences have sometimes contributed to theological controversies, though Alister McGrath plays down the doctrinal significance of the differences between Protestant and Catholic canons.[4]

What do we mean, though, by the 'authority' of Scripture? It is sometimes said that all Christian theologies (it might be truer to say most) treat Scripture as *somehow* authoritative. The question is, *how*? What is the nature of its authority? Some authors remain vague about this, but there is a range of clear positions taken by Christians and churches.

At one extreme is what Daniel Migliore calls the 'biblicist' view.[5] (This view could also be called 'fundamentalist', but that word is so often used as a non-specific term of abuse that it seems best to avoid it in this discussion.) Scripture is viewed as authoritative because it is divinely inspired – biblicists understand this to mean that the written words of the Bible (as originally written down, in the original manuscripts and languages) are the very words of God. The human authors wrote down the words that the Holy Spirit moved them to write, as a result of a kind of divine dictation. Claims of infallibility follow from this, with some biblicists holding that nothing the Bible says can err in any respect and others saying, more modestly, that the Bible cannot err in relation to any matter of Christian faith or life.

In sharp contrast to the biblicist view is the notion that the Bible is the 'classic' of the Christian tradition – a term used, for example, by Vincent

MacNamara.[6] This view likens the Bible to those great works of literature, such as the plays of Shakespeare, that give profound and lasting insights into the human condition. It also suggests something about how the Bible should be used as a source of ethics. You might gain important moral insights from a play like *Othello*, but you would not think of using it as a rule book and you would search the text of the play in vain for ready-made answers to your questions about what you ought to do. If the Bible is a 'classic', it should no more be used in these ways than *Othello* should.

Furthermore, describing the Bible as the classic of the Christian tradition seems to suggest some kind of priority for *tradition* as a source of Christian faith. Christians down the ages have wrestled with questions about how they should live in response to the life, death and resurrection of Jesus Christ. The story of that wrestling and deliberation constitutes the moral tradition of the Church. The Bible is important not because its answers are definitive, but because it gives us a view of the earliest part of that tradition – the wrestling and deliberation of those who were closest in time to Jesus himself.

Somewhere between these two is a view that was well expressed by Allen Verhey some years ago.[7] This view draws an analogy with Christology – the Christian doctrine of the person of Christ. In the person of Christ, there is a coming together of the human and the divine, and some of the most important and complex theological debates in the early Church were attempts to find ways of speaking adequately about this union of the human with the divine. The boundaries were set by the Council of Chalcedon (451 CE), which insisted that the divine and human in the person of Christ must not be confused, divided, changed or separated. By analogy, in Scripture there is a coming together of the divine Word and the words of the human writers. In order to speak adequately about *this* union of the human with the divine, we must have an understanding of Scripture in which the divine Word and the human words are not confused, divided, changed or separated.

According to this view, the problem with the biblicist understanding of Scripture is that it *confuses* the divine Word with the human words of the biblical writings. Perhaps some versions of the idea that the Bible is a 'classic' risk *separating* the divine Word from the human words. Karl Barth, the great twentieth- century Protestant theologian, in contrast, understood the Bible in a way that lay firmly within Verhey's 'Chalcedonian' boundaries. Scripture, he said, is a unique witness to God's revelation of himself in Jesus Christ and, in it, we hear the Word of God thanks to the work of the Holy Spirit.[8] It should be emphasized, though, that the 'Chalcedonian' view of Scripture is not restricted to Protestants: a number of Catholic thinkers, including the leading twentieth-century theologian Hans Urs von Balthasar, would hold similar views.

3 How Should the Bible be Used in Christian Ethics?

Some Christians – particularly those of a 'biblicist' mindset – tend to assume that the moral content of the Bible is a set of rules. Using the Bible in ethics means looking for the rule that will tell you what to do in your particular situation. If this is all there is to it, then David, the minister in our first case study, might find a rule that seems to tell him what to do about marrying divorced people – though, as we shall see, even this might not be as straightforward as it seems. However, Christian doctors and scientists wondering whether or not they should get involved in human stem cell research and churches wondering whether to support or oppose it will look in vain for guidance.

   In fact, the moral content of the Bible is much richer and more varied than a set of rules could ever be. There are rules and commands, to be sure. Most famously, there are the Ten Commandments (Exodus 20.1–17; Deuteronomy 5.1–21), though even they are found in a 'narrative context' – that is, they come in the middle of the story of God's covenant with Israel. However, in Scripture, we find not only rules but also, as Richard Hays puts it, principles, paradigms and a symbolic world.[9] By *principles*, he means general guidelines for conduct, such as the command to love God and your neighbour (Mark 12.28–31 and parallels, quoting Deuteronomy 6.4–5 and Leviticus 19.18). *Paradigms* are stories that give examples of conduct to either imitate or avoid. For example, Acts 4.36–7 tells the story of Barnabas' generosity to his fellow believers; 5.1–11 tells the cautionary tale of Ananias and Sapphira, who pretend to be generous like Barnabas, but are in fact trying to deceive the church, and come to a very bad end. Part of the message seems to be 'Be like Barnabas, not Ananias and Sapphira'. A *symbolic world* gives us the big picture of God, the world and ourselves. This big picture does not include any specific moral guidance, but does show us the general direction in which to find our moral bearings. For example, Matthew 5.43–8 shows us what God is like – indiscriminately generous to the good and the bad alike. Christian discipleship must respond to, and reflect, that generous love of God, but we have to work out for ourselves the details of what that might mean.

How, if at all, should this rich variety of ethical material guide Christians' moral lives, decisions and actions? Many writers on the Bible and ethics have been willing to look to the Bible for guidance at the levels of principle, paradigm and symbolic world, but have been extremely cautious about appealing directly to biblical rules. For example, in the 1970s, Leslie Houlden wrote that the New Testament 'yields certain perspectives, patterns and priorities, and it forms the Christian mind which then turns to the examination of contemporary issues – perhaps to apply central New Testament principles more rigorously than any of the New Testament writers'.[10] One difficulty with appealing directly to biblical rules or commands is that the Bible does not speak with one voice. There are rules and commands that say very different things and some even seem to contradict one another. Even the apparently clear teaching of Jesus on divorce and remarriage comes in significantly different versions in different Gospels, as we shall see later. Faced with the diversity of biblical material, those who take a 'biblicist' approach to scriptural rules and commands either have to select some and ignore others or find themselves doing intellectual gymnastics to try and show that apparently contradictory texts really mean the same thing.

The other major problem with appealing directly to biblical commands is that they come from places and times so different from ours. Attempting to read moral answers directly from the texts seems to ignore these great differences of context. For example, even if the New Testament prohibited divorce in the first century, it could be argued that changes in the status of women, the nature and purpose of marriage and the wider social context between the first century and the twenty-first mean that the prohibition simply does not apply any more. Perhaps, as Houlden argues, the same reasons that led New Testament authors to prohibit divorce in the first century should lead us in the opposite direction now.[11]

Richard Hays takes a different view on biblical rules and commands. He argues that the presence in the canon of all four kinds of moral discourse – rules, principles, paradigms and symbolic worlds – suggests that all four are relevant to the Christian community. If we grant any text authority, it must be in the mode in which it speaks, so we should treat a rule *as* a rule rather than try to squeeze a principle out of it. However, although all four are needed, he believes that ethical material in *narrative* form should take precedence because the New Testament is, above all, the *story* of God's work in Jesus Christ.[12] (Hays' focus on narrative reflects a broader movement in recent theology, which has emphasized that some kinds of theological truth are best communicated in narrative form. Initially this may seem strange as we sometimes tend to think that 'story' means 'fiction' and that truth comes in the form of facts that can be stated in scientific propositions. Narrative theologians, however, argue that, on the contrary, stories can be every bit as true as propositions and, indeed, can communicate kinds of truth that propositions are ill-adapted to convey.)

If we are to treat the ethical material of the Bible in this way, how are we to deal with the two problems I have highlighted – the diversity of the biblical texts and the differences between their context and ours? Hays sets out what he calls the 'fourfold task' of New Testament ethics, which, among other things, includes ways of dealing with these problems.[13] The first part is what he calls the *descriptive* task. This is a matter of careful biblical exegesis, which involves reading the texts, paying attention to all of them, not selecting out the ones we prefer, recognizing their genres (the kinds of literature they are) and taking note of what they actually say, not distorting them to make them say what we think they should.

The next task he describes as *synthetic*. This means asking whether or not there is any overall message or coherent picture that emerges from all these diverse texts, without trying to squeeze them all into one mould.

The third stage is the *hermeneutical* task (the task of interpreting the texts), which involves crossing the divide between the biblical writers' worlds and ours, asking what these ancient texts say to us in our modern world. Like other scholars (including Allen Verhey), Hays stresses the crucial importance of the Christian community and its faith traditions in this task. As the community reads these texts carefully and prayerfully together, it can make creative and imaginative connections between the texts and the new situations that it faces.[14] This is a risky enterprise, for which there are no set rules, but the Church has never been able to avoid it. Even the New Testament authors make these creative leaps of imagination by applying texts from the Hebrew Scriptures to new situations. A Christian community that does this humbly and prayerfully, says Hays, can trust in the Holy Spirit's guidance. The final task is closely linked to the third. Hays calls it the *pragmatic* task of acting on what we have learned and decided: no ethical deliberation is complete unless it results in action and affects the way we live.

Other scholars are more sceptical about many of the ways in which the Bible is used in Christian ethics. A good example is Tom Deidun.[15] He points out the same problems that others, including Hays, recognize – the diversity of the biblical material, the time- and culture-bound nature of the writings, the fact that some of them were written to address very particular situations and needs, as well as the great gap between their worlds and ours. He makes more of these problems than Hays does and criticizes ethicists for ignoring them or failing to take them seriously enough. He doubts that Hays' 'synthetic task' – finding a coherent overall message – is possible, and believes that those who look to the Bible for moral rules or principles tend to end up picking and choosing between texts in an arbitrary way.

Deidun himself is sympathetic to the 'Autonomy' school of Roman Catholic ethics, which I described in Chapter 1. According to this school of thought, Christian sources such as the Bible do not teach us anything new about the content of ethics, but might supply a specifically Christian context and motivation for our moral decision making. For example, one thing that the New Testament can do, according to Deidun, is remind us of the connections between Christian faith-experience and morality. Christians might come to the same moral conclusions as others, but those conclusions will be based not only on right reason but also on their experience of God in Christ through the work of the Holy Spirit. Again, the New Testament gives a picture of the ways in which early Christian communities resolved their moral disputes and dilemmas and Deidun suggests that this picture might challenge the authority structures and decision-making processes of some present-day Christian Churches. (It is worth noting in passing that different views about the use of the Bible in Christian ethics do not divide neatly along the lines of different Christian traditions. Though Hays is a Protestant scholar and Deidun a Catholic, some Protestant thinkers would be sympathetic to Deidun's view, while some Catholics might well be closer to at least some aspects of Hays' position than to Deidun's.)

Hays and Deidun are both professional New Testament scholars who would presumably agree on many technical questions about the study of the Bible, yet they come to radically different conclusions about its use in ethics. This is a reminder that Christians who agree about the problems and challenges in using the Bible may nevertheless disagree sharply about its status as a source of Christian ethics. These differences might not only be based on technical questions of biblical scholarship but also be related in complex ways to much deeper theological and Church commitments.

Most of us will be instinctively drawn to one or other of the various positions in the debate about the Bible and ethics, but it is worth stepping back and taking a questioning look at our instincts. Someone like me, who tends to stress the authority of Scripture for Christian ethics, may need to be reminded by Deidun not to gloss over the difficulties. In contrast, someone who is inclined to stress the continuity between Christian ethics and the ethics of 'any reasonable person' may need to be reminded by Hays that the Church is sometimes called to be a countercultural community, witnessing to standards and ways of life that look decidedly *un*reasonable to the surrounding culture.

4 The Case Studies Revisited

Divorce and Remarriage: Jim and Helen

In our first case study, you will recall, David, the minister, needs to decide whether or not he will marry Jim and Helen.

If he is looking for guidance from the Bible, he may well think first of all of the five texts in the New Testament that prohibit divorce and remarriage: Matthew 5.31–2; Matthew 19.3–12; Mark 10.2–12; Luke 16.18

and 1 Corinthians 7.10–16. This is presented as a saying of Jesus' in the four Gospel accounts and, in 1 Corinthians, Paul says that he is quoting Jesus' teaching ('not I but the Lord', 7.10). The background to this saying is that the Torah (the Jewish 'Law') allowed for a man to divorce his wife under some circumstances (Deuteronomy 24.1–4) and this was apparently taken for granted in the Israel of Jesus' day. Jesus appears to be reversing this permission to divorce.

However, that is not all there is to say about this teaching of Jesus: a careful reading of the texts shows that there is more to them than meets the eye.

Exercise

Carefully read the five texts listed above and summarise in your own words what is said in each of them. Note particularly the ways in which they differ from one another.

There is not space to point out all the differences here, but they are important and interesting.[16] For example, in Mark, Jesus' opponents seem to be trying to trap him into opposing the law of Moses, whereas in Matthew 19 they are inviting him to take sides on an issue debated among rabbis in Jesus' time: what count as proper grounds for divorce? In both versions, Jesus refuses to answer the question directly, but instead reframes the issue. He appeals to the Genesis creation stories (Genesis 1.28; 2.24) to show that God, in creating humans as sexual beings, intended marriage to be a permanent union in which two people become 'one flesh'. The permission in Deuteronomy, he says, was a concession to human sinfulness, to our 'hardness of heart'. Mark's version, unlike the others, allows for the possibility that a woman might divorce her husband and that a woman could be the injured party in adultery. In its context, this is startling, because it radically undermines the patriarchal (male-orientated) view in which the wife is the husband's property. The logic of Mark's account is that marriage must be rethought as a partnership of male and female.

Mark and Luke present Jesus' rule without any exceptions, but Matthew and Paul both seem to allow exceptions to the rule. Matthew prohibits divorce 'except on the ground of unchastity' (*porneia*, in the original Greek). Various meanings of *porneia* have been suggested, some quite narrow and specific. For example, some scholars have suggested that Matthew is allowing for divorce where the husband discovers that his wife was not a virgin when they married. Others argue that he means a marriage can be dissolved if the partners are found to be close blood relatives. Hays, however, argues that Matthew is not using *porneia* in such a narrowly restricted sense, but as a 'catch-all' word for various kinds of sexual immorality. Paul, in 1 Corinthians, states another exception: if a member of the church is married to a non-Christian who wants a divorce, the Christian partner 'is not bound' to the marriage.

Christians have sometimes treated these texts as standalone legal rules, but, in order to work out how they should guide our practice, we need to put them in the context of a biblical and theological understanding of marriage. This is not a simple task as marriage is a complex social, legal and religious entity. It seems to be present in some form in many – some would say all – human cultures. Christians have usually agreed that, as Helen Oppenheimer puts it, the Church 'has no exclusive rights in it',[17] remembering Jesus' argument that it was part of God's purpose for human beings in creation. Some Protestant theologians have described it as one of the 'orders of creation' – that is, roughly speaking, part of the way God has set up the world to protect human life and enable it to flourish.[18] In this sense, you could say that marriage is 'natural' for humans – living like this is good for us because it goes with the way God has created us – but, in another sense, it obviously does not 'come naturally'. The New Testament texts make it clear that it will be hard to live up to the standard Jesus sets for marriage and his followers will need God's help to do so.

Christian thinkers have identified various purposes or 'goods' of marriage.[19] One, perhaps the most obvious, is that it is seen as the *proper context for sexual expression*. The Church has often been rather grudging about this. For example, the 1662 Book of Common Prayer of the Church of England describes marriage as 'a remedy against sin, and to avoid fornication'.[20] However, the point can be put more positively by saying that marriage provides the context in which sex, one of our most powerful drives, can be expressed most creatively rather than destructively. This is one way of reading Paul's comment that 'it is better to marry than to be aflame with passion' (1 Corinthians 7.9).

Another obvious purpose is *the birth and nurture of children*, and Christians often argue that the stability of marriage provides the most secure context in which children can grow and flourish. A third is to provide committed *love and companionship* between the partners, companionship which can begin before children are on the scene and endure long after they have flown the nest. This love and companionship are both expressed and strengthened by sex, but also by the many other aspects of the partners' shared life. There is a long tradition of describing this committed relationship of love and companionship as a *covenant*. This language draws a parallel between the love and commitment of the partners and the 'steadfast love' God showed to the people of Israel by making a covenant with them. Indeed, some of the Hebrew prophets used marriage as an image of God's faithful love for Israel, even when Israel was unfaithful to God (Hosea 2—3, for example) and this brings us to a further purpose.

Marriage has often been treated, fourthly, as a *sign and symbol* of God's love for humanity. In Scripture, this can be seen both in the Hebrew Bible, in texts such as the one already quoted from Hosea, and in the New Testament. In Ephesians 5.22–33, marriage is used as an image of Christ's relationship with the Church. Scholars comment that the analogy seems to go both ways – that marriage acts as a picture of Christ's love for his people, but, at the same time, Christ's relationship with the Church becomes a pattern for the relationships of husbands and wives. The writer's picture of marriage remains hierarchical, with women subject to men, but Hays and others argue that Ephesians begins to undermine this patriarchal picture radically by making Christ's self-sacrificial love the pattern that husbands are to follow.

Some Christian traditions describe marriage as a *sacrament*. In Roman Catholicism, it has traditionally been considered one of the seven sacraments.[21] Although Protestant traditions usually only recognize two sacraments – baptism and Holy Communion – some Protestant writers still describe marriage as 'sacramental' in character. Traditionally, a sacrament is both a sign of God's grace (that is, God's saving love towards us) and a means by which we receive that grace. So, when Christians call marriage a sacrament, part of what they mean is that it is a sign and symbol of God's love, as I have already outlined. They also mean that it can be a way in which we receive God's love and are transformed by that love. Recent discussions have made the point that, in a sacrament, God uses physical and material things to bless humans. Thus, if marriage is described as a sacrament, the couple's physical lovemaking can be a means by which God blesses them, in more or less the same way as physical bread and wine become the means of God's blessing in a Communion service.[22] Furthermore, it is worth remembering that the sacraments belong in the life and worship of the Christian *community*; they are ways in which God blesses the community, not just isolated individuals. If marriage is sacramental in character, this presumably means that it should benefit the whole community, not only the husband and wife. Thus, a marriage that truly reflects something of God's faithful love will help others in the community to understand God's love better. The couple's love for one another should not keep them completely absorbed with one another to the exclusion of everyone else, but should enable them to turn outwards towards others in hospitality, friendship and welcome. The love that they extend to others in the community can be a channel of God's love and blessing.

How might all these thoughts help David to make up his mind whether or not to marry Jim and Helen?

A wide range of Christian writers take their cue from *the Bible* and *Christian tradition* in arguing strongly that marriage is meant to be lifelong, monogamous and faithful. The biblical arguments include not only Jesus' rule against divorce but also the 'symbolic world' of texts, such as Ephesians 5.22–33, in which marriage is meant to be a sign and symbol of God's unending, faithful love. Some Christians go so far as to rule out divorce and remarriage altogether. For example, Roman Catholic Church law prohibits remarriage after divorce, partly on the grounds of Jesus' rule, though, on the strength of 1 Corinthians 7, it allows a Christian who has been divorced from a non-Christian partner to remarry. Protestant traditions have often been more ready to allow for 'hardness of heart' and permit divorce, though it has not been commonplace until relatively recently. In England and Wales before 1857, for example, any divorce required a special Act of Parliament and so would only be possible for those with money and influence.

Recently, *experience* has come to play a more openly acknowledged role in both academic argument and popular assumptions about divorce. Some appeals to experience have a deadly serious purpose. Stories of physical, psychological and sexual abuse in marriage and family life are now taken more seriously than they once were, though, many would argue, still not seriously enough. The experience of those on the receiving end of such abuse, usually women and children, is a powerful indictment of those who have used biblical texts to persuade vulnerable people to remain in destructive and dangerous situations.[23]

Of course, Christians who oppose remarriage after divorce, or even divorce itself, on biblical grounds, are not thereby committed to the view that abused people should remain in abusive situations. It is perfectly possible to oppose divorce but still agree that sometimes, for their own safety, people need to leave dangerous domestic situations, but the stories of women and children who have suffered domestic abuse suggest that the texts have, at times, been used – or misused – in this way.

Appeals to experience in less extreme situations have been roundly criticized by some authors. For example, Hays complains that some churches have uncritically accepted the 'pop psychology' view that marriage vows can be regarded as dispensable if the partners cease to find their marriage personally fulfilling. He argues that the Christian Churches must resist this easygoing attitude to the marriage commitment and should reaffirm their teaching that marriage is a covenant before God, not to be broken except in extraordinary circumstances. However, at the same time, the New Testament itself tempers this teaching with pieces of pastoral improvisation in response to the hard cases that the early Church faced: Matthew's clause 'except for *porneia*' and Paul's teaching about Christians with non-Christian partners. According to Hays (and others), the Churches today can take their cue from this pastoral flexibility in discerning other exceptional situations where divorce might also be justified. He believes violent abuse would be another such case. In common with others, he also concludes that divorced persons must be loved, supported and welcomed as full participants in the life of the Church and that remarriage cannot be ruled out.

One further question concerns the relationship between the Church's discipline and the civil law. Most writers seem to agree that there is not such a thing as 'Christian marriage', distinct and different from 'marriage' pure and simple. At the same time, as we have seen, the New Testament texts present the vision of lifelong faithful marriage as a demanding aspect of Christian discipleship. Accordingly, when the Churches have expected their own members to live up to this high standard, they have sometimes supported less rigorous civil laws on divorce. As David reflects on the story of Jim and Helen, who are on the fringe of his church, he might be asking himself if he should have different expectations of them than of people who are fully part of the church's life and fellowship.

> ## Exercise
>
> Lookagain at the notes you made for the Jim and Helen case study. What would you add or change in the light of your reading about the use of the Bible and Christian understandings of marriage and divorce? Would your advice to David, the minister, now be different in any way from what it was before?

Human Cloning and Stem Cell Research

At the beginning of this Chapter, I drew attention to the very obvious fact that the Bible has nothing directly to say about human cloning, stem cell research or a whole host of other ethical problems with which Christians are faced in the twenty-first century. Furthermore, it might seem that the Bible is so far removed from the intellectual, social and cultural context that makes human cloning and stem cell research possible that it cannot contribute anything relevant to these debates. However, Christians do in fact have plenty to say about cloning, stem cell research and other new problems, drawing, in various ways, on the Bible as well as Christian tradition, reason and experience.

Most Christians who comment on human reproductive cloning agree that it would be wrong and this echoes a fairly widespread opposition to it in wider public and political debates. Much of the opposition in public debates, and to some extent in Christian arguments, stems from concerns about harmful consequences. As things stand with cloning technology at present, it is likely that a high proportion of human clones would either be stillborn or born with serious congenital health problems.

For some people, such arguments about consequences are more or less the only things that need to be said. They take a *consequentialist* approach of the kind that we explore in Chapter 4, which evaluates actions solely in terms of their good and bad consequences. According to this view, if human cloning could be made reasonably safe and we could be satisfied that it would not result in other kinds of unacceptably harmful consequence (such as a diversion of healthcare resources away from more urgent needs), then it could be justified. However, many disagree. It is often said, both in Christian discussions and in wider debates, that, even if reproductive cloning could be made safe, it would still be wrong because it would somehow threaten the worth and dignity of human beings.

This concern about human dignity is sometimes expressed rather vaguely, and writers such as John Harris who support reproductive cloning question this line of argument.[24] There are Christian versions of it, however, that can be more precisely stated. Many Christian objections to reproductive cloning see it as a way of taking excessive control of human procreation and identity. In common with current reproductive technologies such as *in vitro* fertilization (IVF), it would introduce a large measure of technological control into procreation. In addition, it would allow us to determine fairly precisely the genetic make-up of the human beings produced by cloning. (It is worth stressing that this would not amount to anything like total control over the clones' personal identities. A human person's identity is the product of an almost unimaginably complex interaction between genetic inheritance, environmental factors that influence physical characteristics, a unique personal history of relationships, a social, cultural and political context and so on. Even though cloning might allow us to control the genetic component of this mix, many of the other factors would almost certainly be impossible to control. This means that science fiction storylines about cloning great leaders, outstanding thinkers or tyrannical dictators are sheer fantasy. We might be able to replicate the *genotype*,[25] but we could never replicate the *person*.)

Technological control of procreation and identity is seen as problematic in at least two ways. First, it marks a shift in our relationships with our fellow human beings. A number of years ago, Oliver O'Donovan borrowed the language of the Nicene Creed to draw a distinction between 'begetting' and 'making'.[26] Those whom we *beget* are like us – they are fellow human beings who share our nature and command our respect. However, we do not have the same kind of relationship with things that we *make*, as we can own and control them in ways that we cannot own or control our fellow humans. If we try to control human procreation technologically – particularly if we try to determine aspects of the identity of other humans – we are in danger of coming to regard them less as fellow humans who command our respect, and more as products or commodities that we can own and control. This would be bad, not only for those who were regarded as commodities, but for human society as a whole, because it would be a radical distortion of the ways in which Christian faith teaches us to relate to one another.

Second, some Christians see this kind of technological control as an attempt (conscious or otherwise) to make ourselves like God the Creator, forgetting that we are not gods but God's creatures. Christians sometimes express this argument by referring to two texts from the book of Genesis, namely, the creation story, in which God commands the human being to cultivate the garden of Eden (Genesis 2.15) – in effect, a mandate to human beings to make something of the created world – and the story of the Tower of Babel (Genesis 11.1–9), in which humans use their technological skill to try and become like God, but fail and end up 'scattered . . . over the face of the earth'.

Many aspects of medicine and technology could, in principle, be like cultivating the garden of Eden – part of our human calling by God to make something of the world. However, it is argued, reproductive cloning would be more like building the Tower of Babel. In effect, we would be trying to make ourselves into creators of human beings and would be in danger of deceiving ourselves that we can become like God by means of our own skill and cleverness.[27] This will have the effect of alienating us from God because, if we try to become like gods ourselves, we shall be unable to respond to God with the love, trust and worship that are the characteristics of a right relationship with God.

So-called 'therapeutic cloning' and stem cell research, however, would not necessarily be subject to these objections. There is a long tradition that sees medicine as a proper human and Christian calling, a way of following in the footsteps of Jesus the healer. Disease and suffering are contrary to God's loving purpose for human life – they are signs that things have gone badly wrong with the world. (This is not the only thing to say about them, as

they can also be opportunities for us to come to know God's love and goodness more fully, but this does not detract from the point that they are evils
that can and should be resisted.)[28] When we use our knowledge and skill to
resist the power of disease and suffering, we are doing the kind of work that
God has given humans to do. When stem cell research is directed at treating serious diseases, its aims and goals would seem to be in line with this
Christian calling to heal. However, even though the aims and goals of stem
cell research may be good, many Christians have concerns about the means
used to pursue those goals. In particular, embryonic stem cells cannot be
obtained without destroying human embryos. Therefore, we cannot decide
on the morality of stem cell research without judging if, and under what circumstances, it might be morally acceptable to destroy human embryos. To
make that judgement, we shall need to think a little further about the human
embryo itself.

The term 'embryo' refers to an individual during the first eight weeks of
development after conception – from week nine onwards, it is referred to as
a 'foetus'.[29] In Britain, the law only allows experimentation (including stem
cell research) on embryos up to 14 days old, which is the time after which the
nervous system begins to form and also the last point at which the embryo
can split to form identical twins.

It is clear that the early embryo is, genetically, a human individual.
Although its genetic material is derived from both parents, the embryo is
genetically distinct from them and, except in the case of identical twins,
unique. Furthermore, it has started out on a developmental path that, if
nothing interrupts it, will result in the formation of an adult human. (It must
be said that a high proportion of embryos fail to implant in the mother's
womb and many pregnancies spontaneously terminate in their early stages,
so, quite apart from any human intervention, many embryos do not become
adult humans.) However, these facts by themselves do not tell us how human
embryos should be treated.

To know how we should treat human embryos, we need some understanding of their *moral status*. What kind of entity is the embryo and what moral
responsibilities do we have concerning it? Broadly speaking, five answers to
these two linked questions can be found in Christian (and other) writing on
the embryo.[30]

i The embryo is a person

Here, 'person' is a kind of philosophical shorthand for a being with the same kind of moral status that we accord to human children and adults. To say that the embryo is a person is to say, among other things, that it has the same kind of moral claims on us that human children and adults have. If there are ways in which we should never use children or adults (for example, deliberately killing them in order to harvest their organs for transplantation), then neither should we use embryos in equivalent ways (for example, destroying them in order to obtain stem cells for the medical treatment of others).

Christians who hold this view might argue that the embryo is in the early stages of a personal history that begins with conception, the individual's life at every stage of that history is a gift from God and God loves and values the individual at every stage of her life, regardless of his or her characteristics, properties or abilities. There is no point after conception at which a line can be drawn that marks the beginning of a new stage when the individual acquires a new kind of status or value in God's sight.

It is worth saying a little more at this stage about the concept of 'the person'. Its roots are in pre-Christian Greece and Rome, but it was first developed into a philosophically and theologically significant term by the thinkers of the early Church, who needed to find a language for speaking about the triune God and the person of Jesus Christ. However, the concept has gone through many twists and turns in Western thought and some philosophers now use it in ways that are very different from the ways in which earlier thinkers would have spoken of either a divine or human person.[31] Some of these characteristically modern ways of thinking about the person lie behind the next two positions on the status of the embryo.

ii The embryo is no more than a piece of human tissue

Those who hold this view might argue that the early embryo (certainly in the first two weeks after conception) has none of the abilities or properties that normally lead us to recognize human children and adults as persons.

For example, it is not aware of itself, cannot suffer, cannot have relationships with others and cannot have interests, desires or plans. It should be regarded, morally speaking, in much the same way as we would a human organ or sample of tissue. We should be free to use it for the benefit of others in ways that we would not be free to use a human child or adult. For example, if we are free to use a human blood sample as a source of cells for medical research or treatment, we should be free to use a human embryo in the same way.

iii The embryo is a potential person, with a status somewhere between that of human tissue and that of a person

Those who hold this view might agree that the embryo cannot be counted as a person because it lacks the properties and abilities that normally lead us to recognize an individual as a person. Nonetheless, they might argue, it has the *potential* to develop into a person and it is this potential that entitles it to a special moral status – not as high as a person, but higher than a piece of human tissue. This might mean that it is morally justified to use embryos in medical research and treatment, but only if the benefits of the research or treatment are great and cannot be obtained in other ways. Something like this view was expressed by the majority report of the Warnock Committee, on which British legislation on reproductive technology and embryo research is based.[32]

iv We do not know the status of the embryo

Those who take this view might simply mean that the status of the embryo is a complicated issue about which we have not yet found a position that we can all agree on. However, they might mean, more fundamentally, that it is an issue that *cannot* be decided on in a way that would help us rule on how embryos should be treated, because there is no consensus on the meaning of the basic concepts and assumptions that we would have to use in order to decide whether or not the embryo is a person. Sometimes, this view – that we do not, and perhaps cannot, know the status of the embryo for certain – is used to support conclusions similar to position (iii) – the embryo is entitled to some protection, but not as much as a human child or adult. However, Robert Song and others have argued that if we do not know the embryo's status, then we should err on the side of caution and treat it as a person. If we do not, we are opening ourselves to the possibility of committing a grave moral wrong. As Song puts it, quoting Germain Grisez, 'To be willing to kill what for all one knows is a person is to be willing to kill a person.'[33]

v The question 'Is the embryo a person?' is the wrong question to ask

This argument can be found in a number of Christian discussions. For example, Richard Hays argues in this way about the moral status of the foetus in relation to abortion and what he says can easily be extended to relate to the embryo.[34] He draws an analogy with the exchange between Jesus and the lawyer in Luke 10.25–37. Referring to the command to love your neighbour as yourself, the lawyer asks, 'And who is my neighbour?' Luke comments that he '[wants] to justify himself', to place limits on the range of people to whom he is obliged to show care and concern. Instead of answering him directly, Jesus replies with the parable of the Good Samaritan, which unsettles any attempt to draw a line between those who are, and those who are not, our neighbours. In the same way, Hays suggests, the question 'Who is a person?' functions as a self-interested way of setting limits to our moral concern. The parable of the Good Samaritan should unsettle those limits and force us to find different ways of thinking about our moral obligations regarding embryos and foetuses.

It should be clear from this discussion that even when Christians are faced with new issues, such as human cloning and stem cell research, that could not have been imagined by the biblical writers, they still find many ways in which to use the Bible as a source for their moral deliberation. Using Hays's terminology, there may not be any biblical *rules* that apply directly, but Christians do appeal to *principles*, such as the command to love our neighbours, *paradigms* (as in Hays's use of the Good Samaritan story), and the *symbolic world* evoked by passages such as the Genesis 2 creation narrative and the story of the Tower of Babel in Genesis 11. These biblical images and insights interact with themes from the Christian *tradition*, such as the complex history of the concept of 'person', the insights of *reason*, including relevant scientific information, and *experience*, including the experience of patients who might benefit from the treatments offered by stem cell research. Some of these themes recur in later chapters, so, for example, in Chapter 5 we explore the ways in which scientific knowledge might influence Christian ethical thinking and in Chapters 4 and 9 we return to the ethical significance of patients' experience of suffering.

Questions

- Of the five possible answers outlined above to the question about the status of the human embryo, which do you find most satisfactory and why? What does your preferred answer suggest about the morality of embryonic stem cell research?
- Return to your earlier conclusions about human reproductive cloning. In the light of the discussion in this section, how, if at all, would you now add to, or change, those conclusions?

Suggestions for Further Reading

The Bible and Christian Ethics

There is a big body of literature on this topic, the works listed below forming only a small selection from it. The discussion in this chapter has focused on the New Testament, saying little about the use of the Hebrew Bible in Christian ethics. It has also said little about the ethics of Jesus and has not dealt directly with the distinctive ways of using Scripture in the liberationist and feminist theologies, which are introduced in Chapters 7 and 8. The following works should help to fill some of these gaps.

John Barton, *Ethics and the Old Testament*, London: SCM Press, 1998.

Tom Deidun, 'The Bible and Christian Ethics', in Bernard Hoose (ed.), *Christian Ethics: An Introduction*, London: Cassell, 1998, pp. 3–46.

Robin Gill (ed.), *The Cambridge Companion to Christian Ethics* Cambridge: Cambridge University Press, 2001. Chapters 2—5 discuss the Bible and Christian ethics.

Colin Hart, *The Ethics of Jesus*, Grove Ethical Studies no. 107, Cambridge: Grove, 1997.

Richard B. Hays, *The Moral Vision of the New Testament*, Edinburgh: T & T Clark, 1997.

The New Testament Gateway at: www.ntgateway.com (accessed 9 September 2005). A valuable collection of online resources on the New Testament, including material on the canon and the historical Jesus.

Thomas L. Schubeck, *Liberation Ethics: Sources, Models and Norms*, Minneapolis, MN: Fortress, 1993.

Allen Verhey, *Remembering Jesus: Christian Community, Scripture, and the Moral Life*, Grand Rapids, MI: Eerdmans, 2002.

Marriage and Divorce

Again, there is a massive amount of literature on this topic, so in my selection I offer a variety of theological perspectives.

Stanley Grenz, *Sexual Ethics: An Evangelical Perspective*, 2nd edn, Louisville, KY: Westminster John Knox, 1997.

Kevin T. Kelly, *Divorce and Second Marriage: Facing the Challenge*, Lanham, MD: Rowman & Littlefield, 1997.

Dave Leal, *On Marriage as Vocation*, Grove Ethical Studies no. 100, Cambridge: Grove, 1996.

Helen Oppenheimer, *Marriage*, London: Mowbray, 1990.

Elizabeth Stuart, *Just Good Friends: A Lesbian and Gay Theology of Relationships*, London: Mowbray, 1995.

Adrian Thatcher, *Liberating Sex: A Christian Sexual Theology*, London: SPCK, 1993.

Human Cloning and Embryonic Stem Cell Research

Ron Cole-Turner (ed.), *Human Cloning: Religious Responses*, Louisville, KY: Westminster John Knox, 1997.

David Albert Jones, *The Soul of the Embryo: An Enquiry into the Status of the Human Embryo in the Christian Tradition*, London: Continuum, 2004.

Neil Messer, *The Ethics of Human Cloning*, Grove Ethical Studies no. 122, Cambridge: Grove, 2001.

Brent Waters, *Reproductive Technology: Towards a Theology of Procreative Stewardship*, London: Darton, Longman & Todd, 2001.

Brent Waters and Ronald Cole-Turner (eds), *God and the Embryo: Religious Voices on Stem Cells and Cloning*, Washington, DC: Georgetown University Press, 2003.

3

Natural Law

1 Case Studies

Read the two case studies below and make brief notes in answer to the questions that follow. You may wish to keep your notes as you will be invited to revisit them at the end of the chapter.

Homosexuality: The Civil Partnership Act[1]

In November 2004, the Civil Partnership Bill, giving legal recognition to same-sex couples in the UK, received Royal Assent and became law. The Act gives lesbian and gay couples the opportunity to go through a civil registration process similar to that of marriage and to make a formal lifelong commitment to one another. The partners in a civil partnership have a range of rights and responsibilities similar to those of partners in a marriage, covering such areas as property, finance, inheritance and child support. There is also provision for a dissolution process similar to divorce, to deal with cases where a civil partnership breaks down.

When the Bill was first proposed, the Roman Catholic Church in England and Wales opposed it on the grounds that the Government's proposals were not necessary to defend the fundamental human rights of gay and lesbian people and that they would undermine marriage and the family. The Church of England does not allow its buildings to be used for the registration of civil partnerships, but there are reports that Anglican priests, in common with ministers of some other Christian denominations, frequently conduct unofficial blessing services for gay couples.

Early in 2005, it was reported that the Diocese of Lincoln had produced a draft service of thanksgiving for non-marriage relationships. While it might be used by same-sex couples, it could also be used by close friends who are not in a sexual relationship. Bishop John Saxbee said that the service would be consistent with Anglican guidelines because it would not be the blessing of a union, only a thanksgiving for a friendship. The service was welcomed by a spokesperson for the Lesbian and Gay Christian Movement, but greeted with suspicion by the chairman of the evangelical pressure group Reform.

Questions

- Should the traditional Christian prohibition of sexual activity between partners of the same sex be maintained, revised or jettisoned altogether?
- Should Christians support or oppose civil legal provisions for same-sex partnerships?
- Should Christian churches offer services for the blessing of same-sex partnerships?

The 'War on Terror'

September 11th, 2001, is a date that no reader of this book is likely to have forgotten. On that day, four airliners were hijacked over United States airspace by terrorists linked to the Al-Quaeda network. Two of them were flown into the twin towers of the World Trade Center in New York, one into part of the Pentagon and the fourth was diverted from its target by some passengers who resisted the hijackers. The crews, passengers, hijackers and thousands of people in the targeted buildings were killed in the attacks.

Since 2001, other high-profile terrorist attacks linked to Al-Quaeda have included the bombing of a nightclub in Bali, in which many Australian tourists were killed and injured, the coordinated bomb attacks on a number of commuter trains in Madrid and the attacks on London's transport system in July 2005.

Some commentators have argued that these attacks should be regarded as criminal acts and those responsible should be pursued through international criminal justice processes. However, the government of the United States quickly took the view that the September 11th attacks amounted to an act of war and that the USA and her allies were now engaged in a 'war on terror'. One of the first actions in this 'war' was the US-led military action in Afghanistan, which resulted in the Taliban regime being deposed and democratic elections being organized. Hundreds of prisoners, including nationals of many Western nations, were taken in Afghanistan and imprisoned by the US military at Guantanamo Bay in Cuba. Controversially, they were classified by the American authorities as 'enemy combatants', which meant that they were treated neither as civilian criminal suspects nor as prisoners of war under the terms of the Geneva Convention.

The action in Iraq in 2003, in which Saddam Hussein's Ba'athist regime was deposed, was presented as another part of the 'war on terror', although some critics argued that it was a distraction from the fight against Al-Quaeda as Saddam had no clear links with that network.

The 'war on terror' has also included stringent homeland security measures in some Western countries. In Britain, these have included a system of 'control orders' under which those suspected of supporting terrorism can be electronically tagged, banned from using the telephone or Internet and forced to remain in their homes under curfew.

Questions

- From a Christian ethical standpoint, is it ever justified to use violent force in defence of peace, security or justice? If so, under what circumstances should force be used and what restraints, if any, should be placed on its use?
- Is the 'war on terror' really a war? Does it matter whether we call it a war or not?
- Do you consider the various actions in the 'war on terror' to be morally justified?

A great deal of Christian teaching on questions of sexuality, war and many other ethical matters has its roots in the so-called *natural law* tradition. Natural law thinking has been very influential in Catholic theology for many centuries and is the focus of lively contemporary discussion and debate.

It is a tradition that places a strong emphasis on the ability of human reason to discern the good and the right. For that reason, many Protestant theologians have been suspicious of it, arguing that reason, like other human faculties, is too radically distorted by sin to be a reliable guide as to what is good and right.

2 The Roots of the Natural Law Tradition

Part of the background to natural law thinking can be found in the Bible. In the Hebrew Scriptures, the Wisdom literature – especially the book of Proverbs – contains sayings, advice and instruction that do not appeal to Israel's distinctive traditions, such as the stories of the patriarchs, exodus and giving of the Law at Sinai. Instead, they have a markedly international flavour and there are close parallels between them and texts from other ancient Near Eastern nations. In other words, there is teaching and instruction within the canon of Scripture itself that does not seem to rely on any special revelation from Israel's God, but is accessible to human reason and experience. Also in the Hebrew Bible, parts of the prophetic tradition, such as Amos' oracles against the nations (Amos 1.3—2.8), seem to assume that Gentile nations as well as Israel are accountable to Israel's God for their behaviour and can be judged by the same standards as Israel. Some New Testament texts, too, seem to claim that all people, whether or not they have the Scriptures, can have some kind of natural knowledge of God's law. For example, Paul famously writes, 'When Gentiles, who do not possess the law, do instinctively what the law requires, these, though not having the law, are a law to themselves' (Romans 2.14).

Another part of the background to natural law theory can be found in various strands of ancient Greek philosophy. For the Stoics, the good life was one that was lived in submission to the divine ordering of the world – as it were, living with the grain of the way the world was made. Stoic philosophy had a significant influence on early Christianity, which can be seen, for example, in Paul's speech at the Areopagus in Athens (Acts 17.22–31) and in the moral teaching in many of the New Testament epistles.

The philosophy of Aristotle and his followers was another important influence, particularly on Western Christianity in the Middle Ages, when many Aristotelian texts were rediscovered and had a profound influence on Christian philosophy and theology. An Aristotelian theme that became important in natural law thought was the notion that the good life is one that conforms to the proper 'ends' – goals or purposes – of human beings and these ends can be discovered by rational reflection on human nature. (The idea that the good consists in living according to our proper ends is sometimes referred to as a *teleological* view of ethics, from the Greek word *telos*, meaning 'end' or 'goal'. There are close links here with *virtue theory*, which we explore in Chapter 6. It, too, has some of its roots in Aristotelian thought and was developed by medieval Christian theologians.)

3 Thomas Aquinas and Natural Law[2]

Probably the greatest medieval Christian thinker in the West was Thomas Aquinas (*c.* 1225–74), whose massive final work the *Summa Theologiae* brings together Aristotelian philosophy and a Christian theological tradition shaped by the Bible, the Church Fathers and earlier medieval theologians.

Navigating around the *Summa Theologiae*

The *Summa Theologiae* or *Summa Theologica* – sometimes just referred to as the *Summa* or abbreviated as *ST* – is divided into three parts, which are traditionally numbered in Latin. These are the *prima pars*, or first part (1a), the *secunda pars*, or second part (2a), and the *tertia pars*, or third part (3a), which was unfinished at Thomas' death in 1274.

The *secunda pars* is subdivided into the *prima secundae*, or 'first of the second' (1a2ae), and the *secunda secundae*, or 'second of the second' (2a2ae). Thus, the numbering of the parts, in order, is *prima pars* (1a), *prima secundae* (1a2ae), *secunda secundae* (2a2ae), *tertia pars* (3a).

Various different conventions are used for the numbering – some using Roman numerals, some Arabic, some following the Latin order for numbering the subdivisions of the *secunda pars* (1a2ae; 2a2ae), some numbering the subdivisions in a way that would be more natural in English (2-1; 2-2). In this book I shall follow the convention I have already introduced – that is, 1a, 1a2ae; 2a2ae; 3a.

The structure of the book is shaped by the conventions of teaching and debate in medieval universities. Each part is divided into many *quaestiones*, which means questions (q.), and each question is sub-divided into articles (art.). The structure of each article is the same. It begins with a set of objections to a traditional position, then the traditional position is stated in a section known as the *sed contra* ('on the other hand'). Next comes the 'reply', which sets out Thomas' own assessment of the debate, and finally a series of answers to the objections.

The standard English translation, made in the 1960s, runs to 60 volumes.[3] There is a user-friendly abridged edition in one volume, translated by Timothy McDermott, which converts the medieval format of the *Summa* into continuous prose and avoids technical language as far as possible.[4] Quotations from the *Summa* here and elsewhere in this book are from McDermott's translation. Confusingly for the purposes of this chapter, though, one of the technical terms McDermott avoids using is 'natural law', which he prefers to translate as 'the law we have in us by nature'.

Thomas' discussion of law is in *ST* 1a2ae, qq. 90–108 (pp. 280–307 in McDermott's translation). He identifies four kinds of law, generally known as eternal law, natural law, positive divine law and positive human law.

The *eternal law* is 'the plan by which God, as ruler of the universe, governs all things' (p. 281). Thomas says that all created things follow God's eternal law, in that they have 'a natural tendency to pursue whatever behaviour and goals are appropriate to [them]' (p. 281). However, humans, being rational creatures, 'follow God's plan in a more profound way' (p. 281). This is because we have some (partial) understanding of the eternal law and this enables us to reason about the goals or ends that are appropriate for us and other creatures to pursue. In other words, we can make plans both for ourselves and other creatures, and Thomas describes this rational planning as a way of sharing in God's eternal reasoning and planning for the creation. This participation in the eternal law is what Thomas means by *natural law*.

How do we go about this process of practical reasoning (or 'reason planning action' as McDermott translates it)? We have to start somewhere, so we need a first principle that is self-evident, not needing to be proved first before we can begin building arguments on it. Thomas says that all practical reasoning depends on a notion of the *good*. Thus, the self-evident starting point for practical reasoning is that 'good is to be done and pursued and evil to be avoided' (p. 287). By 'good' he means 'whatever man naturally seeks as a goal' (p. 287) – whatever is in accordance with our natural ends or purposes. He identifies three groups of natural ends or purposes and, from each group, general moral principles can be worked out. These are often known as the *primary precepts* or *first premises* of natural law.

First of all, there are the ends that we share with all beings. Anything that exists, including us, has a natural tendency to go on existing, so natural law commands 'whatever conserves human life and opposes death' (p. 287). Second, there are the ends that we share with all animals. All animals, says Thomas, have a natural tendency to mate and bring up their young, so natural law commands us to act in line with this natural tendency. Third, there are ends that are distinctively human, not shared with other animals or other beings. These ends have to do with our rational nature, which inclines us, for example, to know the truth about God and live in an ordered social structure. So, natural law commands 'whatever is relevant to these inclinations, like avoiding ignorance and not offending those we live with' (p. 287). These first premises all follow from Thomas' starting point – that good is to be done and pursued and evil avoided – but he says we know the truth of the first premises intuitively: we do not have to work them out by deductive reasoning.

From these first premises follow *secondary precepts* or *injunctions*. These are more detailed rules about the kinds of behaviour that conform to the three groups of ends. They can be deduced from the first premises and are less general in their application. From the first group of ends, which have to do with preserving our existence, we can derive secondary injunctions that, for example, forbid the taking of innocent human life. From the second group, that have to do with mating and parenting, we can derive rules about sex and family life, such as that extramarital sex and adultery are forbidden. From the third group, rules governing social life can be derived. For example, Thomas says that secondary injunctions about property, such as the rule that goods held in trust should be returned to their owner when required, follow from the premise that we should act according to reason. Although the first premises of the natural law are self-evident, the secondary injunctions are not, so there are rules required by the natural law that are not recognized by everyone. Thomas gives the example of theft. It is contrary to the natural law, but, at one time, according to Julius Caesar, it was not thought wrong by some German tribes.

Can the natural law ever change? Positive divine law (for example, the commands of God given in the Scriptures) and human law can and do *add* 'many things helpful for human living' to the natural law (p. 288). This is particularly important as Thomas does not think that the natural law alone can teach us everything we need to know about our moral obligations. It can show us 'the acts to which nature immediately inclines us' (p. 287), but there are other good acts that we can only learn about by a process of rational investigation. Human laws can develop the natural law by spelling out the conclusions that follow from its premises or specifying in more detail what the natural law requires in particular circumstances. Human law must be in accordance with the natural law, otherwise it is not really law and we are not bound to obey it.

Can anything be *subtracted* from the natural law? Thomas believes that the first premises are absolute – they apply to everybody and can never change. However, the secondary injunctions are not absolute in the same sense. As they are more specific, they do not apply in all situations and, of course, the more specific they become, the more situations will arise to which they do not apply. For example, as we have seen, Thomas thinks that the premise 'act according to reason' gives rise to the injunction 'goods held in trust ought to be returned', but there will be occasions when returning someone's goods would be *un*reasonable. Suppose a friend lends me his car keys and then has too much to drink. I would be wrong to give the keys back if he demands them. In this case, the secondary injunction that normally follows from the premise does not apply. Furthermore, Thomas thinks that the command of God can make a difference to secondary injunctions. He refers to examples from the Hebrew Bible where God appears to command things that are contrary to the natural law, such as Abraham's sacrifice of Isaac (Genesis 22.2), Hosea's relationship with 'a woman who has a lover and is an adulteress' (Hosea 3.1) and the plundering of the Egyptians by the Israelites (Exodus 12.35–6). Such acts would normally be examples of murder, adultery and theft, but they are not if God, who is the creator and owner of the world and all living things, commands them.

Though Thomas' examples might seem difficult and perplexing to modern readers, the main point is that there is some flexibility in his system. The most general moral principles that we learn from the natural law are absolute and unchangeable, but when we try to work out how the general principles apply in particular situations, the answer is bound to depend on the many factors that shape the situation.

4 Natural Law Since Thomas Aquinas[5]

According to Ian Fairweather and James McDonald, Thomas' doctrine of natural law became distorted and was misused in various ways by some strands of Catholic thought in the later Middle Ages and after. Thomas' distinction between primary and secondary precepts and his emphasis on self-determination were sometimes lost sight of. Natural law also became increasingly tied to the Magisterium (teaching authority) of the Church. The result, at times, was that quite specific rules and prohibitions were enforced by Church authority and were claimed to be universally and eternally valid.[6]

However, this was by no means the whole story. Natural law thinking has had a varied and creative history since the Middle Ages. Although it is mostly associated with Catholic thought, it entered Anglican moral theology through the work of Richard Hooker,[7] who was greatly influenced by Thomas. In the early modern period, natural law theory also gave rise to the beginnings of international law and the development of modern theories of rights. Some of these developments came from a group of highly influential Catholic philosophers, theologians and legal theorists in sixteenth-century Spain, including Francisco de Vitoria and Francisco Suárez.

One important effect of this thinking was seen in the work of Bartolomé de las Casas. He argued powerfully on natural law grounds against the forced conversion, enslavement and exploitation of native South Americans by Spanish colonial forces. As a result, he is still something of a hero to some Latin American liberation theologians (see Chapter 7).

Another important figure in international law was the Dutch Protestant Hugo Grotius. He attempted to use natural law thinking to overcome some of the religious divisions and conflicts of seventeenth-century Europe. He gave the first systematic account of how international conflict should be regulated and laid the foundations for the modern notion of individual rights. Ironically, given his own Christian faith, he is also credited with the secularization of natural law thinking, since he argued that the natural law would be obligatory for us even if there were no God. This move had the effect of cutting natural law theory loose from the theological framework in which it had been firmly located by earlier thinkers such as Thomas Aquinas and paved the way for later philosophers such as Thomas Hobbes to produce more openly secular versions.

The twentieth century saw a great revival of interest in the work of Thomas Aquinas. This has led, among other things, to a wide variety of natural law theorizing in Roman Catholicism and a vigorous argument within Catholic moral theology about the way in which Thomas' thinking should be understood and used. In official Church teaching, natural law arguments have been used to ground specific rules and precepts. One well-known example is the prohibition of artificial contraception on the grounds that sex is for procreation and contraception frustrates this God-given purpose. However, natural law arguments have also influenced a range of social teachings on matters such as workers' rights, political subsidiarity and international development.[8]

Among professional theologians, one school of Catholic thought, described as 'revisionist' or 'proportionalist', thinks about right and wrong in terms of what leads to the human good and human flourishing. In that respect, it takes its cue from Thomas and, like him, also holds that anyone who will use their reason rightly can gain moral understanding. We do not depend on divine revelation for what we need to know about the good. Revisionists, though, resist the idea that natural law generates universal, exceptionless moral rules. For example, even if artificial birth control is usually wrong, there might be circumstances in which it is justified.

A contrasting approach to natural law is associated with Germain Grisez, John Finnis and others. Finnis claims that there are certain basic goods or values that are self-evident – life, knowledge, marriage, aesthetic experience, friendship, practical reasonableness and religion.[9] From these basic goods we can deduce moral obligations, including some absolute rules and prohibitions.

As well as its role in official Church teaching and academic theology, natural law thinking continues to have a wider influence in international law and politics. For instance, the language of 'crimes against humanity', used in the Nuremberg trials after World War II and more recent genocide trials, has roots in natural law ideas. The notion of universal natural human rights also owes much to this way of thinking. However, these modern uses of natural law and natural rights language seem to have much more in common with Grotius than Thomas. (For more on rights in general and natural rights in particular, see the Appendix at the end of this chapter.)

5 The Case Studies Revisited

Homosexuality

Official Roman Catholic teaching on questions of sexual ethics, including homosexuality, has deep roots in natural law thought. The argument is that our sexual organs and sexual drives are naturally directed towards the goal of procreation, and that this is part of the order built into creation by God. As we saw earlier, this argument supports the prohibition of contraception in *Humanae Vitae*. Same-sex intercourse cannot possibly have procreation as a goal and, for this reason, it is contrary to the natural law.

This line of argument goes a long way back in the natural law tradition. Thomas followed earlier writers in describing homosexual acts as 'unnatural' because they 'run counter to the natural mode of intercourse between male and female'.[10] Recent Vatican documents echo this view, describing homosexual acts as 'intrinsically disordered'.[11] It should be stressed that this natural law argument does not require the view that procreation is the *only* proper purpose of sex, though at various times in history some Christian thinkers have come close to claiming this. It is perfectly possible to argue that sex is naturally ordered towards loving relationships *and* procreation and these two goals are both so important that sex excluding one or the other is 'intrinsically disordered'.

Critics sometimes reply that it is unnecessarily 'biologistic' to insist that procreation is the primary purpose, or an essential purpose, of sex. Sex can have many purposes, they argue, including pleasure and the expression of love as well as procreation; and it is not necessarily the case that procreation *has* to be one of the goals of each act or even of each relationship. Other critics question the natural law approach to sexual ethics more generally. They accuse natural law thinkers of simplistic attempts to read off divinely established laws from observations of nature. For example, Thomas thought (mistakenly) that there was no 'homosexual' behaviour in the animal world and concluded from this that homosexual acts were against the natural law. However, say his critics, concepts of what is 'natural' or 'unnatural' are socially constructed by humans. We observe the world, classify it and invest our classifications with meaning. So when Thomas concluded that the only kind of sex permitted by the natural law is between male and female for the purpose of procreation he was reading this conclusion *into* his observation of nature rather than finding it there.[12]

This may not be entirely fair to Thomas as his natural law theory is firmly set in a sophisticated theological framework and he is not doing anything as naive as reading moral prescriptions straight from the natural world. As Stephen Pope acknowledges, however, natural law thinking has sometimes assumed too easily that there is something fixed and universal called 'human nature', which can be the subject of timeless, exceptionless moral rules. He believes, though, that it is possible to develop a natural law theory that avoids such pitfalls.[13]

Another major source of Christian teaching about homosexuality is the biblical texts that appear to refer to it.[14] These texts have been influential on Catholic as well as Protestant teaching. The biblical writers do not seem to be highly preoccupied with homosexuality as only around half a dozen texts refer directly to it. Those texts, though, do seem to disapprove unequivocally of same-sex sexual acts.

First, there is the story of Sodom and Gomorrah (Genesis 18.16—19.29), in which the men of Sodom are punished for attempting to gang-rape Lot's angelic visitors. It is widely agreed that this story is irrelevant to the debate about homosexuality as, elsewhere in the Bible, Sodom is a byword for inhospitality and indifference to the needs of others, not sexual misconduct (Ezekiel 16.49, for example).

Next, two texts in Leviticus (18.22; 20.13) forbid men from '[lying] with a male as with a woman', which is described as 'an abomination'. Some writers argue that Leviticus uses the same language for regulations about diet and ritual purity. Christians have almost always disregarded the dietary laws, so it is inconsistent to insist that the prohibition of homosexuality must still be obeyed. Others argue that the laws governing sexual conduct *were* retained by the early Church (for example, at the Council of Jerusalem, Acts 15.20) and should remain binding on Christians.

In the New Testament, the Greek words *malakoi* and *arsenokoitai* appear in lists of 'wrongdoers' whose lives are contrary to the gospel and who 'will not inherit the kingdom of God' (1 Corinthians 6.9–11; 1 Timothy 1.10). The meaning of these words is not entirely clear, but they seem to refer to the partners in sexual intercourse between males.

The most influential text is Romans 1.18–32. (It is also the only biblical text to refer to female same-sex intercourse.) These verses obviously do not state a simple rule against homosexual acts. Instead, as Hays puts it, they function in the mode of the 'symbolic world'. Paul is attempting to show that humanity as a whole is sinful and 'fallen', that we have turned away from the true God and preferred idols. This rejection of God results in all kinds of disordered behaviour, including homosexual acts. Paul presents homosexual behaviour as a consequence and a symptom of humanity's alienation from God. It is a *result* of God's wrath, not the *cause* of it: he writes that 'God gave them up to degrading passions' (1.26). As he writes of people 'exchanging' natural for unnatural desires, some writers believe that this text must be referring to heterosexual people who perversely engage in same-sex intercourse contrary to their natural orientation. From this point of view, it is irrelevant to gay and lesbian people, who experience same-sex desire as natural. Others, including Hays, argue that Paul does not make this distinction. For one thing, the notion of sexual orientation is a modern one that probably would not have been understood in the ancient world. For another, Paul is offering a diagnosis of the condition of sinful humanity as a whole – the text does not operate at the level of individuals' stories and experiences.

Many writers set these texts in the wider context of biblical teaching about male–female *complementarity*. In the creation stories, God made humans male and female (Genesis 1.27) and when the man in the second creation story needed a companion, God created a woman, not another man. Neither a being identical to the man, nor one who is wholly different from him, would allow for true companionship. As Karl Barth puts it, 'What is sought is a being resembling man but different from him.'[15] Heterosexual marriage reflects this complementarity, as Jesus seems to suggest by quoting the creation stories in his own teaching on marriage (see Chapter 2). Barth thinks homosexual relationships reject this complementarity and are therefore 'sexual [unions] which [are] not and cannot be genuine'.[16] Others, though, question the importance of male–female complementarity. For example, they point to the close bonds of single-sex companionship that are also portrayed in the Scriptures, notably within Jesus' inner group of 12 disciples.

It is often said (for example, by Hays) that whenever the Bible mentions homosexuality, it disapproves of it, but others argue that some biblical texts at least hint at homosexual relationships in more approving ways. For example, the story of David and Jonathan depicts powerful, covenanted love between two men (1 Samuel 18.1–5). Again, in the story where Jesus heals a centurion's servant (Matthew 8.5–13; Luke 7.1–10), it is sometimes suggested that the 'servant' (*pais* in Greek) is in fact the centurion's male slave lover and that Jesus tacitly approves of this relationship.[17]

More generally, the Gentile crisis in the early Church is sometimes seen as a precedent for changing attitudes to homosexuality in the Church today. The first followers of Jesus had to go through a massive shift of attitudes in order to allow Gentiles to enter the Church without first converting to Judaism. Traces of this upheaval can be seen in many parts of the New Testament, particularly in the story of Peter and Cornelius (Acts 10.1—11.18) and the Council of Jerusalem (Acts 15.1–35). As it is presented in the New Testament, this was not an arbitrary decision by the early Church, but a considered response to the experience of God's Spirit at work among

Gentiles. Some would say that the Church today is called to make a similar imaginative leap in its attitude to Christians who are in same-sex relationships.

So far, I have discussed natural law arguments and biblically based arguments about homosexuality. However, in this, more than in most ethical debates, *experience* is appealed to as a source of authority. Many gay and lesbian people experience same-sex desire as a deeply rooted part of their identity, something that they did not choose, but that seems to be part of the way they are made. This is by no means a universal experience, however. Some (perhaps more often lesbians than gay men) believe their relationships to be consciously chosen, sometimes as a form of opposition to patriarchal marriage.

Some ethicists also point to the experience of committed gay or lesbian relationships. Such relationships, they say, can and do manifest the Christ-like qualities of self-giving love and faithfulness at least as powerfully as most heterosexual marriages. Just as the early Church responded to the experience of the Spirit among Gentile Christians, as I noted above, so the Church today might be called to respond in a similarly open way to the experience of the Spirit among gay and lesbian Christians. More negatively, the experience of being oppressed and marginalized by the mainstream Churches leads many lesbian and gay Christians to challenge established Christian views. Somewhat like liberationist and feminist theologians (see Chapters 7 and 8), they choose to read the Bible and interpret Christian tradition 'through the spectacles' of their own experience. This leads them to be highly critical of the Church's traditional negative view of homosexuality. It may also lead them to put forward the kinds of arguments about the Bible summarized above, playing down the texts condemning homosexual behaviour and arguing that, properly understood, the Bible challenges the Church to become far more accepting of same-sex unions.

It is time to return to the Civil Partnership Act. In relation to the question of same-sex relationships in general, a range of Christian views has been expressed by the Churches.[18] At one end of the spectrum is the view that such relationships are '*intrinsically disordered*' and can never be a morally or pastorally acceptable option. This is the view expressed, for example, in official Roman Catholic teaching. Then there is the view that same-sex unions *fall short of the ideal*, which is lifelong heterosexual marriage, but that they may be the best that some people can attain in an imperfect world and are certainly better than some of the alternatives, such as promiscuous and casual sex. Something like this view is found in the Church of England report, *Issues in Human Sexuality*. This report argues that committed homosexual relationships may be an acceptable pastoral option for lay people in the church, but not for clergy. A third view is that the mere fact that a relationship is homosexual is *morally irrelevant*, that both homosexual and heterosexual relationships are to be judged by the qualities they display. Good relationships, for example, might be characterized by faithfulness, stability and self-giving love; bad ones by exploitation or abuse. An early expression of this position in a Church document was the *Quaker Report on Sex*, published in Britain in 1963.

These different positions could be related in complex ways to questions about civil partnerships and church blessings of gay and lesbian unions. If homosexual relationships are always destructive of proper human flourishing, then presumably it would be pastorally as well as theologically irresponsible for churches to bless such relationships. The Church might also be required to oppose civil legislation allowing for same-sex partnerships, as Vatican documents argue. Presumably, though, there could be situations in which Churches, while refusing to bless or sanction same-sex unions, might nevertheless support civil legislation on the grounds that it would help protect gay and lesbian people from discrimination and financial hardship. A Church that believed homosexual unions fall short of the ideal, but can still be pastorally justified, might be more ready to support civil legislation. It might or might not believe that church blessings of those unions are pastorally appropriate. That decision would require the weighing up of many different considerations, some of which are in the background of the case study. Churches that took the third view, represented by the Quaker report, would presumably not object either to civil partnership laws or church blessings of same-sex partnerships.

Questions

- Which of the various positions outlined in this section do you find most persuasive and why?

- Return to your answers to the case study questions at the beginning of the chapter. How, if at all, would you change or add to them in the light of your reading in this chapter?

War[19]

In a classic study from 1960, the historian Roland Bainton classified Christian attitudes to war into three types: pacifist, just war and crusading.[20] The last of these can be fairly swiftly disposed of. It is the view that a military action can be a holy war, commanded by God and fought against God's enemies. Although there have been all too many examples of this attitude in Christian history – such as the medieval Crusades and the wars fought by New England Puritans against Native Americans – few serious Christian thinkers would now defend a crusading view of war.

Just War Theory

In one form or another, just war theory is the majority Christian view today. Its roots predate Christianity, with versions of it being found in the work of Greek philosophers such as Plato and Aristotle and in Roman legal codes. The Christian Church, which appears to have been largely pacifist at its beginnings (but see below), began taking a serious interest in just war theory in the fourth century. The conversion of the emperor Constantine in 312 was the culmination of a process by which Christians had moved from being a tiny, persecuted minority to having great political power and influence. In this new situation, Christian thinkers such as Ambrose of Milan and Augustine of Hippo drew on pre-Christian just war traditions in order to address moral questions about war and military service. Christian just war thought was developed and elaborated during the Middle Ages by canon (Church) lawyers such as Gratian and theologians such as Thomas Aquinas.[21] It was further developed in the early modern period by natural law theorists – Vitoria and Grotius, for example – in response to new challenges such as colonial expansion and the European religious wars of the sixteenth and seventeenth centuries.

For much of its history, just war theory has been set within a natural law framework – the natural law precept that I should defend both my own and others' lives could, under some circumstances, require a community to go to war. In this tradition, the term 'just war' is somewhat misleading. War, as it causes terrible destruction and suffering, is never a *good* thing – at best, it might be a tragic necessity to prevent a worse evil. 'Justifiable war' might be a better term than 'just'. From this point of view, just war theory is an attempt to limit the physical and moral damage of war: it provides rules for judging when it is right to go to war and sets limits on what may be done in war. These two sets of rules are often referred to as conditions for *jus ad bellum* (justice in going to war) and *jus in bello* (justice in [the conduct of] war). A standard list of just war conditions is given in the box.

Just War Conditions

Jus ad bellum

1 It must be waged by a lawful authority.
2 It must be for a just cause (to put right an undoubted wrong).
3 It must be a last resort – all peaceful means of resolving the conflict must have been exhausted.
4 The harm likely to be done by the war must be proportionate to the good that is aimed for.
5 It must be waged with a right intention.
6 There must be a reasonable hope of success (otherwise it is likely that great harm will be done for no benefit).
7 The war should contribute to a new state of peace.

Jus in bello

1 Non-combatants must not be directly attacked (the principle of *discrimination*).
2 The means used in fighting the war should be proportionate to the goals.

These criteria are still widely accepted by Christian thinkers and have been used to assess many recent conflicts. For example, during World War II, George Bell, the Bishop of Chichester, protested in the House of Lords against the bombing of German cities because it breached the principle of discrimination. More recently, Christian thinkers have criticized the policy of nuclear deterrence on the grounds that tactical nuclear weapons are neither proportionate nor discriminate.[22] Just war arguments have been used in debates about the NATO action in Kosovo in 1999 and, in 2003, the Bishop of Oxford argued against war in Iraq on just war grounds.[23] Some thinkers, however, argue that traditional just war theory no longer works as the criteria were developed in premodern times, usually to regulate conflicts between paid volunteer armies, using relatively low-tech military hardware, under conditions where combatants and non-combatants could be easily distinguished. The same criteria may simply not apply under conditions of modern warfare, particularly if the major threats to peace and security are no longer from aggression by nation states, but from civil wars (as in the Balkans and Rwanda) or international terrorism (as on September 11th and afterwards). Defenders of the theory reply that it is needed more than ever in the unstable conditions of the twenty-first century.[24]

Just war theory has often been criticized (for example, by Richard Hays) as a theory, developed independently of the New Testament, that cannot be justified by reference to it. One notable exception to this criticism (as Hays acknowledges) is the account given by Protestant theologian Paul Ramsey.[25] His starting point is the fundamental principle of love of neighbour, which is said by Jesus in the Gospels to be one of the two greatest commandments (Mark 12.28–34 and parallels). Ramsey argues that the shift from pacifism to just war theory in the early centuries of the Church was not a change of principles, but only (as it were) of moral tactics. When Christians were a powerless and marginalized group, love of neighbour prohibited them from retaliating for the violence done to them. When they came to hold political power, however, that brought with it the responsibility to defend their people. Ramsey's argument can be understood in this way. If I am attacked, my attacker is still my neighbour, and love of neighbour probably forbids me from injuring or killing that neighbour even in defence of my own life. (He does not absolutely rule out self-defence, but is highly suspicious of it as a motive for the use of force.) In contrast, if I see someone else being attacked, love of my neighbour who is under attack demands that I defend him or her and, if the only way to defend the victim's life is to use lethal force against the attacker, love requires me to do so. Now, if I am a political leader and my people arc under attack, love of my neighbours – the population of my country – could require me to use force to defend them.

Pacifism

Though the majority Christian tradition for most of the Church's history has almost certainly been some form of just war theory, there has been a strong and persistent 'minority report' in favour of pacifism. This 'minority report' is rooted firmly in the New Testament. Richard Hays argues persuasively that the consistent witness of the New Testament is that the followers of Jesus should not use violence, even in defence of justice.[26]

There are *rules* and *principles* forbidding violence, notably in the Sermon on the Mount, where Jesus tells his followers not to resist evildoers, to turn the other cheek when they are struck in the face, give more than is demanded of them and love their enemies (Matthew 5.38–48).

The supreme *paradigm* for Christians is Jesus Christ himself. According to Paul, God in Christ responds to human enmity not by retaliating, but by being on the receiving end of human violence. The followers of Jesus are to live according to this pattern, not repaying evil with evil, but overcoming evil with good (Romans 12.14–21). In the *symbolic world* of the New Testament, says Hays (alluding to Ephesians 6.10–17), 'the real struggle is not against flesh and blood, [and] the only weapons that the church wields are faith and the Word of God'. Hays argues that this powerful witness of the New Testament should 'trump' the Hebrew Bible texts that advocate violence and the majority Christian tradition of the just war.

In response to this New Testament witness, pacifism has re-emerged at many points in Christian history, notably in the Radical Reformation traditions of the sixteenth century. The Churches rooted in those traditions, such as Anabaptists, Mennonites and Quakers, are today among the most active Christian groups in promoting non-violent means of resolving conflicts. Some of the most powerful theological advocates of pacifism in recent years have either come from those traditions, such as John Howard Yoder, or been strongly influenced by them, such as Stanley Hauerwas.[27]

Hauerwas' pacifism is related to his ethic of virtue and character, which we explore further in Chapter 6. He argues that the Church is called to be a distinctive community, its character and way of life shaped by the story of Jesus Christ. Central to that story, and equally central to the identity of the Christian community, is an uncompromising commitment to non-violence. Hauerwas, Hays and others argue that, in order to be faithful to this Christian calling, Christians may well have to withdraw from positions of political power and influence, living instead as a counter-cultural community – a 'city built on a hill' (Matthew 5.14) – that practises the new way of life made possible by Jesus. Such a non-violent counter-cultural community will very likely suffer ridicule, marginalization and violence. However, this is the cost of Christian discipleship and the community's willingness to suffer these things without retaliating will be a powerful part of its witness.

Theological ethics in recent decades has seen something of a stand-off between just war theorists and pacifists. In the past few years, there have been attempts to bridge the divide. For example, Glen Stassen and others have produced an account of what they call 'just peacemaking'.[28] They argue that Christians, whether pacifists or just war theorists, should be more committed to developing strategies for peacemaking, and they propose a number of practical approaches. Such a commitment to peacemaking obviously goes with the grain of pacifism. The just war tradition may not always have shown such a commitment in the past – indeed, one of the common criticisms of just war theory is that it can easily become a way of giving a blessing to militarism and violence – but if just war theorists took seriously the 'last resort' criterion, they would be just as energetically committed to peacemaking as their pacifist colleagues.

Questions

- If the New Testament is, as Hays says, unequivocally pacifist in its witness, does this commit the Church to pacifism today or is Ramsey right to think that a different context calls for a different response?
- If there is a conflict between the New Testament and Christian tradition over the question of war, how should the conflict be settled?

- Return to your answers to the case study questions about the 'war on terror'. What, if anything, would you add or change in the light of this chapter?

Suggestions for Further Reading

Natural Law

Nigel Biggar and Rufus Black (eds), *The Revival of Natural Law: Philosophical, Theological and Ethical Responses to the Finnis-Grisez School*, Aldershot: Ashgate, 2000.

Stephen Buckle, 'Natural Law', in Peter Singer (ed.), *A Companion to Ethics*, Oxford: Blackwell, 1991, pp. 161–74.

Stephen J. Pope, 'Natural Law and Christian Ethics', in Robin Gill (ed.), *The Cambridge Companion to Christian Ethics*, Cambridge: Cambridge University Press, 2001, pp. 77–95.

Homosexuality

There are few topics more written about, and talked about, in contemporary Christian ethics. The books edited by Bradshaw and Siker are helpful guides to the debate as they include contributions from both sides of the question. The book by Jordan offers a recent and original approach to a variety of issues in sexual ethics.

Timothy Bradshaw (ed.), *The Way Forward?: Christian Voices on Homosexuality and the Church*, 2nd edn, London: SCM Press, 2003.

Mark D. Jordan, *The Ethics of Sex*, Oxford: Blackwell, 2001.

Jeffrey S. Siker (ed.), *Homosexuality in the Church: Both Sides of the Debate*, Louisville, KY: Westminster John Knox, 1994.

War

Again, there is a big body of literature on this topic. The following sources set out the various positions particularly clearly.

R. John Elford, 'Christianity and War', in Gill, *The Cambridge Companion to Christian Ethics*, pp. 171–82.

Robin Gill, 'The Arms Trade and Christian Ethics', in Gill, *The Cambridge Companion to Christian Ethics*, pp. 183–94.

Richard B. Hays, *The Moral Vision of the New Testament*, Edinburgh: T & T Clark, 1997, Chapter 14.

Appendix: Rights

Rights are often defined as *justified claims* that entitle one individual or group to require certain kinds of behaviour from others. Rights could be *negative* – for example, a right not to be tortured – or *positive* – for example, a right to basic healthcare. They correspond in some way to *duties* (see Chapter 4).

For negative rights, this is fairly simple. If I have a right not to be tortured, then anyone who might be in a position to torture me has a duty not to do so. For positive rights, though, it is more complicated. Even if I have a right to basic healthcare, it might not be clear who has a corresponding duty to provide me with that care. For example, there might be nobody who has the resources (skill, money, time and so on) to provide the basic care to which I am entitled. There are ways round these difficulties, but they illustrate that the relationship between rights and duties is not entirely straightforward.

What is the *basis* for rights? Many theories have been suggested to justify the notion of rights. According to some accounts, rights only exist when they are granted by a political authority (such as a monarch) to that authority's subjects. Most theories, however, hold that rights are prior to political authority and exist whether or not that authority acknowledges them. If I have a right not to be tortured, the government of my country may deny the existence of that right and order the police to torture me, but the right still exists and those responsible for torturing me are doing wrong, whether they acknowledge it or not.

This claim may be justified in various ways. It might be justified *theologically*, on the grounds that all humans have been endowed with certain inalienable rights by God, their creator. Alternatively, it might be justified by a theory of *natural rights*, which says that humans, simply by virtue of their human nature, have certain inviolable rights. The first thinker to set this out systematically was Hugo Grotius, whom we encountered in section 4 of this chapter. He argued that humans are born free and equal, with the right to exercise control over property and the use of force, and governments and legal systems are devices to ensure that these rights are honoured. As we saw in section 4, Grotius took the decisive step of arguing that the natural law and natural rights could be known by human reason independently of belief in God. Theories rooted in his work, therefore, are decisively different from the natural law theory of Thomas Aquinas, which is inseparable from belief in God as creator and lawgiver. The notion of universal, inviolable human rights – now enshrined in many international treaties, declarations and legal frameworks – owes much to the kind of natural rights theory that stems from Grotius.

Rights can also be justified by *social contract* theories, which propose that, in order to create and maintain peaceful and stable societies, humans must enter, explicitly or implicitly, into some sort of agreement about the terms on which they will live together. This is likely to involve accepting some limits to individual freedom (I am not free to take my neighbour's car without his permission when I need transport to work) and some obligations to one another.

Thomas Hobbes was one early social contract theorist. One very influential recent social contract theory is John Rawls' theory of 'justice as fairness'. In order to work out what a just society would look like, Rawls invites us to imagine ourselves behind a 'veil of ignorance', where we do not know our own race, sex, class, religion, natural abilities and so on. If we now try to work out what social arrangements would best enable us to pursue our aims and interests, whatever our race, sex, class and so on turned out to be, this should yield a set of social arrangements that are fair to everyone of any race, sex, class and so on. Rawls argues that, in these circumstances, we would choose a system in which '[a]ll social primary goods – liberty and opportunity, income and wealth, and the bases of self-respect – are to be distributed equally unless an unequal distribution of these goods is to the advantage of the least favored'.[29]

Rights talk in general, as well as particular theories such as Rawls', has been criticized on a number of grounds. One important criticism, from the philosopher Alasdair MacIntyre and others, is that the modern concept of rights is part of the failed 'Enlightenment project', which is the attempt to base ethics solely on human reason in isolation from any tradition.[30] We return to MacIntyre's critique of the Enlightenment project in Chapter 6.

4

Duty, Consequences and Christian Ethics

1 Case Study

Read the following case study and make brief notes in answer to the questions. As in previous chapters, you will be invited to refer back to your answers at the end of the chapter.

Assisted Dying for the Terminally Ill?[1]

In March 2004, the Assisted Dying for the Terminally Ill Bill was given a second reading in the House of Lords of the UK Parliament. It was put before the House of Lords by the cross-bench peer Lord Joffe, a well-known retired human rights lawyer. Moving the second reading, Lord Joffe said, 'The Bill enables a competent adult, who is suffering unbearably as a result of a terminal illness, to receive medical help to die, at his own considered and persistent request.' The Bill, he said, was 'substantially the same' as an earlier Bill that he had introduced, the Patient (Assisted Dying) Bill. However, three changes had been made in response to concerns that had been expressed about the earlier Bill. First, the new Bill only applied to terminally ill patients. Second, it only allowed the physician to supply the patient with the means to end his or her life, unless the patient was physically unable to do so, in which case the doctor was permitted actively to end the patient's life. Third, a palliative care specialist would have to discuss the option of palliative care with the patient before a request for assistance in dying could be agreed to.

In the background to Lord Joffe's Bill were cases such as that of Diane Pretty, who suffered from motor neurone disease and wanted her husband to be legally permitted to help her to die. She took her case to the European Court of Human Rights, which ruled against her in May 2002. She died shortly afterwards.

It is claimed that there has been a shift in public opinion in favour of euthanasia and assisted suicide as a result of the Diane Pretty case. Some surveys suggest that as many as 80 per cent of the public support assisted dying, though these survey results have been contested. There appears to be less enthusiasm among the health professions with, for example, both the Royal College of Physicians and Royal College of Nursing opposing euthanasia and assisted suicide. There are claims that significant numbers of professionals privately favour life-ending interventions and many have helped patients to die, but the accuracy of these claims is hard to gauge.

Not surprisingly, the Joffe Bill was strongly supported by the Voluntary Euthanasia Society. Commenting on the case of Brian Blackburn – who was given a suspended sentence for killing his terminally ill wife at her request – the VES argued that the Bill was needed to prevent traumatic police investigations and trials in such cases. However, the Church of England and Roman Catholic bishops opposed the Bill in a joint submission to the Lords Select Committee that was set up to examine it. They argued that Lord Joffe's proposals were not needed to ensure proper care for terminally ill people and vulnerable people would be put at risk if the Bill became law. They appealed to the principle of 'respect for human life at all its stages' and argued that this would be undermined by a change in the law on euthanasia and assisted suicide.

Questions

- Why might Christians adopt a principle of 'respect for human life at all its stages'?
- Does this principle imply that it is always wrong to take a human life?

- Do you think there are things that it would always be wrong to do, however much good would result? If so, say why and give one or two examples. If not, why not?

You may wish to write down a few sentences in answer to each of these questions as you will be invited to return to them at the end of the chapter.

2 Absolute Duties[2]

In the jargon of moral philosophy, someone who believed that euthanasia is always and absolutely wrong would be some kind of *deontologist*. The words 'deontologist', 'deontology' and so on are derived from the Greek *deon*, 'duty'. Thus, deontological theories are those that say there are absolute moral *duties* I simply must obey. Another way of putting this is to say, as some philosophers do, that an ethical theory must give an account of two different moral concepts; the *right* and the *good*, and their relationship to one another. Whereas consequentialist theories (see section 5 below) give priority to the good, deontological theories give priority to the *right*, so the rightness or wrongness of an action does not depend on how much good it brings about. An action can be wrong, even if it does a great deal of good or averts a great deal of harm, because it violates a moral duty. A deontologist might say, for example, that it would be wrong to kidnap a young child and deliberately endanger her life, even if that was the only way to force her terrorist father to reveal the details of his plot to cause a massive explosion in a busy city centre.[3] A favourite deontological slogan sums this up neatly: 'Let justice be done, though the heavens fall.'

According to deontologists, then, I ought to act according to my duty. Duties, though, can come in different shapes or sizes. I can have duties to myself or others. Kant, whom we shall meet in the next section, thought suicide wrong because it conflicts with a person's duty to him- or herself. I can have duties either to do something ('Honour your father and mother') or not to do something ('Do not murder'). I can have duties that clearly prescribe my actions or those that leave me with a lot of working out to do. For example, if I pull the trigger on someone (in the absence of any of the circumstances that could perhaps justify killing, such as self-defence or military combat), it is fairly clear that I have violated the duty not to murder. However, it may be far less clear whether a particular course of action would or would not violate the duty to honour my parents. Duties can also come, as it were, in different- sized packages. In some theories, duties are concerned with individual *acts*. So, if I meet a homeless person in the street, it could turn out to be my duty to give him my last ten pound note, but I cannot generalize this into a rule that we always ought to give money to homeless people whom we meet (or into any other general rule, however carefully formulated). In other theories, duties are expressed as *rules*. These could be quite specific, such as 'do not murder', or very general, such as 'love your neighbour'.

One difficulty with the notion of absolute duties is that they may conflict with one another, so there may be times when I cannot do one without violating another. Suppose – to borrow a famous example – I have a duty to care for my children, but also a duty not to steal. I could find myself in a situation where the only way to prevent my children from starving is to steal. One way to get round this difficulty is to be careful about drawing the boundaries of different duties. Some philosophers might argue, for instance, that my duty to care for my children does not extend to stealing for them. Another way is to say there are plenty of things that *can* be duties, but not all of them will *actually* turn out to be my duty in a particular situation. When I find myself faced with choosing between stealing and watching my children starve, I may come to the conclusion that I do not in fact have a duty to avoid stealing in this situation. This is roughly what the twentieth-century philosopher W. D. Ross articulated in his theory of prima facie duties. A prima facie duty is something that matters morally – for example, not stealing – but may or may not turn out to be binding on me in a particular situation.[4] A third way of coping with the problem of conflicts of duty is to hold that absolute duties come only in the form of very general principles, such as 'love your neighbour'. All of these proposed solutions have problems of their own, though of course they may not turn out to be insoluble.

3 Kant's Theory of Ethics[5]

Probably the most famous deontological theory of modern times is the one developed by the German philosopher Immanuel Kant (1724–1804). Kant's writing is difficult, sometimes obscure, but has been enormously influential. He wrote many works on ethics, but his basic moral theory is set out in his *Groundwork of the Metaphysic of Morals*.[6] Some of the main features of his theory are as follows.

1. If I want to know what I ought to do, asking a question such as 'What does God command?' will not help me. Kant holds this view at least in part because he believes that we cannot have certain knowledge about any transcendent reality beyond our experience of the natural world. Therefore we cannot know *for certain* whether or not God exists or what God is like: in his *Critique of Pure Reason*, Kant argues that the traditional proofs of the existence of God fail.[7] So we cannot gain any sure knowledge of right and wrong by trying to base it on the will or law of God. (Kant does believe that our experience of the moral law gives an argument for the existence of God, but belief in God's existence is a consequence, not the foundation, of his system of ethics.)

2. Nor will thinking about the consequences of my actions help me. This is, roughly speaking, because actions and their consequences have to do with the physical realm of cause and effect – what Kant calls the *phenomenal* realm – but knowledge of right and wrong belongs to the realm of reason – the *noumenal*, in Kant's language. This is not to say that morality has nothing to do with the physical world of cause and effect – moral reasoning will, after all, give rise to action in the world – but we cannot learn what we ought to do from our experience of the physical world. The best that such experience can do is teach me what I ought to do *if* I wish to achieve certain aims (*if* I want to pass my exams, *then* I ought to revise). Kant calls this kind of 'ought' a *hypothetical imperative*. Experience cannot teach me whether these are things that I *should* be aiming for. To answer that kind of question, I need a different kind of 'ought': not the sort that says, 'If you want to achieve A, then you ought to do X', but the sort that simply says, 'You ought to do Y.' This second, unconditional kind of 'ought' Kant calls a *categorical imperative*. In

fact, it would be more accurate to talk about '*the* categorical imperative' as Kant believes that there is only one – although, as we shall see, it can be stated in several different forms.

3. Kant's starting point in the *Groundwork* is that the only thing we can call 'good' without any qualification or exception is a *good will*. Plenty of other things may be good in some circumstances and may be useful in the service of good, but the same things, if they are not under the control of a good will, may be thoroughly bad. For example, Kant says that self-control may often be a very good thing, but a scoundrel who possesses self-control will not only be more dangerous but also seem more 'abominable' to us than he would without it. In human life, a good will manifests itself by acting according to duty.

4. If I want to know whether or not an action accords with duty, I must ask about the *maxim* of that action. The *maxim* is the principle on which my action is based. For example, suppose I find myself short of money and borrow some from a friend. I promise that I will repay the loan, though privately I have no intention of doing so. The maxim of this action, according to Kant, would be 'Whenever I believe myself short of money, I will borrow money and promise to pay it back, though I know that this will never be done.'[8]

5. Kant says that I act in accordance with duty if the maxim of my action conforms to the categorical imperative. As we have seen, he thinks that there is only one categorical imperative, but it can be stated in a number of different forms. These include the following:[9]

- '*Act only on that maxim through which you can at the same time will that it should become a universal law*'. This is Kant's first, and most basic, formulation. He illustrates it with the example I have just given, of obtaining a loan by making a false promise. If everyone adopted the same maxim, nobody would believe promises of this kind any more. Such a maxim contradicts itself. It is important to underline that Kant does not object to this maxim because it would result in harmful consequences – that may or may not be the case. His objection is, rather, that, in acting on such a maxim, I act in a fundamentally self-contradictory way, simultaneously using and undermining the concept of a promise.

- *'Act in such a way that you always treat humanity, whether in your own person or in the person of any other, never simply as a means, but always at the same time as an end'.* This formula has been highly influential and is often used as a slogan without much reference to its context in Kant's thought. It demands *respect for persons* – that is, for rational agents like ourselves. We must never use persons merely as means to our ends or tools for our projects. To do so would impair their own capacity to make rational moral decisions. For example, if I deceive my friend into lending me money, she cannot share my end or goal. As Onora O'Neill points out, it is not just that she does not consent to my action, but my act of deceiving her makes it *impossible* for her either to consent or dissent. Her status as a rational agent is undermined.[10]

- *'Every rational being must so act as if he were through his maxims a law-making member in the universal kingdom of ends'.* This formula introduces two important notions – *autonomy* and the *kingdom of ends*. 'Autonomy' means making my own laws. As we have seen, Kant does not think that we ought to base our moral decisions on rules that are 'external' to our own reason. If I want to know why I ought not to make false promises, it will not do to say either 'Because God's law forbids it' or 'Because something bad will happen if I do'. Kant calls 'external' reasons like these *heteronomous*. Autonomous morality, by contrast, means that I refuse to make false promises because my reason shows me that false promising is immoral (a maxim of false promising could not be universalized and it would involve treating others merely as means, not as ends in themselves). However, basing my morality on my own reason does not mean that I will be completely individualistic and unconcerned about others' actions. As the moral law is universally valid, a community of autonomous persons who thought and acted rationally would always treat one another as ends in themselves and reach the same conclusions about the maxims that should guide their actions. Such a rationally ordered community of autonomous persons is what Kant means by a 'kingdom of ends'.

Kant believes that these formulations – and the others that he states – are equivalent to one another. It has to be said that not all of his readers have been able to see the connections between them!

Kant's moral theory, as I have said, has been highly influential. It has also been criticized in various ways. First, it is accused of being only a *formal theory* that tells us little or nothing about the content of moral obligation. It may tell us what kind of thing moral reasoning is, but it is not much help if we are trying to work out how we ought to live our lives. This description certainly fits the *Groundwork*, but Kant does not pretend that the *Groundwork* is a full account of ethics. It is what it says – an attempt to lay the foundation of an ethic by giving a description of what it means to act morally. In some of his other ethical writings, Kant discusses the content of morality in considerable detail.

Second, Kant is sometimes accused of *rigorism*, that his system gives rise to rules that are rigid, insensitive and sometimes absurd – we must do justice even if the result is that the heavens do fall. For example, Kant notoriously thought that it would be wrong to tell a lie even in order to prevent a homicidal maniac from finding and killing his victim. It may be, of course, that he was simply mistaken in thinking that his system committed him to such conclusions.

Third, the language of the kingdom of ends leads some of Kant's readers to think that he is hopelessly over-optimistic about the moral capabilities of human beings and cannot give a convincing account of wrongdoing and evil. However, Kant is no naive optimist. While there may be problems with his account of wrongdoing, he can certainly give an account of it. One of his later works, *Religion Within the Limits of Reason Alone*, contains an account of human wickedness that sounds strikingly pessimistic.[11]

A more general criticism is that Kant's whole project – to base morality on autonomous human reason alone – is fundamentally flawed. One version of this criticism is made by Alasdair MacIntyre and other 'virtue ethicists' and we encounter it again in Chapter 6.

4 Christian Deontology

Kant's thought has influenced Christian thinkers in complex ways. For example, even the work of Karl Barth, who was highly critical of Kant and reacted against his thought in quite fundamental ways, still shows many traces of his influence. However, in other Christian thinkers, the debt to Kant is more obvious. Many Christian ethicists hold that ethics includes absolute duties – laws that must never be transgressed – and Kantian themes, such as respect for persons and the universalizability of moral principles, have proved attractive to Christian writers.

One example is Paul Ramsey, the American Protestant ethicist whom we met in the discussion of just war theory in Chapter 3. His writing is rich, complex and – again – difficult, so we should be careful to avoid oversimplification. However, it is probably fair to say that Ramsey is a good example of a Christian deontologist. By contrast with Kant, who wishes to *avoid* basing his ethic on claims about God, Ramsey's ethic is explicitly theological. It is based on the conviction that God has made a *covenant* – a relationship of love and faithfulness – with humankind. The love and faithfulness that God shows to humans are to be the pattern for our relationships with one another. Accordingly, Ramsey places the command to love your neighbour at the heart of Christian ethics and comments that, in this sense, 'Christian ethics is a deontological ethic.'[12]

Unlike Joseph Fletcher, whom we shall meet at the end of this chapter, and who also bases his ethic on love of neighbour, Ramsey believes that this generates absolute moral principles and rules. In other words, Christian ethics does include principles and rules that may never be broken and are always binding. For example, in his best-known book on medical ethics, entitled *The Patient as Person* – an interesting echo of the Kantian language of respect for persons – he argues that our response to God's covenant love requires 'canons of loyalty' or moral principles that express our faithfulness to one another. In medicine, one of the most important 'canons of loyalty' is the requirement that the patient must give his or her *informed consent* to medical treatment or research. There are situations where the consent requirement cannot apply. For example, if children who are too young to give informed consent need medical treatment, their parents or guardians must give it on their behalf. However, this 'proxy consent' is strictly limited to treatment that the child needs. For Ramsey, one implication of the consent requirement is that children must not be used as subjects of clinical research that does not directly benefit them. This is a rule that must never be broken, however greatly the research might benefit others in the future. To use Kantian language, such research would use children merely as means to an end, not as ends in themselves. Unlike Kant, however, Ramsey grounds this rule in specifically Christian convictions about God and the way God acts towards humankind.

5 Consequentialist Theories

Consequentialist theories, as the name implies, say that actions should be judged according to their consequences. In section 2 above, I contrasted deontological and consequentialist theories and suggested that they differ in their accounts of the relationship between the *right* and the *good*. Deontological theories give priority to the right, so, as we saw in section 2, a deontologist would say that an action could be wrong even if it resulted in great good. Consequentialists, in contrast, give priority to the good and define the right in terms of the good. The right action, according to a consequentialist, is the one that will bring about the greatest good (however 'good' is understood – on this consequentialists vary widely, as we shall see). This may mean, in extreme circumstances, that it is right to do something very nasty if that is the only way to prevent a much greater harm. To return to the example I used in section 2, a consequentialist would say that it could conceivably, under some circumstances, be right to kidnap a child and endanger her life in order to prevent a terrorist outrage. Earlier I quoted the deontological slogan 'Let justice be done, though the heavens fall'; probably the best-known consequentialist slogan is 'The end justifies the means'.

Consequentialist theories are also sometimes described as *teleological*, or goal-directed, from the Greek word *telos*, meaning 'end' or 'goal'. This is a somewhat confusing and probably unhelpful description, as the word 'teleological' used in this sense could describe a much wider range of theories than consequentialism and so would end up lumping very different approaches together under one heading. For example, at least some versions of virtue theory (see Chapter 6) are concerned with the *telos* – the end or purpose – of human life, but, if they are 'teleological', it is in a very different sense from a theory such as utilitarianism and it does not seem very illuminating to use the same word to describe both.

There are many different consequentialist theories of ethics, but the best known and probably the most influential are the different varieties of *utilitarianism*. In order to get an idea of how consequentialist theories work, we shall look in a little more detail at utilitarianism in its various forms.

6 Utilitarianism

Classical Utilitarianism

The theory of utilitarianism was first set out systematically by the philosopher and social reformer Jeremy Bentham in his *An Introduction to the Principles of Morals and Legislation*, first published in 1789.[13] As the title suggests, Bentham was at least as interested in legal and political theory as ethics and wanted to set both ethics and law on a sound, rational footing.

One of his aims was to make the case for the humanitarian reform of the criminal justice system. The *Introduction to the Principles* was intended to be the foundation for a comprehensive new penal code, drawn up on rational principles, which would do away with what he saw as the anomalies and excesses of English law in the eighteenth century. He never completed this project, but the theory of punishment contained in the *Introduction* has been influential in legal theory as well as ethics since Bentham's time.

Bentham's reforming project depended on building a system of morality and law on rational, quasi-scientific lines, starting from self-evident first principles and proceeding by means of clear, logical reasoning without any mystifying appeals to the will of God, tradition or other sources of received wisdom. This approach to ethics is a classic example of what Alasdair MacIntyre has called the 'Enlightenment project' in ethics (MacIntyre's critique of the Enlightenment project is explored in Chapter 6). It could be seen as an attempt to apply to other areas of human life and thought the approach that had been so spectacularly successful in the physical sciences since the beginning of the seventeenth century.

Accordingly, Bentham begins his argument with an empirical observation – that is, a statement about what is the case, based on experience and observation: 'Nature has placed mankind under the governance of two sovereign masters, *pain* and *pleasure*.'[14] In other words, we all naturally try to maximize our *happiness*, which Bentham defines simply as pleasure and the absence of pain. On the basis of this observation, Bentham proposes the moral principle that we ought to act so as to maximize happiness – others' as well as our own. When we have a decision to make, we should choose whatever course of action will bring about the *greatest happiness of the greatest number* of those affected by our action. Bentham calls this the 'principle of utility' or the 'greatest happiness' principle. (Bentham did not invent either the term 'the principle of utility' or the 'greatest happiness' formula, but he was the first to deploy both in a fully worked-out system of ethics.) Of course, in order to know which actions will maximize happiness, we need to be able to measure it. Bentham offers a 'hedonic calculus' to enable us to do so. A pleasure can be quantified according to seven measures, which are its:[15]

- intensity
- duration
- certainty or uncertainty
- 'propinquity' (nearness) or remoteness
- fecundity – the likelihood of its being followed by other similar sensations
- purity – the likelihood of its *not* being followed by opposite – painful – sensations
- extent – the number of people affected by it.

Bentham's account runs into a number of fairly obvious difficulties, some of which were pointed out early on by his critics. One has to do with the justification of his principle of utility. He says that, like the first principle of any argument, it cannot be proved, nor does it have to be. He also claims that no one can consistently deny it and everyone makes use of it at least some of the time. However, his reason for proposing the greatest happiness of the greatest number as the fundamental moral principle of action seems to be his empirical claim that happiness is in fact our fundamental motivation. This has led some commentators to accuse him of committing the 'naturalistic fallacy' – drawing a conclusion about what *ought* to be the case from a premise about what *is* the case. (The term 'naturalistic fallacy' was invented early in the twentieth century by G. E. Moore, but, before Bentham was born, David Hume had already questioned the validity of moving from 'is' to 'ought' in moral argument.[16] The naturalistic fallacy is discussed further in Chapter 5.)

Another problem for Bentham's theory is that it seems to assume that pleasure is a kind of universal moral currency in which any kind of human good or goal can be expressed. Bentham's early critics worried that this was a low, ignoble view of human motivation. It may also be misleadingly simplistic. The assumption that all pleasures are different instances of the same thing seems problematic. It is not obvious that all the countless different pleasures that humans experience – from eating a good meal to falling in love, from watching your children grow up and flourish to contemplating a great work of art – can be measured on the same moral scale. The variety and diversity of human goods may make this impossible.

One of the things that makes Bentham's system seem attractive is its simplicity, but it could be a false simplicity that fails to do justice to the complexity and subtlety of human motivation and experience. In his 1861 book *Utilitarianism*, John Stuart Mill (who was Bentham's pupil, but later reacted against some aspects of his thought) develops and refines the theory and attempts to deal with some of the difficulties of Bentham's version.[17] To the objection that utilitarianism reduces all human ends to the base desire for pleasure, he responds by acknowledging that there are different kinds of pleasure and some are more intrinsically valuable than others. The more valuable pleasures are those that employ the 'higher faculties' of human beings. Even a little of the higher pleasures is worth more than a great quantity of the lower and, to know which are the most valuable, we should ask those who have experienced the different kinds of pleasure. Mill says:

> It is better to be a human being dissatisfied than a pig satisfied; better to be Socrates dissatisfied than a fool satisfied. And if the fool, or the pig, are of a different opinion, it is because they only know their own side of the question. The other party to the comparison knows both sides. (p. 10)

Note that Mill expresses his own thought rather carelessly here when he compares the experience of two human individuals, 'Socrates' and 'the fool'. He makes it clear elsewhere that we can only be confident in counting one pleasure higher than another if that is the judgement of the overwhelming majority of people who have experienced both.

This account of happiness is richer and more plausible than Bentham's. It also, of course, makes the latter's 'hedonic calculus' much more complicated and perhaps completely unworkable.

Armed with this account of happiness, Mill also attempts to address the problem of justifying the 'greatest happiness' principle (or the principle of utility, as he also calls it). Like Bentham, he acknowledges it is impossible to prove that we ought to promote happiness. He simply observes that 'people do actually desire it' and says this demonstrates effectively enough 'that each person's happiness is a good to that person, and the general happiness, there-fore, a good to the aggregate of all persons' (p. 36). He also claims that hap-piness (understood in the rich and diverse way he has earlier argued for) is the ultimate end people desire – everything else they desire, such as virtue, is desirable either because it is a form of happiness or because it is a means to happiness. Therefore, the 'greatest happiness' principle can be accepted as the fundamental principle of morality because it is in line with the ultimate end towards which humans direct their lives. As Mill's understanding of happiness is more complex and richly textured than Bentham's, he can claim this more plausibly than Bentham could, though Mill's account still seems to involve claims about human nature that not everyone finds convincing.

Contemporary Utilitarianism

There are many different versions of utilitarianism on offer in contemporary literature, some of which have been developed in an attempt to address some of the problems of earlier versions. First, there are different views as to the standard by which actions should be judged. Classical utilitarianism, as we have seen, took *happiness* as its ultimate standard – we should act so as to maximize the happiness of those affected by our actions. However, even the richer account of happiness offered by Mill seems to some utilitarians to take too narrow a view of the human good. Some therefore argue for *preference-*

utilitarianism – that is, we should act so that the preferences of all concerned are satisfied as far as possible. This can take account of a wider range of motivations, including charity, selfless devotion to a good cause and even laying down one's life to save others. Some critics still worry, though, that it has a rather consumerist flavour: the good consists in satisfying whatever preferences people happen to have, and the theory has nothing to say about the preferences people *should* have – what it is *good* for us to prefer. Others, therefore, argue instead for *welfare-utilitarianism*, which proposes that we should act so as to satisfy people's (long-term) interests or welfare, not just their (possibly short-term) preferences.[18]

There is also a difference of opinion about the shape and size that utilitarian judgements should come in. The simplest version is *act-utilitarianism* – whenever I have a decision to make, the right course of action is the one that will maximize happiness (or welfare or preference-satisfaction). This has met with various objections. One is that it might require us to do deeply repugnant things if they were the way to maximize happiness. Thus, the end could justify (and indeed require) some thoroughly nasty means, as in the example of the terrorist and his daughter that I mentioned in section 2. Act-utilitarians concede that repugnant acts could in principle be required, but only in such extreme circumstances that the alternative is even more unpalatable. Another objection to act-utilitarianism is that it is impracticable. It seems to require us to calculate the consequences of all our options before we make any decision, but life is too short to do this and, anyway, some of the relevant consequences may be literally impossible to foresee. Some theorists therefore prefer *rule-utilitarianism*, which says that when I have a decision to make, I should act on the rule that, if everyone obeyed it, would maximize happiness (or welfare or preference satisfaction). This is obviously more feasible than calculating the consequences in advance of every decision as we can work out and learn the rules in advance and, anyway, many of them will probably turn out to be well-known pieces of moral wisdom, such as the Ten Commandments. It also seems to deal with the problem of repugnant conclusions. For example, even if kidnapping and endangering the life of a child would maximize utility in one isolated case, it seems pretty clear that the rule 'Never kidnap children' would maximize utility overall, if everyone obeyed it. However, rule-utilitarianism may not in fact get us out of this bind. If we make the rules general enough to avoid the repugnant cases, they will become the sort of harshly inflexible rules that can give repugnant results of their own, as we saw when discussing Kant's ethics in section 3. If, on the other hand, we make them specific enough to deal flexibly with the hard cases, they will end up commanding the same repugnant actions as act-utilitarianism.

7 Christians and Consequentialism

Many Christians have been suspicious of consequentialism in general and utilitarianism in particular. There are many grounds for this suspicion. One is that Christian ethics seems to have a stake in the existence of absolute laws and commands – do not murder, do not steal and so on. (As we saw in Chapter 2, there is a great deal more to biblical ethics than the Ten Commandments and the Sermon on the Mount, but, nonetheless, the moral content of the Bible does seem to *include* absolute rules and commands.) Consequentialist theories would seem to call such rules into question: it might generally be wrong to murder, but there could be situations in which consequentialism would require it.

Another difficulty for Christians is that some consequentialist theories – certainly classical utilitarianism – deliberately give an account of moral decision making that is independent of any religious or theological frame of reference. The criteria for right action are defined in purely this-worldly terms – maximizing happiness, welfare or the satisfaction of preferences, for example. Many Christian thinkers find this odd, to say the least.

A related difficulty is that theories such as utilitarianism seem to operate with a fairly restricted notion of human nature and the good. In Mill's version of utilitarianism, for instance, the ultimate end for human beings is happiness, understood in this-worldly terms. Contrast this with the view of Thomas Aquinas. In his system, human beings do indeed have this-worldly ends (existence, procreation and living according to our rational nature), but our *ultimate end* is eternal life with God.[19] Furthermore, the notion that human life has certain proper ends, both in this world and beyond, would lead many Christians to think that not all preferences, nor all kinds of happiness, should be given equal weight. Utilitarian theories tend to call for the maximization of happiness or the satisfaction of preferences without expressing an opinion about what *should* make us happy or what we *ought* to prefer. By contrast, Christians influenced by Thomas, for example, might want to ask what preferences we ought to have or what kinds of happiness might contribute to a fully human life as God intends it to be.

Both Bentham and Mill argued that utilitarian theory is compatible with Christianity. A loving God, they said, presumably desires the happiness of his creatures, so, if we want to know what actions will be in line with God's will, the principle of utility offers us the surest way of finding out. It is doubtful that these arguments should be taken at face value as both Bentham and Mill were hostile to established religious traditions. However, some Christians have embraced various forms of consequentialism, including utilitarianism. For example, around the same time as Bentham, Archdeacon William Paley (better known for his *Natural Theology*, which proposes a famous version of the 'design argument' for the existence of God) argued for a form of utilitarianism.

In the nineteenth and twentieth centuries, various Christian thinkers have argued that utilitarianism is, in effect, a philosophical version of the Christian command to love your neighbour as yourself. Most famously, in the 1960s, American Anglican Joseph Fletcher put forward a theory of 'situation ethics', which is essentially a version of act-utilitarianism.[20] Fletcher wants to get away from 'legalism' – by which he means any system that has rigid, absolute rules – without falling into the opposite trap of 'antinomianism', which is complete moral lawlessness. He seeks a middle way in which the only absolute is the command to love your neighbour as yourself. While laws and moral traditions might guide us, we cannot know for certain in advance what love will require of us in a particular situation. As Fletcher puts it, 'Love's decisions are made situationally, not prescriptively.'[21] Now, loving your neighbour means seeking his or her good, so, in order to discover what love requires in our situation, we must work out which course of action will bring about the greatest good for the greatest number.

Fletcher's situationism has not worn well and many Christian ethicists now regard it as little more than a historical curiosity. It obviously suffers from the same difficulties as other versions of utilitarianism, which, of course, from a philosophical point of view, might or might not be soluble. However, as a *theological* theory of ethics, it looks distinctly thin. Despite the impressive line-up of theologians Fletcher claims, rightly or wrongly, as fellow situationists, it seems fairly clear that he more or less lifts a secular philosophical theory off the shelf in order to spell out what might be understood by Christian love. This, not surprisingly, leaves large gaps in his understanding both of love and of the human good.

Despite its problems, situationism's basic assumptions have come to seem attractive to many Christians – particularly those active in pastoral care, who know from experience how harsh rigid rules can seem to vulnerable people. If situationism is indeed inadequate as a theological ethic, Christian communities will need to find better alternatives that meet the same pastoral needs. Some possibilities are explored in Chapter 9.

8 The Case Study Revisited

The Ethics of Assisted Suicide and Euthanasia – Definitions and Distinctions

It is worth beginning with some important definitions and distinctions as discussions of euthanasia and assisted suicide often suffer from muddle and confusion about the meanings of key words (as well as other kinds of confusion, which, of course, will not be sorted out by careful definitions alone).

Suicide is the direct and intentional killing of oneself.

In *assisted suicide*, someone else provides help to the person committing suicide. For example, a doctor might supply a lethal dose of a drug, but it is still suicide as the person who dies kills *him* or *herself* – he or she is not killed by the one who assists.

Euthanasia means killing someone else whose life is thought to be not worth living. Various distinctions are made between different types of euthanasia. One set of these is between *voluntary*, *non-voluntary* and *involuntary* euthanasia. *Voluntary euthanasia* is done at the request of the person who is to be killed or with his or her consent. *Non-voluntary euthanasia* is done without the request or consent of the one who is killed, because he or she is not capable of giving consent. Examples might be the killing of a very severely disabled newborn infant or a patient with advanced Alzheimer's disease. *Involuntary euthanasia* is the killing of a person who is capable of consent, but has not given his or her consent to be killed. The Nazi euthanasia programme in Germany in the 1930s and 1940s is the best-known historical example of involuntary euthanasia.

Another distinction sometimes made is between *active* and *passive* euthanasia. *Active euthanasia* means doing something to cause or hasten the death of the person to be killed, such as administering a lethal dose of a drug. *Passive euthanasia* means causing or hastening death by omitting or ceasing to do something, for example, removing a patient from a ventilator that is keeping him or her alive. Many authors (particularly those who are against euthanasia) argue that 'passive euthanasia' is not really euthanasia at all – it is simply the good clinical practice of not giving medical treatment that would be futile and/or excessively burdensome to the patient.

The law varies from one jurisdiction to another. In Britain, suicide was decriminalized in 1961, but, at the time of writing, assisting suicide remains a criminal offence. Active euthanasia is regarded as murder in UK law. However, withholding or withdrawing life-prolonging treatment, where it is judged clinically appropriate to do so, *is* permitted. In the case of Tony Bland – who was in a persistent vegetative state (PVS) following the Hillsborough football stadium disaster of 1989 – the House of Lords ruled that artificial feeding and hydration could be counted as medical treatment and could be withdrawn. This was accordingly done, with the result that Bland died. The Joffe Bill mentioned in the case study is intended to change British law, legalizing both assisted suicide and (more exceptionally) voluntary euthanasia in certain limited circumstances. If it were passed, Britain would not be the first jurisdiction in the world to do this. Voluntary euthanasia and assisted suicide are legal in the Netherlands and Belgium, while the State of Oregon in the USA has a law permitting assisted suicide.

The Value of Human Life

The prohibition of assisted suicide and euthanasia reflects a notion of the value of human life that has deep roots in the Christian tradition. That tradition understands human life as a 'gift' or 'loan' from God, who created all things, including human life, and pronounced them 'very good' (Genesis 1.31). Christians have taken this view of human life to mean, first, that we should cherish and treasure it and do all we can to protect it. Second, our life is not our own – God is, in an important sense, the true 'owner' of all life, including ours. If that is so, then there are limits to what I may do with either my own life or someone else's. I may not dispose of anyone's life, including my own, in just any way I want to. This explicitly theological view of the value of human life is reinforced in some Christian traditions by the natural law precept that life is to be protected (see Chapter 3).

From this Christian viewpoint, the value of life is reckoned to be *unconditional* – that is, every individual's life is to be valued, regardless of status, condition, age or anything else. This unconditional value is some-times described as the *sanctity of life*, though, as we shall see, some Christians question whether or not 'sanctity' is an appropriate term to use. The Anglican and Catholic bishops' submission to the Select Committee on the Joffe Bill, referred to in the case study, appeals to this theologically grounded notion of the value of human life.

In accordance with this view, the Christian Church since at least the fourth century has fairly consistently disapproved of suicide. Thomas Aquinas, in the thirteenth century, held that it is wrong for three reasons:

- it is contrary to natural law
- it harms the human community to which the person belongs
- 'it wrongs God whose gift life is and who alone has power over life and death'.[22]

Official Roman Catholic teaching has held consistently to this view. One well-known recent expression of it is in Pope John Paul II's encyclical letter *Evangelium Vitae*, which appeals to the Bible, Christian tradition and natural law to support the claim that suicide 'is as morally objectionable as murder'.[23]

The Protestant tradition has largely agreed. Karl Barth, for example, also argues that suicide is 'self-murder', a violation of God's command 'Thou shalt not kill'. Characteristically, Barth will not rule out the possibility that, in some quite exceptional case, God might command someone to take his or her own life as God is sovereign and God's command cannot be second-guessed by human beings. However, that exceptional possibility is right on the margins of his account.[24]

When Christians and the Churches have thought about assisted suicide, it has been widely agreed that, if suicide is wrong, it is also wrong to help someone else commit suicide. This is spelled out, for example, by John Paul II in *Evangelium Vitae*.

There have been secularized versions of this rule against suicide, too. Kant, for example, thought that suicide is forbidden by the categorical imperative. He argued that the maxim, 'From self-love I make it my principle to shorten my life if its continuance threatens more evil than it promises pleasure', could not be universalized without self-contradiction, so if I commit suicide to save myself from pain and suffering, I am using my own humanity merely as a means, not as an end in itself.[25]

While the Christian tradition has generally prohibited the killing of humans, most Christians have allowed exceptions to that prohibition. For example, the majority Christian tradition has permitted killing in self-defence, war and capital punishment (though there have been powerful Christian voices raised against all of these). So, more precisely stated, what the Christian tradition has generally prohibited is *the direct killing of an innocent human being.* 'Innocent' in this context does not mean one who is free from all moral guilt, but one who has done nothing to justify his or her being killed. Neither a violent assailant nor the members of an invading army would be considered 'innocent' in this sense. (The other important qualification introduced in this formula is the word 'direct'. Later in this section, I shall say a little about the significance of this for the euthanasia debate.) Unlike self-defence, war and capital punishment, however, euthanasia has not been recognized as an exception to the general rule against killing. John Paul II in *Evangelium Vitae* regards it as a 'grave violation of the law of God',[26] morally equivalent to either suicide or murder. Barth, too, regards it as murder and, by contrast with his discussion of suicide, does not allow even the possibility that it could, in an exceptional situation, be commanded by God.[27] (It may seem odd, by the way, to regard voluntary euthanasia as a form of murder as the major and obvious difference between voluntary euthanasia and most murders is that, in the former, the 'victim' *wants to be killed*. Yet, consent does not necessarily make a crucial difference here. In those rare and bizarre cases of murder in which the victim consents, his or her consent is not accepted in law as a defence.) In line with this broad stream of tradition, the bishops' submission on the Joffe Bill resists euthanasia and assisted suicide.

Although mainstream Christian tradition has placed a great and unconditional value on human life, it has been wary of claiming that this value is *absolute* or *infinite*. To make that claim would be to turn human life into an 'idol', to treat it with the kind of devotion that should only be given to God. As Joseph Boyle, a Roman Catholic, observes, the Christian tradition has often recognized that trying to preserve your life at any cost is spiritually dangerous.[28] It can distract you from far more important matters – in particular, the need to be in a right relationship with God. The fact that the Church has made a habit of honouring its martyrs indicates that, in the Christian tradition, it is better to die than deny or betray your faith in Jesus Christ. For this reason, some Christians argue that it is misleading to talk about 'the *sanctity* of life', words such as 'respect' or 'dignity' capturing the Christian position better. Stanley Hauerwas puts the point well (if, perhaps, with just a touch of hyperbole):

> Put starkly, Christians are not fundamentally concerned about living. Rather, their concern is to die for the right thing. Appeals to the sanctity of life as an ideology make it appear that Christians are committed to the proposition that there is nothing in life worth dying for.[29]

Modern Challenges

Possibly throughout human history – if not, certainly for a very long time – there have been people who have suffered slow and painful deaths and those who have experienced their lives as a burden and a curse, not a blessing.

However, modern technological medicine seems to have made these things a much bigger problem for us than they were for most of our ancestors. Many of us are now living longer than our grandparents did, and high-tech medical care enables us to survive illnesses and injuries that would almost certainly have killed our forebears.

For many people, of course, these developments are a huge blessing, but for some the lives that have been prolonged by medical care seem painful, limited and sometimes overwhelmed by suffering. This experience – of being kept alive, but with a terribly poor quality of life – is one reason for the traditional rules against suicide and euthanasia being increasingly challenged. These challenges have come particularly (but not only) from secular philosophers, many of them using *consequentialist* approaches of the sort outlined earlier in this chapter.

Christian appeals to the notion of *life as a gift* have been challenged. Critics argue that, if I am given a gift, it becomes mine and I can use it or dispose of it as I choose. My gratitude to the giver might put limits on what I do with it. For example, I might feel obliged to keep a gift if I know that the giver would be very hurt to find out that I had got rid of it. However, it is hard to see how gratitude obliges me to keep a gift that causes me unbearable pain and torment. By the same token, the view of life as a loan from God may not support the traditional prohibition of suicide and euthanasia. As philosopher David Hume argued in the eighteenth century, if artificially ending my life trespasses on God's position as the giver and owner of life, the same could be said about artificially *prolonging* someone's life by, for example, giving life-saving medical treatment.[30]

More generally, many philosophers challenge arguments based on the *sanctity of life*. They argue that this concept comes from a Christian belief system that the majority of people in Western societies today do not hold, so public ethical decisions and laws cannot be based on it.[31]

In place of Christian ethical approaches, many philosophers argue for various kinds of *utilitarian* approach to these questions. Some argue that allowing assisted suicide and euthanasia would result in more benefit, and less harm, than continuing to prohibit it. Others, such as Peter Singer, argue that, in our decision making, we should seek, as far as possible, to satisfy the *preferences* of all concerned. So, if some people experience their lives as a terrible burden, and have a strong desire to end them, permitting assisted suicide and euthanasia could be the decision that most fully satisfies the preferences of the interested parties.

Ironically, in view of Kant's opposition to suicide, another popular argument for euthanasia and assisted suicide is based on *autonomy*, which, as we saw earlier, is an important part of Kant's moral theory. However, the notion of autonomy deployed in the euthanasia debate seems to have relatively little to do with Kant. I said in section 3 that autonomy for Kant does not mean permission to act completely individualistically. Rather, it has more to do with each person's responsibility to work out the demands of the moral law for him- or herself. The version of autonomy in play in arguments about suicide and euthanasia probably owes more to the utilitarian philosopher John Stuart Mill, who held that adults should be free from interference by others in the way they live their lives, so long as their choices do not cause harm to others.[32]

The autonomy argument for suicide and euthanasia is that I should have the freedom to direct my life as I see fit, provided my choices do not interfere with the freedom of others. That freedom includes the right to die at the time and in the way that I choose. (Part of Diane Pretty's argument, which was rejected by the European Court, was that, if her husband was not allowed to help her die, she would be deprived of the right that able-bodied people have to choose the time and manner of their death.)

These arguments are not deployed only by secular thinkers – some Christians, such as Paul Badham, also argue in favour of voluntary euthanasia, sometimes making use of broadly similar consequentialist and autonomy-based arguments.[33]

It would be overly simple, though, to imagine that the consequentialist arguments are all on the pro-euthanasia side of the debate. It is quite possible to make a consequentialist case *against* legalizing assisted suicide and voluntary euthanasia. For example, a consequentialist could argue that, while euthanasia or assisted suicide might well be justified in some individual cases (such as that of Diane Pretty), legalization could allow various harmful consequences. It could give rise to a 'slippery slope' situation in which vulnerable people were put under pressure to ask for euthanasia. If voluntary euthanasia became routinely accepted, society might in time come to accept non-voluntary euthanasia and perhaps even, eventually, involuntary euthanasia.

Legalization might also undermine the relationship of trust between patients and the health professionals who care for them. Furthermore, if euthanasia and assisted suicide were available as easy and cheap options, this might be a disincentive for hard-pressed health services to develop proper terminal and palliative care. The result could be that *more* people ended up dying in avoidable pain and distress. In short, it can be argued that, although assisted suicide and euthanasia would be good in some individual cases, legalizing them would, in the long run, do far more harm than good and that, overall, the good would be maximized and harm minimized by continuing to prohibit them. Those – particularly consequentialists – who argue in favour of euthanasia and assisted suicide find themselves having to show that slippery slopes and other seriously harmful consequences would not be at all likely to follow from legalization. Both sides in these arguments look to Oregon, the Netherlands and Belgium for evidence as to whether or not legalization has resulted in any kind of abuse, erosion of trust or other harmful consequences that people fear.

It is also worth noticing that arguments about slippery slopes, the dangers of abuse and other harmful results are not only used by consequentialists. The bishops' submission for the Joffe Bill uses several of these arguments in an attempt to show that the Bill would undermine the fundamental principle of respect for human life. Robin Gill, a Christian theologian who is not a consequentialist, argued in his evidence to the Select Committee scrutinizing the Bill that, although euthanasia might be justified in individual cases, such as that of Diane Pretty, legalizing it would create a serious risk that vulnerable people would be made even more vulnerable.[34]

Responses to the Challenges

Christians and others who wish to maintain their opposition to euthanasia and assisted suicide respond to these challenges in various ways. One is to reassert traditional Christian claims about the value of human life and the wrongness of killing. This is what the papal encyclical *Evangelium Vitae* sets out to do. It draws a fundamental contrast between the 'Gospel of life', announced by Jesus Christ and entrusted to the Church, and the 'culture of death' which can be seen in many aspects of modern society. Euthanasia and assisted suicide are seen as aspects of the 'culture of death', fundamentally opposed to the 'Gospel of life'.

An argument that is similar in many respects is advanced by Michael Banner, who holds that the practices of euthanasia and assisted suicide betray a fundamental lack of trust in the hope of eternal life offered by God through the resurrection of Jesus Christ. Christians should never countenance such a move.[35]

Some Christian ethicists also challenge the assumption that release from suffering must always be the overriding aim. Nobody denies that reducing suffering is an important goal, but some authors point out that the Christian community has traditionally tried to train and equip its members to *endure* suffering and hardship. For complex historical and cultural reasons, it has become difficult for us in Western societies to find value or meaning in enduring suffering and now our culture has a powerful assumption that the relief of suffering is an overriding aim that should trump almost all others. However, say some Christian thinkers, if we accept this assumption, we may lose sight of some important aspects of what it means to live a good human life. Setting up a legal situation where there is the escape route of a quick and painless death may encourage us to forget about other important human goals and values.

Having said that, Christians and others are quick to point out that suffering can be minimized without euthanasia and a pain-filled life need not be prolonged at all costs. The Christian warning that I mentioned earlier – about making an idol of bodily life – supports this point. Many Christians and others point to the hospice movement and the development of palliative care (the branch of healthcare that aims to relieve the pain and suffering of patients with incurable or terminal diseases) as alternatives to euthanasia. It is sometimes said that if good palliative care were available to all who needed it, this would make euthanasia and assisted suicide unnecessary in virtually all cases. Those who argue for euthanasia reply that, as things stand, the majority of patients do not have access to proper palliative care and that, in any case, there may be a minority for whom pain relief just does not work.

While thinking about pain relief and palliative care, it is worth returning to the formula I stated earlier, that Christian ethics has traditionally prohibited the *direct* killing of innocent human beings. A terminally ill patient may need large doses of analgesic (pain-relieving) drugs to manage his or her pain and these could have the side-effect of shortening his or her life. Christian ethicists often appeal to the so-called 'doctrine of double effect' to reassure patients and professionals that giving such drugs is justified. The doctrine of double effect is that it is morally justified for me to do something in order to achieve a good result, *even if I can foresee that my action will also have an evil consequence*, provided that I do not *intend* the evil and that the evil 'side-effect' will be outweighed by the good I am aiming for. (To understand the distinction between 'foreseen' and 'intended' effects, consider the following example. I am expecting a phone call about an urgent and complicated matter. While I am eating my meal, the phone rings. I answer it, expecting to be in for a long conversation. In answering the phone, I do not *intend* to let my food go cold – I *intend* to try and sort out the business that the phone call is about – but I can *foresee* that my food is very likely to have gone cold by the time I get off the phone.)

The doctrine of double effect has long been used in just war theory (see Chapter 3) to say that the intentional killing of non-combatants is prohibited, but actions that will have the foreseen but unintended side-effect of causing civilian casualties may be justified. In the case of palliative care, the good aim is relief of the patient's pain and the foreseen but unintended evil is the shortening of his or her life. The doctrine of double effect is used not only in moral arguments but also in law, so that health professionals who give large doses of analgesics with the intention of relieving pain are not prosecuted for murder or manslaughter if those drugs also shorten their patients' lives. Critics sometimes argue that it is a moral and legal fiction to say that I can foresee, but not intend, a result of my action. In effect, they say, both law and clinical practice already sanction some forms of euthanasia under the cloak of 'double effect' and it would be better to be honest about it and do it more effectively.

Another relevant distinction here is between active and passive 'euthanasia'. Critics of the traditional view argue that there is no moral difference between a deliberate act and a deliberate omission that have the same result.

If I see my enemy drowning and, because I want him dead, do nothing to save him, I am as guilty of his death as if I had pushed him in. To switch off a ventilator, withdraw a feeding tube or refrain from resuscitating a terminally ill patient, they say, is just as much a form of euthanasia as administering a lethal dose of a drug. As professionals are already practising 'passive euthanasia', so the argument goes, they should also be willing, and permitted, to practise active euthanasia, which offers more effective and humane ways of achieving the same goal. However, many health professionals and Christian ethicists argue that there is a real distinction, even though it may be hard to state. Not every medical intervention, they point out, is obligatory or even desirable, and a wise doctor knows when to stop intervening because he or she can do nothing more to cure the patient. This situation is a far cry from actively seeking his or her patient's death.

Questions

- Is Christian ethics committed to the view that there are absolute moral duties? If so, how might Christians know what those duties are?
- How well do you think the principle of 'respect for human life in all its stages' expresses the Christian understanding of the value of human life? What practical moral obligations might follow from this principle?
- Should the Christian Churches maintain or revise the traditional prohibition of assisted suicide and euthanasia? Should they support or oppose legal changes such as those proposed by Lord Joffe?
- Compare these answers to your responses to the case study questions at the start of the chapter. How, if at all, has your thinking changed as a result of your work on this chapter?

Suggestions for Further Reading

Deontological Ethics

Immanuel Kant, *Groundwork of the Metaphysic of Morals*, London and New York: Routledge, 2005.

Paul Ramsey, *The Essential Paul Ramsey: A Collection*, William Werpehowski and Stephen D. Crocco (eds), New Haven, CT: Yale University Press, 1994. (A collection of Ramsey's writings on a variety of subjects, together with a helpful introduction to his life and thought.)

Peter Singer (ed.), *A Companion to Ethics*, Oxford: Blackwell, 1991. (Contains several useful and relevant chapters, particularly Chapters 14, 17 and 18.)

Consequentialist Theories

Robert E. Goodin, 'Utility and the Good', in Singer, *A Companion to Ethics*, pp. 241–8.

Richard M. Hare, 'Utilitarianism', in John MacQuarrie and James Childress (eds), *A New Dictionary of Christian Ethics*, London: SCM Press, 1986, pp. 640–3.

J. J. C. Smart and Bernard Williams, *Utilitarianism: For and Against*, Cambridge: Cambridge University Press, 1973.

Euthanasia and Assisted Suicide

The following are very useful books.

Nigel Biggar, *Aiming to Kill: The Ethics of Suicide and Euthanasia*, London: Darton, Longman & Todd, 2004. (A careful and closely argued re-examination of the traditional Christian position and the standard criticisms of it.)

Robin Gill (ed.), *Euthanasia and the Churches*, London: Cassell, 1998. (A multi-author collection in which three authors respond to each main essay and the writer of the main essay then replies to these responses.)

5

Critical Voices: Science, Technology and Christian Ethics

1. Case Studies

Read the following case studies and make brief notes in response to the questions. You will be asked to refer back to your answers later in the chapter.

Human Genetics, Evolution and Ethics

In 2001, a massive and expensive scientific collaboration, involving scientists from many different countries over more than a decade, culminated in the publication of the first sequence of the human genome.[1] In effect, this is a 'readout' of all the genetic material that is passed on from one generation to the next when humans reproduce and new individuals are conceived and that helps to determine the physical characteristics of each individual.

   The genetic information of humans, like that of most living things, is encoded in sequences of *deoxyribonucleic acid (DNA)* – a large biological molecule made up of a long sequence of small building blocks strung together end to end. These building blocks come in four different types – known as A, C, G and T – and it is the precise sequence of these that encodes the information carried in a stretch of DNA – just as the sequence of letters on a printed page encodes the information carried in a sentence. The human genome contains around 30,000 *genes*, or lengths of DNA that code for particular *proteins*.

Proteins are another class of large biological molecule and come in many thousands of different shapes and sizes. They perform many of the biological functions needed to build and maintain a living organism, such as a human body. Some regulate the individual's growth and development from embryo to adult, others form parts of the structure of the body's many different kinds of cells, tissues and organs, still others carry out the many different chemical processes within living cells that keep the body functioning, and so on. Each protein has a specific three-dimensional shape that is precisely adapted to its function. The shape of a protein depends on its chemical composition and this is controlled by the gene that codes for it. Small variations in a gene sequence from one individual to another can result in differences in the structure and function of the protein coded for by that gene and these changes can result in variations in characteristics such as hair colour, eye colour, physical stature and so on. Some genetic changes can cause the loss of important biological functions, resulting in inherited diseases such as cystic fibrosis. Others can have more subtle effects, which may include increased susceptibility to conditions such as heart disease and cancer. In some cases (including single-gene disorders such as cystic fibrosis), there is a simple connection between a single genetic change and a particular biological effect. However, in the vast majority of cases, the relationship between genetic variations and biological effects is less straightforward because most biological characteristics are the result of complex interactions between many different genetic and environmental factors. For example, a person's risk of developing some kinds of heart disease may be influenced by a number of different genes, but also by aspects of lifestyle, such as diet and exercise, the conditions in which he or she lives and works and other environmental factors besides.

In recent years, there has been increasing interest in the field of *behavioural genetics*, which studies genetic influences on aspects of human psychology and behaviour.[2] The assumption is that, as the brain's structure and function are determined partly (but only partly) by genetic factors that influence the individual's development, genetic variations between individuals may contribute to differences in psychological and behavioural traits.

This area of research hit the news in the early 1990s when geneticist Dean Hamer and his colleagues found that men who possessed a particular genetic factor were more likely to be homosexual than those who did not. The popular press headlined this as the discovery of a 'gay gene'. There has also been popular speculation about 'genes for' violence, sexual promiscuity, addiction and other kinds of behaviour. Professional biologists are quick to point out that this language is a gross oversimplification as most aspects of human behaviour are highly complex phenomena in which genes, other biological factors and social and cultural influences all interact.

The human genome project has provoked great interest in the possibility of changing people's physical characteristics or even behaviour by manipulating their genes. At the most basic level would be *gene therapy* for single-gene diseases, such as cystic fibrosis. Where a disease is caused by a single faulty gene, it might be possible to treat the disease by introducing a properly functioning version of that gene into the affected cells, tissues and organs. There have been a number of clinical trials of gene therapies in the past decade, but so far with limited success. Some biologists believe that more therapeutic benefits will come from the genome project by way of a better understanding of disease mechanisms, allowing the design of more effective drugs, than by gene therapy.[3]

There is also speculation about *genetic enhancement*, which means using genetic manipulation to alter characteristics that are not associated with disease – attempting to improve on nature, as it were. A relatively simple example is 'gene doping', which would involve giving athletes an extra copy of the gene for a growth hormone in an attempt to promote greater muscle growth. It is not clear whether or not this would succeed, but the International Olympic Committee was apparently worried enough to have funded research into ways of testing for gene doping, in advance of the 2008 Beijing Olympics. More far-reaching speculations about genetic enhancement include thoughts of raising levels of intelligence, making people less violent, enhancing musical ability and so on. Professional biologists, however, tend to be extremely sceptical about the feasibility of ever doing these things.[4]

A more indirect way of manipulating the genetic make-up of human individuals is by *preimplantation genetic diagnosis (PGD)* in combination with *in-vitro fertilization (IVF)*. When human embryos are created by IVF or similar techniques, it is now possible to remove a single cell from each embryo and test that cell for a range of genetic characteristics before implanting the embryo in the mother's womb. This makes it possible to select embryos that have the desired characteristics and discard the others. This technique is already used in a number of countries to screen embryos for certain genetic diseases of which there is a family history – only those embryos lacking the genetic marker for the disease in question being selected for implantation.

When the technique was first introduced in the UK, it was only permitted to use it to screen for disease, but, in March 2005, the House of Commons Science and Technology Committee controversially recommended that parents undergoing IVF should also be permitted to select the sex of their embryos, even when there is no medical reason for doing so.[5]

Another controversial development in human biology is the attempt to apply *evolutionary* theory to aspects of human psychology, behaviour and the social sciences.[6] Human beings, like other living things, are the product of a long process of evolution by *natural selection*. This process relies on the fact that, in any population, there will be variations in all kinds of physical characteristics, caused by randomly occurring genetic changes. If any of these variations make their owners more likely to survive to reproductive age, they are more likely to be passed on to future generations and, over time, will become increasingly common in the population. Over long periods of time, this process can result in changes in the characteristics of a species and in the emergence of new species.

This theory was first worked out in the nineteenth century by Charles Darwin and has been developed and extended by many other biologists since Darwin's day. The term *neo-Darwinism* is sometimes used to describe the more developed version of the theory that has been in use since the early twentieth century. Few scientists dispute that humans have evolved in this way, but some make the more controversial claim that not only our physical characteristics but also details of our psychology, social behaviour and culture can be explained by neo-Darwinism. Those who make this claim identify themselves by various names, such as *sociobiologists* and *evolutionary psychologists*. Among the features that they aim to explain are:

- gender differences, including differences in sexual behaviour between men and women
- aspects of male violence, including the physical abuse of stepchildren
- the existence of morality – in particular, altruism (that is, behaviour that promotes someone else's interests at the cost of damage to my own)
- the existence of religion.

The basic argument is that all these characteristics reflect forms of behaviour that were advantageous to our ancestors during the evolutionary history of our species. Therefore, natural selection has left us with brains that are strongly predisposed to these kinds of behaviour when presented with certain environmental conditions or triggers. If we understand the mechanisms that trigger certain kinds of behaviour, say evolutionary psychologists, we may be able to intervene more effectively to change them. For example, we could then remove the environmental conditions that trigger stepfathers' violence towards their stepchildren. Critics respond with many charges against evolutionary psychology, including the following:

- it oversimplifies complex aspects of human nature, presenting a picture that is initially appealing, but, in fact, highly misleading
- many of its claims are highly speculative, lacking solid scientific support
- some of these poorly supported claims reflect social stereotypes and prejudices (for example, about gender differences) and do harm by giving an appearance of scientific respectability to those prejudices
- it may do damage by falsely promising simple solutions to complicated social problems.

Questions

- To what extent, and in what ways, should the biological sciences influence our thinking about Christian ethics?
- What challenges does the picture of human nature presented by genetics and evolutionary biology pose to Christian ethics? How might Christian ethicists respond to those challenges?

Genetically Modified Crops[7]

Few ethical issues in recent years can have provoked more heated debate in Britain than the question of whether or not *genetically modified (GM) crops* should be grown and marketed in the UK.

The same research that made the human genome project possible has also enabled scientists both to understand and to alter the genetic 'blueprints' of other living things, including some plants that are grown extensively as crops. By means of a variety of molecular biological tricks, new DNA sequences can be introduced into plant cells in such a way that they give rise to new characteristics as the plant grows and develops. In this way, it may be possible to make many changes that could make crops more attractive to consumers, producers or seed companies. For example:

- crops could be made more tolerant of herbicides (weedkillers), making it easier to control weeds when the crops are cultivated
- they could be made resistant to some diseases, pests and environmental stresses, such as drought, salt or frost, which could reduce farmers' costs and might also enable marginal land in developing countries to be cultivated
- they could be made to contain products that are valuable to health, such as vitamins and vaccines – this could be especially beneficial to the health of some populations in developing countries
- features attractive to consumers, such as flavour or shelf-life, could be enhanced
- plants could be made sterile, so that farmers are obliged to keep buying seed from seed companies rather than saving seed from one harvest to sow the next season.

This last example would affect farmers in developing countries, who tend to save seed, much more than farmers in industrialized countries, who tend to buy new seed each season anyway. A few years ago, the biotechnology company Monsanto drew back from this line of research in response to public protests.

In some parts of the world, particularly the United States, GM crops are already grown on a large scale without causing much public concern. In the UK and elswhere in Western Europe, however, environmentalists and the public have been more hostile. A number of concerns has been raised:

- the use of herbicide-tolerant GM crops might result in increased herbicide use, which would be harmful to wildlife and possibly to human health
- GM plants could cross-pollinate with wild relatives to produce herbicide-resistant 'superweeds' that would disturb the ecological balance
- foods made from GM crops might turn out to be harmful to human health
- the growing use of GM in agriculture could be a way in which powerful business corporations exploit vulnerable and powerless communities, particularly in developing countries.

Before deciding whether or not to permit the commercial growing of any GM crops, the British Government ordered a three-year period of farm-scale evaluations. During this time, a range of crops were scientifically tested in conditions like those under which they would be farmed. It also carried out an economic assessment of the likely benefits of GM crops and a public consultation exercise.

The economic assessment suggested that there would be little short-term benefit to the British economy, but there might be much greater benefits to both producers and consumers in the longer term. In the consultation exercise, the majority of those who responded were opposed to the introduction of GM crops. The scientific assessment suggested that one of the crops, a GM variety of maize, had a beneficial effect on biodiversity, while the GM sugar beet and rape that were also tested appeared to have a harmful effect. At around the same time, the British Medical Association stated that GM crops were highly unlikely to harm human health, though their effects on health should continue to be surveyed.

In March 2004, the Government agreed in principle that the maize variety that had been tested could be grown commercially in England, but withheld permission for commercial growing of the beet and rape varieties. This decision only applied to the one variety in each case that had been tested – any other GM crop would have to go through a similar scientific assessment before it could be grown commercially. However, the company that had produced the maize variety subsequently decided not to go ahead with the commercial cultivation of the crop, saying that government restrictions made it 'economically non-viable'.

Opinion in Britain remains as divided as ever. Environmental groups have criticized the farm-scale evaluations for being scientifically flawed and only studying a few of the possible environmental effects of GM crop cultivation, while industry spokespeople and lobbyists expressed frustration at the tight regulation and slow pace of change in European countries.

Questions

- What responsibilities do humans and human societies have concerning the natural world and why?
- What kinds of technological manipulation of nature (if any) are morally acceptable, where (if anywhere) should a line be drawn, and why?
- Is the commercial growing of GM crops within the boundaries of what is morally acceptable?

2 Science, Technology and Christian Ethics

In the space of just one chapter, it is obviously not possible to discuss every area of science and technology that raises critical questions for Christian ethics. So, in order to illustrate the kinds of challenges that science and technology might pose, we shall focus on a few specific areas – the aspects of biological science and technology mentioned in the case studies – and look in a little more detail at the following five questions raised by them:

- Does science undermine Christian belief (in which case Christian ethics cannot even get started)?
- Does evolutionary biology explain away morality?
- Do we need to revise any of our moral judgements in the light of our scientific knowledge?

- Is it legitimate to try and 'redesign' ourselves technologically?
- Is it legitimate to try and 'redesign' nature?

3 Does Science Undermine Christian Belief?

The challenge facing us with this question is a very familiar one and many people assume, without really thinking about it, that the natural sciences *do* undermine religious belief in all kinds of ways. In particular, in relation to the areas of science introduced in the two case studies, many people think that evolutionary biology threatens Christianity: if human beings and other living things originated by means of the kind of evolutionary process worked out by Charles Darwin, then Christian belief in a creator God must be impossible. This view is held by both believers and non-believers. Some Christians, who style themselves 'creationists', deny the theory of evolution and hold that the world was made literally as described in the first two chapters of the book of Genesis. On the other side of the argument, some scientists and others argue that Darwinian evolution makes Christian belief both unnecessary and implausible. This has been argued particularly forcefully by biologist Richard Dawkins and philosopher Daniel Dennett.[8]

A great deal has been written about the relationship between science and religion. Many Christian theologians and scientists from a wide variety of disciplines and Church traditions argue that Christian faith is perfectly compatible with a scientific view of the world. In relation to biology in particular, a number of authors hold that evolutionary theory is not in conflict with a Christian doctrine of creation or other aspects of Christian faith.[9] This is not the place to review these debates in any detail, but one point worth making is this. Many arguments against Christian belief on the basis of evolutionary biology are faulty because they rest on basic confusions between different types of cause and different types of explanation. They assume that the Christian doctrine of creation is an answer to the same kind of question as a neo-Darwinian theory of evolution, that the two are rival scientific hypotheses offering alternative answers to questions such as, 'How did there come to be such a variety of living things?' They then go on to think that if there is more scientific evidence for the neo-Darwinian theory than the

Christian doctrine, that makes the Christian doctrine less likely to be true.

'Creationists' who deny the truth of evolutionary theory, of course, make the same assumption as their atheist opponents – namely, that the book of Genesis offers an alternative scientific explanation of the origins of life.

However, it is far from clear that either side is right to make this assumption. They would be if the language used by scientists and theologians were *univocal* – that is, if any word, phrase or statement could only ever mean one thing. Many philosophers and theologians, however, would argue that language is much richer and more complex than this, so apparently similar statements can mean very different things in different contexts. If they are right, then there is much less reason to think that neo-Darwinism and the Christian doctrine of creation are direct rivals. In the rest of this chapter, I shall assume that something like neo-Darwinian evolutionary theory is true, because the scientific evidence in its favour is overwhelming. I shall also assume, though, that, there is no good reason to think that neo-Darwinian evolution calls the Christian doctrine of creation into question.[10]

4 Does Evolutionary Biology Explain Away Morality?

We often tend to assume that *altruism* – sacrificing one's own interests in order to help someone else – is at the heart of morality. The most extreme form of altruism, which we regard as morally praiseworthy and heroic, is when someone lays down his or her life for the sake of others.

The existence of altruistic behaviour is a famous puzzle for any evolutionary biologist who thinks that genetic factors influence behaviour because, on the face of it, it does not look as though a 'gene' for altruism would last very long. A 'gene' that made its possessors likely to lay down their lives for others would seem to damage its chances of being passed on to future generations. It might appear that 'genes' for selfishness and ruthless self-assertion would do better in the process of evolutionary competition. (As the first case study made clear, of course, the language of 'genes for' this or that kind of behaviour is a great oversimplification. It would be more accurate to say something like 'a heritable predisposition to altruistic behaviour'. For our present purposes, though, 'a gene for altruism' will do, provided we remember the caveats in the case study. In this discussion, I shall place the word 'gene' in inverted commas as a reminder that we are probably not talking about a single stretch of DNA that a molecular biologist could extract and sequence.)

Altruism looks like evolutionary suicide. Yet such behaviour is found throughout the animal kingdom – not only in humans and in other primate species with relatively complex social structures, but even in social insects, such as bees. Indeed, in many insect species, all but one of the females in a hive forego their opportunities to reproduce in order to support the queen. This cannot be a matter of conscious choice as insects' nervous systems are far too rudimentary for that. It must be biologically 'programmed' in some way and such behaviour must have been favoured by natural selection.

In the 1960s and 1970s, biologists such as William Hamilton and Robert Trivers proposed the theories of *kin selection* and *reciprocal altruism*, which help to explain this puzzle.[11] According to Hamilton, the key to understanding the altruism of social insects is that all the female insects in the hive are sisters of the queen. This means that they share many of the same genes. Therefore, a gene that leads some of them to sacrifice their own reproductive chances could still spread in the population if it had the effect of improving the queen's reproductive chances as she would be very likely to possess a copy of the same gene. Hamilton worked out the mathematics of this in detail and showed that it could indeed happen.

Although the behaviour of apes and humans is much more complex than that of insects, the same reasoning could apply. 'Genes' that predispose individuals to sacrifice themselves for their kin could spread in the population as those who benefit from the sacrifice, and thereby have their own reproductive chances improved, are likely to have copies of the same 'gene'. Hard-headed evolutionary logic could favour the sort of love that leads parents to sacrifice themselves to save their children, or siblings to risk their lives for one another.

What about altruism towards those who are not close relatives? This is where reciprocal altruism comes in. In species that have relatively complex forms of social organization (including our evolutionary relatives, the great apes), it often turns out that a strategy of cooperating and exchanging favours is better for everyone than hostility and outright competition. If you scratch my back and I scratch yours, we may both get on better than if we refuse to help each other. Therefore, again, 'genes' that promote such behaviour could spread in the population, even though they sometimes lead individuals to sacrifice their own chances. This is because, on average, those who possess these 'genes' will be more likely to survive and reproduce than those who do not.

Evolutionary psychologists speculate that many aspects of social organization, and moral instincts and concepts such as the notion of 'fairness' and our tendency to disapprove of cheating, have evolved as mechanisms for ensuring that co-operative and altruistic behaviour really does work for the reproductive success of those who engage in it. A 'gene' that makes me vulnerable to being taken advantage of, by leading me to sacrifice my interests for the benefit of cheats and free-riders who never give anything in return, is, on average, likely to do less well in the evolutionary competition than a 'gene' that inclines me to disapprove of cheats and help those who help others.

Question

- What problems and challenges, if any, do you think this account of morality poses for Christian ethics? Try to identify the various problems as precisely as you can and distinguish different questions clearly from one another.

One worry that Christians might have about this account is that it seems to debunk aspects of human nature that we tend to admire and value. Thus, generosity, compassion, justice and self-sacrifice are really just sophisticated forms of genetic selfishness: evolution has found more effective ways of promoting individuals' reproductive success than out-and-out competition.

In fact, when pressed, evolutionary psychology writers tend to avoid this kind of extreme debunking, though they sometimes get carried away with their own rhetoric. In more serious moments, they will often say that, although morality originated as a set of behaviours that promoted reproductive success, humans have the capacity to take it further and develop moral behaviour that does not merely serve the interests of their 'genes'. The evolutionary roots of altruism may lie in kin selection and reciprocal altruism, but the moral instincts and concepts that evolved in this way sometimes lead humans to extraordinary acts of genuine altruism and self-sacrifice that have nothing to do with reproductive success. Our sense of justice may have its origins in a psychological mechanism for detecting cheats and free-riders, but that sense of justice can lead us to create legal systems that are designed to ensure fair and equal treatment for all.

Christians certainly have an interest in saying that there is more to morality than sophisticated forms of genetic selfishness. The words of Jesus in Luke's Sermon on the Plain might suggest that true Christian morality starts at exactly the point where kin selection and reciprocal altruism stop:

> If you love those who love you, what credit is that to you? For even sinners love those who love them. If you do good to those who do good to you, what credit is that to you? For even sinners do the same. If you lend to those from whom you hope to receive, what credit is that to you? Even sinners lend to sinners, expecting to receive as much again. But love your enemies, do good, and lend, expecting nothing in return. Your reward will be great, and you will be children of the Most High; for he is kind to the ungrateful and the wicked. (Luke 6.32–5)

Having said that, Christians might also find themselves agreeing with evolutionary psychologists that human goodness is not always as good as we like to think it is. The Christian doctrine of original sin expresses the notion that some forms of wrongdoing and vicious character can go very deep in human nature. Furthermore, we often deceive ourselves into thinking that we are better than we really are. Even when we do good we may not always be doing it for all the best reasons and an evolutionary account of the origins of morality may teach us to have a healthy suspicion of our own and others' characters and motivations.

There is a further question that Christians (and others) might wish to put to evolutionary psychologists: does the picture of morality offered by evolutionary psychology do justice to the richness and complexity of human motivation? Evolutionary psychologists tend to think of particular behaviours and psychological traits as mental 'modules' that operate more or less independently of one another and have developed more or less independently in our evolutionary history. This has been dubbed the 'Swiss Army knife' model of the mind: just as a Swiss Army knife contains a number of relatively simple gadgets, each with one function, so the mind is an assembly of many different mental gadgets or modules, each of which performs relatively simple and well-defined functions. For example, different aspects of morality may be under the control of an 'altruism module' that evolved for the purposes of kin selection and reciprocal altruism, a 'justice module' that evolved to promote social sanctions against cheating and free-riding, and so on. The complexity, power and flexibility of human minds exist because there are very many of these mental modules and they interact with one another and the environment in highly complex ways. However, critics of evolutionary psychology have attacked this modular view of the mind as simplistic, misleading and lacking evidence to support it. Human minds, they say, are simply not like Swiss Army knives.[12]

Certainly some of the approaches to Christian ethics surveyed in this book think of morality as something very different from a set of 'mental modules'. Both virtue ethics (see Chapter 6) and narrative approaches to biblical ethics (Chapter 2) encourage us to think about morality not as a series of distinct psychological functions with specific evolutionary roots, but, rather, in a richer and more integrated way. Our moral deliberations, actions and virtues, from this standpoint, are best understood as parts of the stories of particular human lives, lived in response to God and one another. Moral decisions, actions and characteristics arise out of our fundamental commitments (including faith commitments) and our relationships with God and other people. In turn, our decisions and actions help to shape our basic commitments and relationships.

5 Should Science Make Us Revise Our Moral Judgements?

During the media feeding frenzy surrounding the 'gay gene' in the mid 1990s, both Christians and non-Christians frequently claimed that the traditional Christian prohibition of homosexual behaviour would be unsustainable if homosexuality had a genetic cause. The argument seems to go like this: if it's in our genes, then it's natural and, if it's natural, then it can't be morally wrong. Similar arguments crop up in other ethical debates. For example, it is estimated that anything up to 70 per cent of pregnancies spontaneously abort within the first three months, often before the mother even knows she is pregnant. This statistic is sometimes presented as a reason for allowing both abortion and research on human embryos on the grounds that, if nature destroys human embryos and foetuses in such quantities, we cannot say that it is always wrong for *us* to destroy human embryos and foetuses.

Both these arguments, and others like them, are attempts to base moral judgements on scientific discoveries or theories. As well as these piecemeal arguments, there have been attempts to construct complete moral systems on the basis of science. One of the most famous (or notorious) was Herbert Spencer's attempt in the nineteenth century to build an ethical theory on Darwin's theory of evolution. Spencer argued that 'good' conduct meant 'more evolved' conduct and more highly evolved conduct was that which promoted survival, procreation and permanently peaceful societies.[13]

Both the piecemeal arguments about such things as abortion and the 'gay gene' and the comprehensive theories such as Spencer's are attempts to get an 'ought' from an 'is' – to derive conclusions about what we ought to do from scientific statements about what is the case. Philosopher G. E. Moore, referring directly to Spencer, argued that this is a false move, which he called the 'naturalistic fallacy'.[14]

Moore, as we saw in Chapter 4, was not the first to question the validity of deriving an 'ought' from an 'is'. In the 1730s, David Hume had observed that many moral arguments began with statements about God or human nature, but then 'of a sudden I am surpriz'd to find, that instead of the usual copulation of propositions, *is* and *is not*, I meet with no proposition that is not connected with an *ought*, or an *ought not*'. Hume argued that 'is' and 'ought' were two different kinds of statement and he placed the burden of proof on those who wanted to deduce 'ought' from 'is':

> as this *ought* or *ought not*, expresses some new relation or affirmation, 'tis necessary that it shou'd be observ'd and explain'd; and at the same time that a reason should be given, for what seems altogether inconceivable, how this new relation can be a deduction from others, which are entirely different from it.[15]

Moore goes further, arguing that Spencer's argument depends on defining words such as 'good', which express moral judgements, in terms of factual statements such as 'This will promote human survival'. According to Moore, Spencer thinks that when we say, 'This is good', we simply *mean* something like, 'This will promote human survival', but it is not obvious that we *should* define words like 'good' in such ways and Spencer does not give good reasons for doing so.

If Moore is right, we cannot draw moral conclusions solely from scientific observations about what *is* the case. In itself, the fact that many embryos and foetuses are naturally destroyed early in pregnancy is irrelevant to the question of whether or not we *ought* to destroy embryos in scientific experiments or foetuses by aborting them.

Equally, if homosexuality should turn out to have natural, scientifically discoverable causes (including genetic causes), this fact in itself would be irrelevant to the question of whether or not people *ought* to engage in homosexual behaviour. If Moore is right, it also means that we cannot appeal to evolutionary biology either to justify our morality or call it into question. We may have evolved to think that we should behave altruistically, have a sense of fairness and so on because these ways of thinking and behaving promoted the survival and reproductive success of our evolutionary ancestors, but that fact (if it is a fact) cannot tell us whether or not we are correct in believing that altruism, fairness and so on are good or right.

Not all philosophers agree with Moore that the 'naturalistic fallacy' really is a fallacy. For example, Alasdair MacIntyre, whom we meet again in Chapter 6, holds that Hume's and Moore's arguments assume that *facts* and *values* are distinct and separate things.[16] Facts are objective and value-free, the kind of claim that could be proved by observation and scientific experiment, while values are subjective and non-rational, not matters of fact that could be experimentally tested.

According to MacIntyre, this tendency to separate fact from value took hold in the eighteenth century, though others have argued that its roots go back further than that. Although many thinkers since then have believed that the separation of fact and value is logically necessary, MacIntyre challenges this view. He believes that this separation was a symptom of the major shift in moral thinking that he calls the 'Enlightenment project', which we shall explore further in the next chapter. Before the eighteenth century, it would not have seemed obvious that facts and values are distinct and separate from one another.

Certainly, some of the Christian approaches to ethics surveyed in this book assume a different kind of relationship between facts and values. For example, according to Thomas Aquinas' account of natural law (Chapter 3), we can draw conclusions about how we ought to behave from observations of ourselves and the world. In a sense, natural law arguments move from an 'is' to an 'ought', but they do so in a very different way from Spencer. The crucial difference is that, in Thomas' natural law theory, the facts themselves are not neutral, but value laden. The theory claims that human beings have been created by God with particular ends or purposes. This is a factual claim about the kind of thing a human being is: when we say 'human being', part of what we mean is 'a being that exists for these ends'. This factual claim has an evaluative claim built in, however – that a human being is the kind of being whose good consists in fulfilling these ends, so it follows that right actions are those that help us to fulfil our ends. (Incidentally, Spencer was scathing about both Aristotle and medieval Christian thought. It is therefore interesting and ironic that his description of 'more evolved' conduct was strikingly similar to Thomas Aquinas' list of natural human ends, which was summarized in Chapter 3. Perhaps Spencer's theory should be understood as an attempt to produce a secularized natural law theory, without the philosophical and theological underpinnings of Thomas' version.)

According to MacIntyre's view, there is certainly a relationship between facts about humans and the world and judgements about how we ought to behave. This does not mean, however, as Spencer thought, that we can read moral conclusions directly from a scientific account of human nature. Scientific insights may well inform our understanding of human nature, but they are not the only kind of insights we need. If our moral judgements are to be based on our understanding of the kind of being we are, and the kinds of ends we have, we shall need to consult facts about human nature other than just scientific ones in order to form that understanding. By itself, a scientific account of the causes of homosexuality will not tell us whether or not homosexual behaviour can be in line with our human ends. Nor can a scientific account of the origins of altruism, by itself, tell us whether or not we ought to behave altruistically. Furthermore, it may turn out to be difficult or even impossible for us to discover on our own what our proper ends are. This is partly because we have finite minds and a limited capacity for understanding ourselves and the world, let alone God.

It could also be because we are sinners. Most Christian thinkers agree that sin has a distorting effect on many, indeed perhaps all, aspects of human life, including human knowledge. Some strands of Christian thought, including the natural law tradition derived from Thomas Aquinas, have said that, despite this, we can still have some natural knowledge of our proper ends. Other thinkers, though – particularly those in some Protestant traditions – would say that sin distorts our knowledge of God, ourselves and the world so radically that we cannot have reliable knowledge of the human good unless God reveals this to us.[17]

6 Should We Try to Redesign Ourselves?

As we saw in the first case study, knowledge of the human genome and related areas of science has led to an enormous amount of speculation about the possibilities for controlling and modifying the genetic characteristics of human beings, either directly by means of genetic manipulation or indirectly using such techniques as IVF and PGD. The aims in view range from the relatively modest – such as gene therapy for single-gene disorders – to highly ambitious dreams about the genetic enhancement of people's bodies, minds and personalities. Some of the things that are talked about are already being done, such as the selection of healthy embryos by PGD. Others such as gene therapies for some single-gene disorders, are being developed experimentally, though so far with limited success. Others still, including the more ambitious forms of genetic enhancement, may never become technically feasible. Apart from the question of what is technically feasible, now or in the future, which if any of these forms of genetic control *should* be permitted?

Much of the public debate on this question has centred on consequentialist arguments about benefit, harm and risk. In some cases, the benefits would be obvious. For example, if a lethal disease such as cystic fibrosis could be effectively treated by gene therapy, that would be a massive benefit to patients and their families. In other cases, such as sex selection of babies for non-medical reasons, the benefits would be less clear, though, presumably, the parents who seek to choose the sex of their children perceive some benefit to their children, themselves or both.

The risks, in general, have to do with the fact that many of these techniques are somewhat imprecise and difficult to control, so there is a small chance of bringing about unintended harmful consequences as well as the desired effects. For example, if you were attempting to insert a healthy gene into a patient's genome in order to counteract the effects of a genetic disease, there would be a small but real risk that your intervention would also result in another unintended and harmful genetic change. Furthermore, if the genetic change were made in such a way that it could be passed on to the patient's children, there would be a chance that harmful effects could appear and spread in future generations.

Consequentialist arguments about human genetic manipulation involve balancing the benefits of the desired genetic change against the risk of unintended and harmful consequences and the seriousness of the harm that would be done if those unintended consequences did occur. Largely on the basis of such arguments, UK law currently allows human genetic manipulation for the treatment of disease (gene therapy), but forbids genetic enhancement of characteristics that are not related to disease. It also stipulates that genetic manipulation must be done in such a way that the changes only affect the patient him- or herself and cannot be passed on to future generations (in technical language, it allows *somatic cell* but not *germ line* genetic manipulation).[18]

Some Christians take the view that, beyond risk–benefit arguments, there are no reasons to object in principle to any form of human genetic manipulation. There may even be positive theological reasons to encourage it. Christians might argue that God's call to human beings to have 'dominion' over the created order (Genesis 1.26–8) encourages us to use technologies such as genetic manipulation to take control over our own nature and destiny. (Of course, other forms of genetic control such as PGD also raise questions about the treatment of human embryos as selecting embryos with desired characteristics will often mean destroying those that are not selected. These issues were discussed in the final section of Chapter 2, so I shall not say more about them here, but it is important to remember that they arise in this context as well. Christians who take a highly permissive view of genetic manipulation would probably also be inclined to take a permissive rather than restrictive view about the ways in which human embryos may be used.) An early expression of this view, written at a time when many of the developments described in the case study were still in the future, comes from Joseph Fletcher:

> The future is not to be sought in the stars but in us, in human beings. We don't pray for rain, we irrigate and seed clouds; we don't pray for cures, we rely on medicine ... This is the direction of the biological revolution – that we turn more and more from creatures to creators.[19]

Other Christians are highly suspicious of this view, fearing that it represents an arrogant attempt to put ourselves in the place of God, the inevitable result of which will be that we become alienated from God and fail to fulfil our true role in the created order. This kind of warning was sounded by Paul Ramsey, who, like Fletcher, was thinking about technological possibilities that were then still in the future: 'Men ought not to play God', he wrote, 'until they have learned to be men, and after they have learned to be men they will not play God.'[20]

We appear, then, to have two opposite Christian attitudes to the question of 'redesigning' ourselves by using genetics and other technological means. One sees this as a right and proper part of our human calling, while the other rejects it as a foolish and futile attempt to 'play God'. However, the choice is not as polarized as it might seem. Fletcher's extreme view would probably be supported by few Christian thinkers, but some would sign up to a more moderate version of it. They might resist talk of humans 'turning more and more from creatures to creators', but be happy to think of humans as 'created co-creators' with God.[21] This language acknowledges that humans are God's creatures, not gods, but suggests that humans are given a large and active role by God in shaping and developing the created world, including their own nature. However, some Christians would be unhappy even with the language of 'created co-creator' and would be more sympathetic to Ramsey's warnings about 'playing God'. This position may not be as stark as it seems either. It might appear to mean that we should refrain from any kind of interference in the created world, that we should simply let nature take its course. If applied consistently, it would forbid many areas of human activity and culture – no medicine, no agriculture, no technology and much more besides. Some Christians may wish to argue for such a view, but Ramsey certainly did not. The language of 'playing God' is probably best understood as a warning against having an exaggerated view of our own power and authority over creation. According to this view, we deceive ourselves if we come to believe that there are no limits to what we *can* do or what it is *right* for us to do in an effort to improve the world. By developing such an inflated view of ourselves, we risk becoming alienated from God because we assume that we can solve every kind of human problem without God's help. We also fail to fulfil our true human potential and risk behaving inhumanely towards some of our fellow humans. (It is worth pointing out that sometimes when the language of 'playing God' is used by both Christians and others in public debate, it is used in a much less specific way than this and seems to indicate an almost superstitious fear of 'interfering with nature'. 'Playing God' in this sense often becomes a discussion-stopping slogan. It should be clear that I am not using the term in this way, but in a quite specific sense, to describe one kind of distorted view about the possibilities for human action in the world.)

For many Christian thinkers, then, making the right choices about human genetic manipulation means finding the right course between two extremes, which are, on the one hand, 'playing God' and forgetting our human limitations and, on the other, refusing to intervene in the world at all. They differ, though, as to what the right course would permit and forbid. One possible view would be that *all* interventions on the human genome are forms of 'playing God' and should be avoided, though it is hard to find a Christian theologian who takes this view. Most approve of somatic cell gene therapy and some, such as Robert Song, are inclined to draw the line there – not least because other therapeutic procedures, such as preimplantation diagnosis and germ line gene therapy, would involve the destruction of human embryos. Some Christians would draw a line between gene therapy and genetic enhancement. They might argue that both somatic cell and germ line therapy could be in line with God's purposes, but genetic enhancement runs the risk of 'playing God' by deluding ourselves that we can perfect human nature and solve all our problems technologically. Others – particularly those who adopt the 'created co-creator' view of humankind – question this and argue that genetic enhancement, as well as therapy, could be consistent with humanity's God-given role in the world.[22]

Questions

Answer the following questions with regard to the various prospects for human genetic control mentioned in the first case study.

- Which, if any, should Christians welcome as proper expressions of human responsibility in the world and why?
- Which, if any, should they reject as 'playing God' (in the specific sense explained above) and why?

7 Should We Try to Redesign Nature?

To put the question in more general terms, we could ask *how should we understand the relationship between humans and nature and what kinds of human activity in the world would reflect a right relationship between humans and nature?*

At this point, a word of clarification is needed about 'nature'. It is a slippery term that can mean many different things in different contexts. In this section, I shall use it to mean, roughly, the non-human parts of the material world we live in. I shall also use the term 'creation', by which I shall mean everything that God has made, including the material world around us. If we talk about 'creation', as distinct from 'nature', we are making certain claims about the world, such as that it has come into being as the result of God's plan and purpose, and that it has value because it has been created and is loved by God.

Much writing on ecological ethics offers a choice between two different accounts of the relationship between humans and nature: *anthropocentrism* and *biocentrism*. *Anthropocentric* accounts understand the relationship in a human-centred way. At their simplest, they say that humans are the only beings on Earth that have moral value in and of themselves. This might be argued, for example, on the grounds that humans alone are rational beings and it is a rational nature that makes beings morally valuable in and of themselves. (This idea can be traced to Immanuel Kant, among others. It underpins his 'formula of the end in itself', which we met in Chapter 4. According to this view, of course, if it turned out that other beings, such as great apes or dolphins, were also rational beings, we should have to recognize that they too had moral value in and of themselves.)

It is clear that a crude anthropocentrism can lead to ecological damage, the exploitation of animals and other destructive behaviour towards nature. It can encourage us to think of the natural world simply as a pool of resources to be used however necessary to meet human needs or desires by mining, logging, fishing, intensive farming, animal experimentation, hunting for sport and so on.

In a famous article from the 1960s, historian Lynn White Jr – himself a Christian – argued that the Christian Church had created the conditions for the development of a scientific and technological mindset that adopted this kind of attitude to nature.[23] Thus, in White's eyes, the Church was at least partly responsible for the present ecological crisis and should take the lead in finding new ways to relate to the natural world.

Others have argued, against White, that highly anthropocentric and exploitative attitudes to nature developed during a period when the influence of the Church in Western societies was already beginning to wane. According to these thinkers, it was not Christianity, but the rise of science and technology in an increasingly secular culture, that led to the damaging exploitation of nature.

Be that as it may, anthropocentrism does not necessarily lead to the destruction of nature. Much environmentalist campaigning is based on the argument that we need to care for the natural world because human existence and welfare depend on it. For example, we must prevent global warming because of the threat it poses to human settlements, agriculture and ecosystems on which we depend. Also, biodiversity must be preserved because the natural world contains valuable resources that we have not yet discovered, wilderness areas should be preserved because their grandeur enriches human experience, and so on.

Some environmentalists, though, doubt that any kind of anthropocentrism can help us act responsibly towards the natural world as putting human interests first inevitably leads us to exploit nature and create ecological problems. To find solutions to these problems, we shall have to be more radical in our thinking. For this reason, many writers on ecological ethics argue for *biocentric* approaches, in which all life on Earth is considered morally valuable in and of itself, regardless of whether or not it has any value to human beings. When deciding how to act, we should not privilege the needs or interests of humans over other living beings. As far as possible, we should avoid exploiting nature. Biocentric arguments tend to suggest that most living things and ecosystems get on best without any human interference, so, as far as we can, we should avoid interfering with nature.

Celia Deane-Drummond, however, argues that this view depends on out-of-date ecological science. It assumes that the various components of an ecosystem remain in a stable balance unless some external influence, such as human intervention, disturbs that balance. However, more up-to-date ecological research indicates that ecosystems are more unstable and unpredictable than this and are often open to a wide variety of external influences. She suggests that this calls into question the biocentric view that there is a stable 'balance of nature' that is best left undisturbed by humans.[24]

Not all Christian environmental thinking fits neatly into either the anthropocentric or the biocentric category. One very popular Christian model for humanity's relationship to the rest of the created world is that of *stewardship*. Though this term is sometimes used by secular writers and organizations to refer in a fairly general way to care of the environment, Christian uses of the term tend to be more specific.

The idea is that the natural world is owned by God, its creator, who has entrusted humankind with the task of looking after it. One source of this view is the second Genesis creation story, in which God places the first human in the garden of Eden 'to till it and keep it' (Genesis 2.15). Talk of stewardship can be highly anthropocentric – God has placed humanity in charge of the world and given us permission to use it in whatever way we see fit. The notion that God has given humans 'dominion' over the world (Genesis 1.26) fits in well with this view.

Some accounts of stewardship are less anthropocentric than this. They emphasize that God loves and values the whole of creation for its own sake, that humans have been given an active and vital role in caring for creation, and that we are answerable to God for its safekeeping. Such a view of stewardship is sometimes linked to the idea that humankind has a 'priestly' role with regard to creation – to enable the whole created order to fulfil its purposes and glorify God. Such notions of stewardship and priesthood are at least cautiously supported by some Christian environmentalists, such as Ruth Page. Others, such as Stephen Clark, reject Christian talk of stewardship as 'fashionable cant' that tempts us to think of the world in dangerously anthropocentric terms.[25]

Some Christian feminists believe that patriarchy, including patriarchal forms of Christianity, has played a large part in the ecological crisis (see Chapter 8 for more on patriarchy and the feminist critique of it). For them, theological language that stresses God's power, authority and transcendence (that is, God's 'otherness' over against the world) tends to encourage both men's subjection of women and humanity's subjection of nature. We need new language to speak about the world, humanity and God in ways that give due weight to God's immanence – that is, God's close involvement in the world – and do not support relationships of domination. Sallie McFague, for example, has argued that traditional patriarchal and hierarchical theological language is inappropriate for our age and we need to find new 'imaginative pictures' of God's relationship with the world. Rather than imagining the world as the realm ruled by God, she suggests that it is more helpful to imagine the world as God's body. Also, rather than depicting God as 'king, lord and patriarch' of the world, she prefers the metaphors of God as the world's 'mother, lover and friend'.[26]

Other Christians, though, argue that more traditional Christian sources can help us think and act in ecologically responsible ways, even if these sources have been used in the past to justify destructive attitudes to nature. For example, Thomas Aquinas is often regarded as a thoroughly bad influence by environmentalists as his writing seems to support a thoroughly anthropo-centric view of animals and nature. Yet, Michael Northcott has argued that Thomas' natural law theory (see Chapter 3) can be revised and developed so as to offer 'significant resources for an environmental ethic'. Celia Deane-Drummond also draws on Thomas, particularly his account of the virtues (see Chapter 6), arguing that the virtues of *wisdom*, *prudence* and *justice* can enable us to understand the created world and to treat it rightly.[27]

These various Christian accounts of the relationship between humans and the non-human world could lead to widely varying conclusions about practical GM crops. Indeed, there are Christian thinkers vigorously involved on all sides of this debate. For example, Michael Northcott sees the use of genetic engineering in agriculture as the latest development in a long history of increasingly technological, industrialized farming. This sort of agricul-ture, he argues, damages ecosystems, threatens human health and disadvan-tages the poor, both in the West and in developing countries. He believes that genetic engineering will simply continue these trends and is sceptical about claims that it has an important role to play in feeding the world's poor. He acknowledges that genetic manipulation could be used in different ways, so as to support poor farmers and rural communities in developing countries, preserve biodiversity and reduce the damage done by the large-scale use of agrochemicals. However, he argues that this scenario is highly unlikely to become a reality. This is because the technology is largely controlled by multinational companies and their commercial interests will always push research and development in the direction of maximizing profits, even at the expense of environmental damage and exploitation of the poor.

A report sponsored by the Evangelical Alliance, in contrast, takes a somewhat more positive view. The authors argue that responsible steward-ship of the Earth involves innovation and a certain amount of risk, which leads them to conclude that GM crops should be evaluated on a case-by-case basis, not rejected from the outset. They agree with Northcott that current uses of the technology are open to severe criticism – relatively little research and development is directed towards the needs of the poor and GM crops tend to be imposed on the populations of both poor and wealthy countries without sufficient consultation, for example. They believe that major changes are needed, both in the priorities of GM crop research and development and the ways in which decisions are made about GM. However, they are less pessimistic than Northcott about the possibility of making such changes. They also believe that technological developments, such as genetic engineering, will become more and more necessary during the twenty-first century in order to feed the world's population and promote health in poor communities.[28]

Questions

- Write a few sentences to summarize what you believe the relationship between humans and the non-human world should be and explain the reasons for your view.
- What moral conclusions does your view suggest about GM crops?

Suggestions for Further Reading

Stephen R. L. Clark, *Biology and Christian Ethics*, Cambridge: Cambridge University Press, 2000.

Philip Clayton and Jeffrey Schloss (eds), *Evolution and Ethics: Human Morality in Biological and Religious Perspective*, Grand Rapids, MI: Eerdmans, 2004.

Celia E. Deane-Drummond (ed.), *Brave New World? Theology, Ethics and the Human Genome*, Edinburgh: T & T Clark, 2003.

Celia E. Deane-Drummond, *The Ethics of Nature*, Oxford: Blackwell, 2004.

Neil Messer, *Selfish Genes and Christian Ethics: Theological and Ethical Reflections on Evolutionary Biology*, London: SCM Press, 2007.

Michael S. Northcott, *The Environment and Christian Ethics*, Cambridge: Cambridge University Press, 1996.

6

Critical Voices: The 'Recovery of Virtue'[1]

1 Case Studies

Read the following case studies and make brief notes in response to the questions. As before, you will be asked to revisit your answers at the end of the chapter.

Healthcare Rationing and Justice
'Child B' and 'Baby Ryan'[2]

'Child B' was ten years old and very ill with leukaemia. A bone marrow transplant had failed and her doctors believed that further treatment would be futile. However, her father obtained a second opinion from another specialist who recommended further chemotherapy and a second bone marrow transplant. Because this was an experimental treatment that was thought to have only a slender chance of success and guidance from the Department of Health limited the funding of treatments that were unproven, Child B's health authority judged that it would not be an effective use of its resources and decided not to fund it. Her father took the health authority to court and initially succeeded – the High Court placed a heavy burden of proof on the authority to show why other patients should have priority over Child B.

However, the Court of Appeal overturned the High Court's decision, partly on the grounds that courts ought not to get drawn into arguments about resource allocation, but primarily because the experimental treatment was not judged to be in Child B's best medical interests. Subsequently, a private individual came forward and donated the money to fund her treatment, but it proved unsuccessful and she died after a few months.

Arguments about medical futility played a large part in Child B's case and her doctors turned out to be correct, but it should be noted that these judgements are not clear cut and can be very difficult to make. There are occasional surprises, as in the American case of 'Baby Ryan'. He was born prematurely and diagnosed with multiple health problems, including brain damage, blocked intestines and kidney failure. His doctors wanted to withdraw treatment on the grounds that it was futile and prolonging his suffering and a second opinion agreed. However, after his parents obtained a court order to maintain his treatment, a third hospital offered to treat him. Its treatment (including surgery on his intestines) proved remarkably successful and, by the time he was one year old, he appeared to be developing normally with no permanent damage to his brain function.

Drugs for Developing Countries[3]

In 2005, a number of organizations, including the healthcare charity Médecins Sans Frontières (MSF), launched the 'Drugs for Neglected Diseases Initiative'. This is meant to focus increased research effort on drugs, vaccines and diagnostic tests for diseases that mostly affect poor countries and communities – for example, tuberculosis, sleeping sickness and leishmaniasis. For some of these diseases, no effective treatments, vaccines or tests have been developed. For example, the current test for TB only works in about 50 per cent of cases and is even less reliable in children and patients who also have HIV. For some diseases, there are effective treatments that have been withdrawn from the market because they are uneconomic to produce.

One reason for the neglect of these diseases is that the research and development (R&D) needed to bring new drugs to the market is very expensive and, at present, much of it is funded by multinational drug companies out of the sales of their products. This tends to mean that R&D is focused on the diseases common in wealthy countries as treatments for these diseases will bring the best return on companies' R&D investment. According to MSF, redressing the balance will require a massive investment in research into neglected diseases, which will require that big changes are made to the way health R&D is funded and much greater efforts from governments and international organizations (such as the World Health Organization) than they have made to date.

Questions

- Do we have a right to healthcare? If so, what exactly do we have a right to? If we have a right to healthcare, who has a duty to provide it and how far does their duty extend?
- When there are not enough resources to give everyone all the medical treatment they could benefit from, how would you decide which patients and what treatments should have priority?
- Who ought to be involved in making that decision?
- Who might have responsibilities for addressing the global problems raised in the second case study? What responsibilities might they have and why?

2 Healthcare, Justice and the Failure of the 'Enlightenment Project'[4]

Almost certainly, any society equipped with modern medicine is going to face the problem of scarcity. Modern healthcare demands costly resources – highly trained professionals, expensive equipment and drugs, large institutions, such as hospitals – and, in a sense, it is a victim of its own success, in that there is always more that could be done than the available resources allow. So, we are always going to have to face the question of how to allocate these limited resources *fairly* (how to ration them, to use a shorter but less accurate term). To use a piece of moral jargon, this is a question of *distributive justice*, which is the aspect of justice that says how a community's goods should be shared out among its members.

Not surprisingly, public arguments about healthcare resource allocation usually reflect one or other of the philosophical approaches to ethics that we surveyed in Chapter 4. One of the most influential approaches to the problem is based on the *quality adjusted life year* (*QALY*). The idea is to measure the outcome of medical treatment in terms of both the length and the quality of patients' lives. To calculate the number of QALYs a patient enjoys, you multiply the number of years he or she lives by a factor representing the person's quality of life, where 1 represents full health and 0 represents death. (Some versions also allow for negative numbers, representing a quality of life *worse* than death.) The effectiveness of a treatment can be measured by the net gain of QALYs – that is, the number of QALYs patients have after their treatment, minus the number they would have had if they had not been treated. According to this measure, a treatment is effective if it increases length of life, quality of life or both. The cost-effectiveness of treatments can be measured as cost per QALY. Health economists who favour this approach argue that treatments with low costs per QALY should have priority over those with high costs per QALY.

This approach is obviously based on a form of *utilitarianism* (see Chapter 4) as it says that health policy makers, managers and professionals should allocate their resources so as to do the greatest good for the greatest number. It has attracted many critics. Some wonder whether or not it is possible to measure 'quality of life' as reliably and objectively as the method requires (compare the criticism of Bentham's 'hedonic calculus' in Chapter 4). Others complain that it is unjust. For example, some argue that it discriminates unfairly against older people because they have fewer years left to live and therefore stand to gain fewer QALYs than younger people receiving the same treatment. Defenders of this approach sometimes reply that it is perfectly fair to discriminate against the old because they have already had a 'good innings', whereas the young still have much of their lives ahead of them.

Another influential approach, apparently quite different, comes from Norman Daniels, who is influenced by theories of justice such as the one developed by political philosopher John Rawls.[5] Rawls' theory is an attempt to give a sophisticated philosophical account of the commonsense notion of 'justice as fairness'. Among other things, his theory requires *equality of opportunity* – that is, everyone in a society should have the opportunity to pursue their own goals and preferences. It would be unfair if, for some arbitrary reason over which you had no control, you were denied opportunities to pursue your most important goals while your neighbour was given those opportunities.

Now Daniels argues that a certain level of health is necessary if people are to have access to the normal range of opportunities available to people in their societies. If you are too sick, you might miss out, for example, on important opportunities for education and employment. So, to ensure fairness, society is obliged to provide enough healthcare to ensure that, as far as possible, no one misses out on the normal range of opportunities in that society. This level of healthcare is sometimes referred to as a 'decent minimum'. Another way of putting this is that all members of a society have the *right* to a decent minimum level of healthcare. (For more on rights and Rawls' theory of justice, see the Appendix to Chapter 3.)

Whereas the QALY approach is utilitarian, the kind of approach suggested by Daniels seems to have some of its roots in *deontological* theories of the kind we explored in Chapter 4. It uses the language of obligations, rights and principles, such as justice. However, this kind of approach also has its critics. For example, 'libertarian' political theorists such as Robert Nozick argue that, in order to protect equality of opportunity in the way that Rawls and Daniels want, the State would have to interfere in the freedom of individuals in unacceptable ways. If the State is to provide a 'decent minimum' of healthcare for all, it will have to fund it by taxing the better-off, but, say libertarians, this is unacceptable. The State is not entitled to take people's money away from them for this kind of purpose unless they freely choose to give it.

There are also other quite different critiques of Rawlsian theory. For example, some feminists hold that the arguments Rawls uses to develop his approach depend on a peculiarly male understanding of what it is to be human and ignore women's perspectives and experience. (For more on feminist approaches, see Chapter 8.)

To sum up what I have said so far, there are different, probably incompatible, approaches to the problems of healthcare funding and distribution, no approach seems to command a consensus and each is criticized from a variety of directions. The picture begins to look very confusing.

This is one example of what philosopher Alasdair MacIntyre, in the early 1980s, called the 'interminability' of modern moral debates.[6] By calling them 'interminable' he does not just mean that they go on and on, but also that they cannot be brought to a conclusion, because those holding the different positions argue from such different starting points that they cannot find enough common ground to resolve their disagreements.

According to MacIntyre, this problem is caused by what he calls the 'Enlightenment project' in ethics. By this he means the attempt, from about the end of the seventeenth century, to cut ethics loose from any external sources of authority and base it solely on autonomous human reason working from self-evident first principles.

Though apparently very different from one another, Kant's deontological theory and Bentham's utilitarianism (both introduced in Chapter 4) are classic examples of what he means. According to MacIntyre, this project has failed and, indeed, was bound to do so. This is because the Enlightenment thinkers were attempting to construct rational justifications for a morality that they had inherited from an older tradition within which it made sense. They wanted to hold on to the morality, but reject the tradition. In other words, they had a pretty good idea what a good human life was like – an idea that they owed largely to the philosophical and theological traditions that had shaped Western societies for centuries. They wanted to construct rational justifications for their notions of the good life without appealing to the traditions that had shaped those notions, but the philosophical systems that they used to try and justify their notions were not rich or comprehensive enough to do the job. Each system could give an account of some aspects of the good life, but not others, and so our moral discourse and debate has become fragmented, incoherent and, as MacIntyre says, interminable.

For example, our inherited notions of justice have roots that go as deep as the Hebrew Bible and the philosophy of Plato and Aristotle. The tradition that has come from these sources, among others, has generated a rich and complex notion of what justice is. The different modern approaches that are deployed in arguments about healthcare resource allocation may each capture some parts of that notion, but they miss out other parts. This, from MacIntyre's point of view, is what makes the discussion so confusing and makes it seem difficult, if not impossible, to reach a consensus.

If MacIntyre is right, then we cannot have the morality without the tradition that it comes from. We have two options: discard the morality or try to recover the tradition. The first option he identifies with the philosopher Friedrich Nietzsche, who, he says, was one of the first to realize the incoherence of the Enlightenment project. MacIntyre himself, however, wishes to follow the second course, which means going back to the roots of the tradition in Aristotle and his predecessors.

3 A Brief History of Virtue[7]

The older tradition MacIntyre wishes to recover and develop for our own time is the tradition of *virtue* and the *virtues*. *Virtues* are qualities of character or, as Thomas Aquinas put it, 'dispositions to act well'.[8] This means that, while the modern approaches we explored in Chapter 4 focus on acts and decisions, virtue ethics is at least as interested in moral *character*. In other words, for deontological ethics and utilitarianism, the key questions are, 'What should I do?' and 'How do I know what I should do?' A more fundamental question for virtue ethics is, 'What sort of person ought I to *be*?' My choices and actions will flow from my character (note, though, that my choices will also help to form and develop my character), so, if I have a virtuous character, my judgements about what I should do will be more sound and reliable than if I do not.

Classical Roots

The concept of virtue goes back to ancient Greek thought, in which the word *aretē* (usually translated 'virtue') originally meant any kind of excellence. Thus, the *aretē* of a knife might have to do with its sharpness, the *aretē* of a racehorse with its speed and so on. Later, it came to mean some praiseworthy trait of character or intellect.

Some of the key early contributions to the tradition came from Plato (427–347 BCE) – one of the most important figures in the history of Western philosophy. He held that, in order to become virtuous, we must have some knowledge of what is truly good. We cannot reliably gain this knowledge by observing the everyday world around us, which is subject to change, imperfection and decay. If we wish to acquire true knowledge of the good, we shall have to seek it in the realm of the eternal realities – the so-called 'Forms' or 'Ideas' – from which everyday things get their reality and their characteristics.

The supreme Form for Plato is the 'Form of the Good', and anything good in the world is good in so far as it reflects – or, as Plato puts it, 'participates in' – the Form of the Good. One of the main ways in which we gain knowledge of the good, according to Plato, is through philosophy, which is why his ideal state would be ruled by philosophers.

Among Plato's other contributions to the tradition is an influential list of the most important virtues, which are often called the 'cardinal' virtues:

- courage
- temperance
- prudence
- justice.

('Temperance' here does not mean quite what it meant to the nineteenth-century Temperance Movement, which tried to persuade people to abstain from alcohol. Rather, it means that all your drives and instincts should be held in the right balance and properly controlled by your reason. 'Prudence' here also has a different meaning from its modern one of rational self-interest. The Greek word is *phronēsis*, which can also be translated as 'practical wisdom', and means something like a capacity for sound judgement about practical moral matters.)

Plato is also a source of the idea of the 'unity of the virtues'. This is the notion that, to be virtuous, it is not enough to have one of the virtues in isolation – you need to have them all, in the right balance, and they should spill over into one another, as it were. So, in a situation that demands courage, a truly virtuous person will display not just courage, but the kind of courage that you would expect to see in a person who is prudent, temperate and just.

Further crucial contributions were made by Plato's pupil Aristotle (384–322 BCE), who developed – and in some cases challenged – Plato's thought. In his *Nichomachean Ethics*, Aristotle draws a distinction between *intellectual* and *moral* virtues. *Intellectual virtues* are, as the term suggests, qualities such as intelligence and mathematical skill. They are developed by instruction. *Moral virtues* are praiseworthy qualities of character, such as courage, generosity and self-control, and these are developed by upbringing, example, practice and habit. This is an important point that, as we shall see, has been taken up by modern writers on virtue ethics. In order to develop virtuous habits, you need to *practise*. To use a modern illustration, just as you can only learn to ride a bicycle by practising, so you can only learn to be courageous by acting courageously. Theoretical discussions about either cycling or courage, though they may be interesting and valuable in their own way, will not get you very far by themselves.

Aristotle also develops the so-called 'doctrine of the mean'. This is the notion that any virtue is a sort of middle way between two extremes, which are vices. For example, courage is the mean between cowardice on the one hand and rashness on the other.

Another key idea that the Greeks bequeathed to later thought is the notion that human beings have some kind of end or goal (*telos* in Greek) – human life is *for* something. For Aristotle, the ultimate human goal is *eudaimonia*. This is often translated as 'happiness', but *eudaimonia* is a much richer concept than what we often mean by happiness and certainly richer than Bentham's concept of happiness, which we met in Chapter 4. It is probably better that we understand it as something like 'human flourishing' or 'fulfilment'. The virtues are those qualities that enable us to move towards our goal. As we shall see, Christian thinkers later took up this idea that human life has a goal or purpose, but reworked it in distinctively theological ways.

Early Christian Thought

Though the Bible does not use the language of virtue very much, the New Testament contains lists of characteristics that Christians are supposed to display and these could be called lists of virtues. One is found in

Galatians 5.22–3 and comprises love, joy, peace, patience, kindness, generosity, faithfulness, gentleness and self-control. (Significantly, Paul describes these qualities as the 'fruit of the [Holy] Spirit', which immediately suggests a difference from Greek thought about the virtues, as we shall see later.) Another list, perhaps the most famous, is in 1 Corinthians 13.13 and comprises faith, hope and love.

Early Christian thinkers took up the language of virtue from classical sources and combined it with their reading of the New Testament. In particular, Ambrose of Milan (*c.* 339–97 CE) combined Plato's list of the four cardinal virtues (also known as 'natural' virtues) with Paul's list – faith, hope and love – which are often referred to as the 'theological' or 'supernatural' virtues.

Augustine of Hippo (354–430 CE), whose thought was deeply influenced by Plato and his followers, reflected critically on the ideals of virtue that he found in the society around him. He argued that virtue can only be truly virtuous if it reflects the knowledge and love of God – the source of all true goodness. Pagan virtues, he believed, though they may be praiseworthy in many respects, cannot truly be called virtuous as they are not rooted in the love of God.

The Middle Ages and After

Christian virtue theory was most fully developed in the Middle Ages by Thomas Aquinas.[9]

Thomas follows earlier Christian thinkers in adopting a two-tier scheme of virtues:

- the cardinal virtues of prudence, courage, justice and temperance
- the theological virtues of faith, hope and love.

He also draws a great deal from the Greek philosophers, especially Aristotle, who is one of his chief influences. For example, Thomas takes up the idea that humans have ends or goals and the virtues direct us towards these goals. As we saw when we explored his natural law theory (Chapter 3), he holds that humans have three groups of natural ends, which are to:

- exist and maintain our existence
- mate and rear offspring
- live in ordered societies and know the truth about God.

The cardinal virtues direct our lives towards these natural goals. We have a natural capacity to develop these virtues or, as Thomas puts it, 'acquire' them. If it were not for sin, our acquired, natural virtues would be sufficient to enable us to attain our natural goals. However, because we are sinners, our nature is no longer 'integrated', but 'disordered' and, in this state, our capacity to develop even our natural virtues is impaired. We now cannot achieve even our natural ends or goals by our own efforts – we need God's help to do so.

Furthermore, as well as our natural goals, human life also has a *supernatural* goal that is quite beyond our natural human capacities to attain. It is personal union with God and a blessed immortality. The theological or supernatural virtues of faith, hope and love direct our lives towards this ultimate end, but we do not have any natural capacity to acquire these virtues – they must be 'infused' or 'instilled' in us by God. These virtues, then, are not a matter of human achievement, but God's loving gift to us or the work of God's Spirit in us. (There are echoes here of Paul's description of Christian virtues as the 'fruit of the Spirit'.) In other words, we need God's *grace*, both to repair the damage done to our natural virtue by our sin and to direct our lives towards their ultimate, supernatural goal.

According to MacIntyre, the tradition of the virtues continued to supply the language and intellectual framework for understanding morality into the early modern period. However, as the Enlightenment project gathered pace in the eighteenth century, these older ways of thinking about virtue were increasingly obscured by the new approaches of the Enlightenment thinkers. (Note, however, that the language of the virtues never disappeared entirely. Jean Porter points out that significant contributions to virtue theory from both philosophers and theologians can be found up to the early twentieth century.) MacIntyre argues, as we have seen, that the inevitable failure of the Enlightenment project has left our intellectual and moral life in the mess that it is in now.

If that is so, what can be done about it? In answer to this question,

MacIntyre notes that there have been other times when the language and tradition of the virtues has been threatened, in particular during the 'Dark Ages' following the collapse of the Roman Empire. During that time, the tradition was kept alive largely by the monastic communities founded by St Benedict and others.

This stress on *community* is an important aspect of MacIntyre's thought. The idea is that it is difficult for coherent moral traditions to flourish in a society as large as a modern nation state – they need more local, closely knit forms of community that can develop (and argue about) shared understandings of the good life. So, in the face of the fragmentation of moral discourse following the failure of the Enlightenment project, MacIntyre famously closes his book *After Virtue* by offering an alternative vision: 'the construction of local forms of community within which civility and the intellectual and moral life can be sustained through the new dark ages which are already upon us . . . We are waiting . . . for another – doubtless very different – St Benedict.'[10]

4 Theologians Among the Virtues

Among Christian ethicists, there has in recent decades been a great renewal of interest – largely inspired by MacIntyre – in the ethics of virtue and character. This recent movement in Christian ethics is very diverse and does not conform to any tidy pattern. For example, Christian virtue theorists vary in the use they make of leading figures from earlier stages of the tradition, such as Thomas Aquinas. Some contemporary writers, such as Celia Deane-Drummond, draw heavily on Thomas, and find in his approach a very fruitful resource for addressing many contemporary moral problems.[11] Others, such as Stanley Hauerwas (one of the most prolific and best-known recent thinkers in this area) are more eclectic – that is, they deliberately draw on a wide range of sources from diverse strands of the Christian tradition.

Much recent theological writing about virtue ethics emphasizes the importance of *character*. For a writer such as Hauerwas, for example, character is more fundamental than acts, rules or principles. Thus, the basic questions we should ask are not what we should do, but what sort of people, and communities, we should be. Following Aristotle, many Christian virtue ethicists emphasize that character and moral virtue are developed by example, practice and habit. Following Thomas, they also emphasize that truly virtuous character is not merely a human achievement but also God's gracious gift – it is the result of the Holy Spirit's work in the lives of people and communities.

Moral character, as I have mentioned, is developed by example, practice and habit. Virtue ethicists influenced by MacIntyre stress the importance of *moral communities* in nurturing character. A moral community, in the sense they mean, is shaped by a *tradition* that gives the community a sense of its roots, history, identity and purpose. The tradition even shapes the community's notions of *rationality* as the shared patterns and habits of thought help determine what counts as a good reason for believing or doing something. Such traditions come largely in *narrative* – story – form. That is, a community gets its moral identity from the story or stories that it tells about itself. The members of a community find their own moral identities and roles as they participate in the community and identify themselves with its story.

For Christian virtue ethicists such as Hauerwas, the Church is called to be a 'community of character', which gets its identity from the story of Jesus Christ. As Hauerwas puts it, 'Christian ethics is not first of all an ethics of principles, rules or values, but an ethic that demands we attend to the life of a particular individual – Jesus of Nazareth.'[12] The Church repeatedly retells and re-enacts that story in its worship, so that its members come, as it were, to inhabit the story for themselves. For those who participate in the Church's life and worship, the story ceases to be just a tale of long-past events, and becomes *their* story. Their moral identities and characters – and the character of the Christian community to which they belong – are formed by this story. While this moral formation may include specific instructions, commands, rules and so on, a more fundamental aspect of it is a renewed moral vision that is akin to what Richard Hays calls a 'symbolic world' (see Chapter 2). You see the world, your own place in it and the way of life that is required of you differently once your identity has been shaped by this story. Hauerwas and William Willimon put it vividly:

ethics is first a way of *seeing* before it is a matter of *doing*. The ethical task is not to tell you what is right or wrong but rather to train you to see. That explains why, in the Church, a great deal of time and energy are spent in the act of worship: In worship, we are busy looking in the right direction.[13]

For Hauerwas and others, the character of the Christian community sets it sharply apart from the society in which it is set (this is certainly the case if that society is a Western liberal democracy). For example, as we saw in Chapter 3, Hauerwas believes that a central feature of the Church's character should be a radical commitment to non-violence. He has also argued in many books and articles for a radically countercultural approach to questions of medical ethics, including death, dying and euthanasia.

Hauerwas' stress on the distinctive character of the Christian community as the basis for Christian ethics has gained him many critics.[14] One common criticism is that his ethic is *sectarian* – that is, it makes sense as part of the belief system of the Church, but is incomprehensible to anyone who does not share that belief system and offers no points of contact that would allow for moral dialogue between Christians and non-Christians.

Another objection is that Hauerwas' vision of the Church is a fiction that does not correspond to reality. This charge partly refers to his tendency to borrow from many different Christian traditions, from Anabaptist to Roman Catholic. The result, according to his critics, is an invention that does not correspond to any real Christian denomination. More seriously, as most ministers will tell you, Christian congregations are not always shining examples of moral communities. Many do not look that different from their surrounding culture and a few, at worst, can be quite vicious, dysfunctional groups that actually compare very poorly with secular society.

To some extent, though, the second of these objections misses the point. Hauerwas has no difficulty in acknowledging that the Church often spectacularly fails to be what it is called to be and, indeed, his writing is intended, in part, as a challenge to the Church to be more faithful to its calling. As he put it some years ago, 'I find I must think and write not only for the Church that does exist but for the Church that should exist if we were more courageous and faithful.'[15] Furthermore, defenders of his approach point out that

real, perfectly ordinary Christian individuals and communities do sometimes get it right, living out their Christian calling and displaying Christian
virtues in extraordinarily courageous and faithful ways. If the stories of such
communities are told, they become part of the tradition that can help form
the character of other Christian individuals and communities.[16]

In response to the first charge of sectarianism, Hauerwas and others often
argue that there is no moral 'view from nowhere' – no objective, neutral point
of view from which to think about moral questions. It is not as if everyone else
in a pluralist society were playing the same moral game by commonly agreed
rules that were fair to all and the Church opted out and went off by itself to
play a different game with an idiosyncratic set of rules. Rather, everyone's
moral vision and identity is shaped by some tradition or other (or, perhaps
more often in a modern society, by a confusing and self-contradictory mix
of traditions). The basic assumptions of one tradition can tend to exclude
or marginalize the perspectives of another: if you agree to play the game by
someone else's rules, you may find yourself playing on a field that is tilted
in their favour. According to this view, it is likely to be more fruitful and
helpful to be open about your own tradition and the distinctive perspectives
it gives you than to try and find some kind of neutral common ground for
moral dialogue. However, this does not mean that different traditions are
condemned to be sealed off from one another, talking only to themselves. As
MacIntyre has argued, it is possible (though it takes some effort) for different
traditions to learn one another's moral 'language' and communicate with one
another. Furthermore, Hauerwas has often stressed that the Church's most
important moral contribution to the society around it is not a distinctive
and countercultural moral *argument*, but a countercultural *way of life* that
witnesses to the new possibilities opened up by following Jesus Christ. This
is beautifully illustrated by Hauerwas and Willimon's story of Dorothy, who
was a member of the church in which one of them grew up. In the church,
they thought of her as the Sunday school teacher's assistant. It was only later,
when they were 'nearly all grown up and adult', that the world taught them to
think of her as someone 'afflicted' with Down's syndrome. In the church, she
was not regarded as afflicted or problematic, but was a valued and respected
member of the community. Hauerwas and Willimon connect her story with
the episode in Matthew's Gospel in which Jesus tells his disciples that, unless

they become like children – who were among the most insignificant and powerless members of first-century Palestinian society – they 'will never enter the kingdom of heaven' (Matthew 18.1–4). They comment:

> It is here, in an episode like Matthew 18:1–4, in setting a child in the middle of disciples, that Christian ethics begin. By way of concrete reminders and illustrations, the Church assembles reminders of the kingdom of God in subtle, seemingly trivial and insignificant ways. In placing Dorothy, someone quite insignificant and problematic for the world, in the middle of the third grade Sunday school class, Buncombe Street Church was re-enacting Matthew 18:1–4 and practising ethics in the ordinary, unspectacular yet profound and revolutionary way the Church practises ethics.[17]

5 The Case Studies Revisited[18]

Healthcare Rationing and Justice

As virtue theory has come back onto the agenda of ethics, many secular and Christian ethicists have been eager to explore its implications for medical ethics. There have been virtue-based discussions of particular issues, such as abortion and euthanasia, discussions of the particular virtues that doctors, nurses, patients and others should display and wider-ranging accounts of the practice of medicine as an activity with its own distinctive moral character. However, the more political and economic aspects of medical ethics, such as healthcare resource allocation, have not been given the virtue treatment to anything like the same extent. Discussion of these questions still, by and large, tends to follow deontological or utilitarian approaches, such as the ones described at the beginning of this chapter.

What would happen if we tried to think about healthcare resource allocation in terms of virtue ethics? There are various ways in which this could be done, but we might start by recalling that the question of resource allocation is one of distributive justice and, in ancient and medieval accounts, justice is one of the four cardinal virtues. So, what difference does it make if we think about justice as a virtue in relation to resource allocation?

The first thing to notice is that, although the tradition of the virtues has a great deal to say about justice, it will not give us neatly packaged answers to our questions about healthcare resource allocation. Thomas Aquinas, for example, discusses the virtues – including justice – extensively, but he does not spell out in any detail what counts as a just distribution of goods. We shall not get from him any principles that will tell us how much of a healthcare budget should go on hip replacements and how much on liver transplants, or whether Child B's health authority was right to refuse funding for her experimental treatment. There is a very good reason for this. What counts as a just distribution of goods depends so much on detailed factors that vary from one context to another that no one, not even Thomas, could hope to foresee all the relevant factors and weigh them all up in advance of a particular situation. We shall have to approach the question more indirectly and, for Thomas, this is where another virtue – prudence, or, practical wisdom – comes in.

I said earlier that prudence means something like a capacity for sound practical moral judgement. Thomas identifies one kind of prudence that he calls 'political prudence'. This virtue enables those responsible for making political decisions (which, in a democracy, means every voter, in one way or another) to judge what decisions will best serve the good of all: what will give everyone the best opportunities to flourish and attain their goals. So, the more highly the members of a political community develop the virtue of 'political prudence', the more sound their judgements about detailed questions of resource allocation will be.[19]

How, though, do we develop the virtue of 'political prudence'? Again, there are various ways in which this question could be answered, but one would be to follow the example of Hauerwas and others and look at the distinctive traditions and practices of the Christian Church. If we approach the question this way, we are, in effect, asking, 'From a Christian point of view, how do we know what counts as a just distribution of healthcare resources in a particular situation?' The initial answer to this question is that we need to cultivate a form of 'political prudence', shaped by the Church's traditions, that will give us a sound instinct for justice in the distribution of healthcare goods.

How do we go about cultivating that 'political prudence'? One way, perhaps, is to look for themes in the Church's tradition – stories from its Scriptures, aspects of its practices, and so on – that will give us insights into what the Christian tradition means when it says 'justice'. For example, in the Sermon on the Mount, Matthew's Jesus paints a picture of a God who is indiscriminately generous to all, whether or not they deserve it: 'he makes his sun rise on the evil and on the good, and sends rain on the righteous and on the unrighteous' (Matthew 5.45).

Divine justice, according to this text, does not seem to mean simply giving people what they deserve. If Christians think that the allocation of healthcare goods ought to reflect divine justice in some way, this text might make them suspicious of any policy that regarded some people as more 'deserving' of healthcare than others, either because they had contributed more to society in the past or because they had more to contribute in the future. Again, it seems that one highly important practice of the first followers of Jesus was to share their goods self-sacrificially with those in need (see, for example, Acts 4.34–5). This sharing did not seem to have geographical limits. Paul, for example, tried hard to persuade churches right around the eastern Mediterranean to contribute to a collection for the impoverished believers in Jerusalem (see 2 Corinthians 8, 9, for example). The Christian practice of sharing sacrificially with those in need has often been neglected, but rarely forgotten totally, by the Church. Christians whose understanding of justice has been influenced by this practice might be strongly inclined to think that all the members of a community should be ready to make sacrifices in order to meet the needs of those who are ill. Furthermore, the fact that such sharing crosses geographical boundaries might influence the way that Christians think about international inequalities in healthcare, as in the second of our case studies.

A further aspect of the Church's tradition that might have a bearing on its vision of justice in healthcare has to do with an honest attitude to the limits of human existence. We are finite beings and we have limited resources, so we cannot do all the good that needs to be done. As Allen Verhey points out, this means that, in healthcare, we will sometimes be faced with *tragic* choices – that is, if we cannot do *all* the good things that need doing, the choice of one good is also, necessarily, a choice against another.[20] If we spend part of our healthcare budget on *this* group of patients, the same amount of money will not be available to pay for *that* group's care. It is dishonest to pretend that we can avoid tragic choices or that everyone's disease can be cured. However, as Verhey, Hauerwas and others point out, the Church has a history of enabling its members to find the strength to face tragedy and suffering and continue to care even for those who cannot be cured.

I have sketched out some themes from the Christian tradition that might influence the way that Christian communities think about healthcare resource allocation. How such Christian thinking ought to influence political decision making in secular and pluralist societies is a separate question that we must leave on one side for now, but we return to it in Chapter 9.

Questions

Return to your answers to the case study questions at the start of the chapter.

- What difference would a virtue ethics approach make to your answers?
- What do you think are the strengths and weaknesses of such an approach?

Suggestions for Further Reading

Virtue Ethics

Of the many books by Hauerwas, the ones listed below give a good flavour of his writing. The book by Nation and Wells offers sympathetically critical discussions of his thought by a variety of authors. The article by Porter is a valuable overview of virtue ethics and her book gives a good account of a contrasting Christian approach to that of Hauerwas.

Stanley Hauerwas, *A Community of Character: Towards a Constructive Christian Social Ethic*, Notre Dame, IN: University of Notre Dame Press, 1981.
——, *The Peaceable Kingdom: A Primer in Christian Ethics*, London, SCM Press, 1984.
——and Charles Pinches, *Christians Among the Virtues: Theological Conversations*

with Ancient and Modern Ethics, Notre Dame, IN: University of Notre Dame Press, 1997.

Mark Thiessen Nation and Samuel Wells (eds), *Faithfulness and Fortitude: In Conversation with the Theological Ethics of Stanley Hauerwas*, Edinburgh: T & T Clark, 2000.

Jean Porter, *The Recovery of Virtue: The Relevance of Aquinas for Christian Ethics*, London: SPCK, 1994.

Jean Porter, 'Virtue Ethics', in Robin Gill (ed.), *The Cambridge Companion to Christian Ethics*, Cambridge: Cambridge University Press, 2001, pp. 96–111.

Healthcare Resource Allocation

Tom L. Beauchamp and James F. Childress, *Principles of Biomedical Ethics*, 5th edn, New York: Oxford University Press, 2001, pp. 225–82. (A standard work on medical ethics, widely used by health professionals and others. The chapter cited here covers a wide range of secular approaches to healthcare resource allocation.)

H. Tristram Engelhardt, Jr, and Mark J. Cherry (eds), *Allocating Scarce Medical Resources: Roman Catholic Perspectives*, Washington, DC: Georgetown University Press, 2002.

Stephen E. Lammers and Allen Verhey (eds), *On Moral Medicine: Theological Perspectives on Medical Ethics*, 2nd edn, Grand Rapids, MI: Eerdmans, 1998, pp. 943–1004.

7

Critical Voices: Liberation Theologies and Christian Ethics

1 Case Study

Read the following case study and make brief notes in answer to the questions. You will be asked to refer back to your notes at the end of the chapter.

The Trade Justice Campaign[1]

In 2001, a number of non-governmental organizations, including Christian Aid, launched the Trade Justice campaign to draw attention to some of the problems and issues associated with international trade and global capitalism.

The industrialized countries of the world tend to argue strongly in favour of free trade between nations and oppose import tariffs and other economic barriers that individual nations might put up to protect their own producers from foreign competition. The policy of free trade is enforced through the World Trade Organization (WTO) and the international negotiations that it sponsors.

Historically, many of the world's poorer nations have not operated free trade policies, but have been obliged to move in a free trade direction due to pressure from the richer nations brought about via the WTO and other channels. The International Monetary Fund (IMF) and the World Bank also put pressure on developing countries to adopt free market policies, both domestically and in their international trading relationships, on the grounds that such policies will be the most effective way of enabling their economies to grow.

In the post-war period, so the argument goes, newly independent nations in Africa and elsewhere developed economies dominated by State-run industries. These centrally controlled economies tended to stagnate rather than grow, partly because they were inefficient and partly because corruption was also widespread. It is often claimed that trade liberalization and the adoption of free markets, among other things, are needed to enable these countries to move out of poverty.

Trade Justice campaigners, however, question the wisdom of some of these arguments. They concede that the centrally controlled, protectionist economies of the 1960s and 1970s were inefficient and this inefficiency was one factor in the failure of these economies to prosper. However, they argue that international free trade unfairly disadvantages poor nations for a variety of reasons. One is that producers in wealthy nations often enjoy more stable conditions and a better infrastructure (road and rail networks, energy supplies and so on) than their competitors in developing countries, which allows them to produce and distribute their goods more efficiently. Another is that wealthy nations or blocks of nations (for example, the USA and the European Union) sometimes subsidize their producers heavily, enabling them to produce cheap goods that can be dumped on markets in the developing world, forcing producers in these countries out of business. Trade Justice campaigners argue that, where developing economies have been successful (for example, in the Far East, at least until the slump of the late 1990s), they have benefited from protectionist barriers that shielded their growing industries from competition until they were sufficiently robust to compete on the world stage.

The campaign calls for a range of measures, including:

• stopping economic partnership agreements requiring free trade policies and the opening up of markets between European countries and their former colonies – instead, there should be agreements that do not enforce trade liberalization on developing countries where it is likely to hinder poverty reduction

- stopping the IMF and World Bank from making free trade policies a condition for development loans and debt cancellation for poor countries
- strengthening and enforcing the principle that poor countries should receive special treatment, 'biased' in their favour via the WTO
- cutting subsidies paid to producers and exporters in rich nations
- increasing international aid and debt cancellation in order to allow poor countries to develop the infrastructure that will make their economies more secure.

Questions

- In thinking about the ethics of international trade, what kinds of insight might Christians expect to gain from:

  - the Bible and Christian theological tradition
  - economic experts
  - producers and consumers in wealthy countries
  - producers and consumers in developing countries?

- What is your initial response to the Trade Justice campaign – how persuasive do you find its diagnosis and prescription and why?

2 Starting with Experience

This chapter and the next introduce a range of approaches to theology that focus on the experience of oppressed people and groups and seek to provide resources for their liberation. Because of this focus on the liberation of oppressed people, some of these theological approaches are known as *theologies of liberation*, a term that was first applied to the radical theological movement emerging from the Latin American churches in the late 1960s. Because poverty and economic inequality are among the forms of oppression that liberation theologies address and some Church campaigning on global trade and economics is influenced by liberationist approaches, I have linked the discussion of liberation theologies in this chapter with a case study about international trade. However, it is worth underlining that the various theologies of liberation are concerned with many other problems besides economic inequality, as we shall see. Accordingly, sections 3–5 of this chapter introduce liberationist approaches in a fairly general way and indicate something of the range of concerns that they address. Liberationist approaches to economics are discussed alongside other theological approaches in section 6. In the next chapter, we explore some varieties of *feminist* theology, which has important features in common with the theological approaches introduced in this chapter.

The first thing to say (in general!) about these theologies is that it is dangerous to generalize about them, because they are *contextual*. Any one of these theologies takes as its starting point the concrete experience of a particular group of people in a particular situation and its theological approach is shaped by that particular context and experience. It is *not* a matter of first sorting out your basic theological principles and then applying them in turn to the situations of Latin American peasants, black communities in urban Britain, women in rural India, people with disabilities and so on. Rather, the way you read and interpret the Bible, the way you engage with Christian tradition and the use you make of other areas of thought (such as the social sciences) will all be shaped and filtered by your concrete experience in a particular context. This should become clearer as we look in more detail at particular examples.

Having said that it is dangerous to generalize, the theological approaches that are introduced below and in the next chapter do have certain other features in common. One is a focus on *praxis* – a Greek word meaning 'practice'. Thus, the most important thing is right action, not right theory. Latin American liberationists sometimes quote Karl Marx: 'philosophers have only *interpreted the world*, in various ways; the point, however, is to *change it*.'[2] Theory – including theological 'theory' – is supposed to be the servant of practice, not the other way round. So, once you are already committed to right action, theory can help you understand more clearly what needs to be done, but the commitment to right action comes first. (Tim Gorringe, a

British theologian highly sympathetic to liberation theology, points out that the relationship between theory and praxis may be more complex than liberation theologians sometimes suggest. Theory may sometimes play a role in creating a commitment to right action, so it may in fact be more accurate to speak of a 'dialectic' or interplay between theory and praxis.)[3]

Another thing these theologies have in common is that they are *critical* of established attitudes and practices, including those of established theological traditions. These traditions are seen as having been controlled by the powerful, who have used them to give legitimacy to practices that oppress the powerless. There is a fair amount of variation in the way this critical attitude to established traditions works out. Some Latin American liberationists, for example, draw extensively not only on the Bible but also on many of the major figures in the Church's theological tradition, including the Fathers and medieval theologians such as Thomas Aquinas. Some feminists, by contrast, are much less inclined to build on the work of the 'dead, white males', who have been largely responsible for the Church's theological tradition, and regard the writings of the Bible itself with a high degree of suspicion, too, as most biblical writings reflect male perspectives from cultures in which women were given little status or value.

To get more of an idea of how such theological approaches work in practice, in the next section we look in a little more detail at Latin American liberation theology.

3 Latin American Liberation Theology

The term *liberation theology*, as noted earlier, originated in Latin America in the late 1960s, growing out of the widespread experience of poverty and political oppression. Some theologians and Church leaders, mostly (though not all) from the Roman Catholic Church, became increasingly critical of forms of economic development that trapped the poor in poverty and governments that used extreme force and violence to maintain social order. They also became critical of the way in which the Church had often colluded with this political and economic oppression and been used in one way or another as an ally by oppressive leaders and governments. They encouraged the development of grassroots communities of Christians – the so-called *base communities* – in which the poor could read the Bible together and use it to challenge the situation they found themselves in.

Liberationists became increasingly involved in many kinds of action for social transformation and their theological work has been a search for the theological resources that will support, inform and guide this struggle for social change. Key figures in the movement, such as Gustavo Gutiérrez, Leonardo and Clodovis Boff and Juan Luis Segundo, have become influential far beyond Latin America via the translations of their writings and have often found themselves in conflict with their Church authorities.

Thomas Schubeck – a North American Jesuit sympathetic to liberation theology – draws attention to some of its important features:

- it uses *distinctive sources*
- it has a *distinctive theological method*
- it looks at theology and ethics from a *new perspective*
- it is guided by an *ultimate standard*.[4]

Distinctive Sources

As mentioned earlier, *praxis* is very important to liberation theologians and I said that its basic meaning is 'practice'. However, in Latin American liberation theology, it tends to be used in a more specific, almost technical, sense, though its exact meaning varies from one writer to another.

In general, 'praxis' is used to mean committed action, in solidarity with the oppressed and directed towards social transformation. To liberationists, praxis is the starting point for theological reflection, as we shall see in the next subsection.

In order to understand the causes of oppression, liberation theologians have also made distinctive use of the *social sciences* – particularly sociology and economics. They have often had a preference for Marxist-inspired methods of social analysis. Thus, they have adopted sociological models that understand society as badly structured, conflict-ridden and needing transformation (so-called 'conflict' or 'dialectical', as opposed to 'functionalist', models).

They have also rejected models of economic development based on capitalist economics – instead adopting the Marx-inspired view that such economics keep the poor dependent on the wealthy and mask the ruthless assertion of the interests of the powerful. Their use of Marx and Marxist theory has been one source of their conflicts with the Vatican. It has also come in for more widespread criticism following the collapse of Soviet-style communism after 1989. However, liberationists stress that they do not swallow Marxist theory uncritically, but find it a fruitful source of insights into the structural causes of poverty and political oppression. We return in section 6 to liberationists' use of Marxist economic analysis.

Scripture is another key source of liberation theology, as is made clear in Gutiérrez's famous definition of theology: 'critical reflection on Christian praxis in the light of the Word [of God]'.[5] However, liberationists use it in distinctive ways. They insist that what you find in the Scriptures and how you understand them depends crucially on the perspective from which you read them – the spectacles, as it were, through which you read the Bible. If you read the Bible from the perspective of the powerful (for example, white, male, middle-class Westerners), you will tend to notice those texts that support the status quo and promote the interests of the Establishment and are likely to filter out – probably unconsciously – the texts and themes that challenge the established order. What is needed is a conscious choice to read the Bible instead 'from below', from the perspective of the poor and the oppressed, somewhat as the base communities in Latin America have read the Bible and brought it into contact with their own situation. If you make this conscious choice to read the Bible through the spectacles of the oppressed, you will find yourself noticing all kinds of things that you might have missed before. It is now almost taken for granted in theology that our perspective plays an important role in influencing the way we read and interpret texts, including the Bible. It is largely thanks to liberation theology that this has become such a commonplace.

A Distinctive Theological Method

Liberationists put these distinctive sources together into a distinctive *methodology* – a way of doing theology. This is often pictured as a so-called *hermeneutical circle*, which is a cycle or spiral in which praxis, social analysis and Scripture constantly interact, inform and challenge one another (see figure).

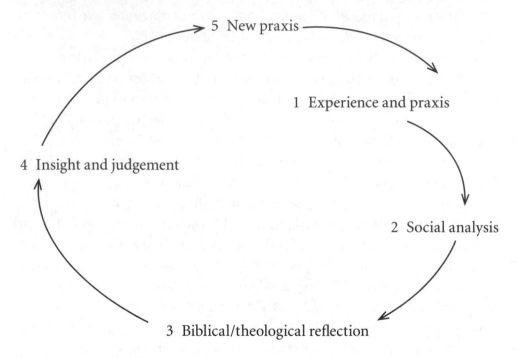

The hermeneutical circle

1   The experience of oppression – and committed action with the aim of challenging oppression – raises questions about the causes of that oppression.
2   Social-scientific methods of analysis are used to understand the political, social and economic factors that bring about and maintain the oppressive situation.
3   The Bible is read in search of theological insights that will guide a Christian response to that situation.

4   In the light of this reading of the Bible, insights and judgements are formed about the situation and the response that is called for.

5   Further praxis, guided and directed by these insights, generates new experience and raises new questions that call for analysis and reflection, and so the cycle continues.

This approach to theology makes possible a complex and subtle interplay between experience, Scripture and tradition, and other analytical tools. Although it begins with experience – in particular, the experience of poverty and oppression – that experience is not treated in any simple way as a kind of scientific datum, but may be analysed, reinterpreted and understood in new and different ways in the light of Scripture and tradition.

A New Perspective

But what gets all of this started in the first place? Liberationists recognize that their distinctive sources and methods depend on a prior choice – to interpret reality and read the Bible from the perspective of the poor and oppressed and do theology in the service of social transformation. This prior choice is often called the *preferential option for the poor*. It is, itself, rooted in Scripture (for example, in Luke's emphasis that the gospel is fundamentally good news to the poor). However, it is not self-evident – this stance of commitment to the cause of the poor has to be consciously chosen. Liberationists sometimes describe the choice as a 'conversion'. An example they use is Archbishop Oscar Romero of El Salvador, who was well known as an advocate of the poor and a critic of military rule and was murdered by a right-wing death squad in 1980. In his early career, he is said to have been conservative in his views and unsympathetic to liberation theology. However, after he had been appointed Archbishop, he underwent a radical shift in his attitudes – said to have been partly prompted by the murder of one of his priests, Rutilio Grande. This and similar events opened Romero's eyes to the injustice and oppression around him, as a result of which he became increasingly committed to the cause of the poor and oppressed.

An Ultimate Standard

For most liberationists, the ultimate standard and goal for human society is the *Kingdom* (or reign) *of God*. This language of the Kingdom expresses the hope that God will 'unblock' the future, as Tim Gorringe puts it,[6] and gives purpose to people struggling for liberation and justice in the present. It is understood, at least partly, in this-worldly terms – that is, the reign of God means God's will being done on Earth, which is understood to some extent in terms of just social, political and economic structures. However, liberationists who use this language stress that no present social reality, however good, can be completely identified with the reign of God – there is always a continuing need for liberation.

4 Black Theologies of Liberation

There are important common features (and, of course, equally important differences) between Latin American liberation theology and other 'local theologies' developed around the world by oppressed social or ethnic groups trying to find resources for their own liberation. Among the most influential have been *black theologies*, which have grown up in various black communities around the world.

For these communities, a major part of the social reality that needs analysing and challenging is racism – a combination of cultural and social attitudes and stereotypes that assume the superiority of one racial group with political, social and/or economic structures that reinforce the power of that group and work to the disadvantage of others.

In South Africa in the apartheid era, the struggle against oppression required opposition and resistance to a legal and political framework that systematically excluded blacks from political power, social opportunity and economic well-being – a resistance that was suppressed with the full force of the law and violence from the security forces. Theological opposition to apartheid also called for resistance to the 'Afrikaner theology' that buttressed the apartheid worldview.

In North America, black theology has been closely linked with the civil rights and Black Power movements. Black theologians such as James Cone have been concerned with the legacy of racism that has been left by the history of slavery in America and sought to work for the liberation of black people from every kind of oppression by white society. They have also been severely critical of white Christianity for being deeply implicated in the racism of society and doing theology in 'eurocentric' ways – that is, in ways biased in favour of white European perspectives to the exclusion of others.

Part of the project of black theology, therefore, is the reconstruction of theology so as to free it from such eurocentrism. Black theology in Britain is similarly concerned with the ongoing effect of Britain's colonial history, which has left a legacy of racist attitudes, practices and structures in British society and the Churches. Black theologians such as Robert Beckford seek to do theology in ways that bring together black Christian identity, a political and social concern for black liberation and attention to cultural expressions of black identity.[7]

5 Other 'Theologies from Below'

Many other people and groups take their cue from liberation theology, doing theology from their own particular perspectives as communities that experience particular forms of oppression and seeking particular forms of liberation and empowerment. It is only possible to give a few examples here to illustrate the diversity of these theologies:[8]

- I mentioned South African black theology in the apartheid era, earlier, but, in many other parts of Africa, theologians have for some time also been developing forms of *African theology* that explore the relationship between Christianity and African traditional cultures.
- There is a growing theological movement in India that does its theology from the perspective of the *Dalits*, who are the 'untouchables' at the bottom of the Indian caste system.
- Those living with various disabilities have begun to develop *theologies of disability*, reflecting on their faith and the society around them from the perspectives of people with disabilities. One example is John Hull,

a blind theologian and educationalist. Some of his writing challenges the assumptions about disability that are found in Christian thought, worship and practice, such as the use of blindness as a metaphor for moral and spiritual failure, the claim by some Christians that anyone with enough faith can be miraculously healed of their disability and the assumption that the ideal human being is able-bodied. In common with the wider disability rights movement, he is also critical of structures and practices (in the Church and in society at large) that tend to exclude and discriminate against people with disabilities.

- I mentioned briefly in Chapter 3 that some lesbian and gay Christians seek to develop *lesbian and gay theologies* from their experience of being an oppressed minority both in society and in the Church. More radically, so-called *queer theologies* aim to articulate the experience of a variety of sexual minorities – not only lesbian and gay, but also bisexual, transvestite and transgendered people, for example. Whereas some gay theologies argue that committed gay relationships should be accepted by Christians as a form of marriage, queer theologies aim to destabilize the whole notion that marriage is the best or only pattern for sexual relationships.

6 The Case Study Revisited: Theology, Economics and Trade Justice

Theologian Stephen Long classifies Christian writing about economics into a *dominant tradition*, an *emergent tradition* and a *residual tradition*.[9]

Christian writers in the *dominant tradition* are those who would broadly agree that *relative scarcity* is a fundamental reality with which economics has to get to grips. By 'relative scarcity' is meant that individuals and societies have finite resources and there are always more things that they could do with their resources than the resources themselves allow. If I have £10 to spare, I could buy a cinema ticket costing £7.50 for a film I have been wanting to see or a book on Christian ethics costing £9.95, or I could donate £10 to Christian Aid. If I choose the book, I cannot see the film or make the donation – these are what economists call the 'opportunity costs' of my decision.

Against this background, economics is the science concerned with the allocation of relatively scarce resources. Theologians in the dominant tradition agree with mainstream economists that the *market* is the most efficient mechanism yet devised for allocating relatively scarce resources in a way that maximizes the satisfaction of human preferences. (When it is put this way, the connections with the utilitarian theories described in Chapter 4 are obvious.)

The notion that the market functions in this way has its roots in the work of Adam Smith in the eighteenth century. Smith argued that those who buy and sell in the marketplace do not act out of benevolence or charity, but out of self-interest. However, their self-interested actions work together for everyone's benefit:

> It is not from the benevolence of the butcher, the brewer or the baker that we expect our dinner, but from their regard to their own interest. We address ourselves, not to their humanity, but to their self-love, and never talk to them of our own necessities but of their advantages.

Someone who pursues his or her own economic self-interest, said Smith, is 'led by an invisible hand to promote an end which is no part of his intention'[10] and when people pursue their own interests they frequently end up doing more good for society than when they are directly pursuing the common good.

This view – that the market is the best device for allocating resources – has been developed in economic thought in various ways, particularly by means of the concept of *diminishing marginal utility*, developed in the 1870s. 'Utility', in this context, means the satisfaction or benefit that consumers gain from goods or services, while 'marginal utility' means the extra satisfaction gained from an additional unit of a good or service. The assumption is that, other things being equal, the marginal utility of a good or service decreases with each additional unit purchased.[11] Consider a simple example. I am hungry after a hard morning teaching Christian ethics. I go for lunch to a sandwich shop where sandwiches cost £1 each. The first sandwich I buy has a high marginal utility – I feel much better after it than I did before. After my first sandwich, I am no longer ravenous, but am still quite hungry, so I buy a second. I get some satisfaction from the second sandwich, but less than I did from the first – its marginal utility is lower. After the second, I am no longer particularly hungry, though I could still find room for a third. At this point, though, I reflect that, instead of having yet another sandwich, I would rather spend the extra pound on a cup of coffee. Before I had had anything to eat or drink, the marginal utility of one sandwich was greater than that of a cup of coffee, but, after two sandwiches, the marginal utility of one more sandwich has fallen – diminished – to the point where it is lower than that of a cup of coffee, so I choose the coffee.

Within this framework, the market is reckoned to be the most efficient mechanism for maximizing the satisfaction of consumers' preferences and responding to the kinds of changes in preferences described by the concept of diminishing marginal utility. However, the market is held to be value-neutral – it cannot guide people to prefer one thing rather than another. Economics, according to this understanding, is the science that describes how markets and economic mechanisms function, but it has nothing to say about what people *ought* to prefer as their decisions about what to prefer will be guided by their beliefs, values and commitments, including their moral and religious commitments. This view of economics, in other words, makes the same sort of sharp distinction between facts and values that we encountered in section 5 of Chapter 5 in the context of the so-called 'naturalistic fallacy'.

Apologists for the market argue that its value-neutrality makes it a useful device for coping with moral plurality. A pluralist society contains people with a great variety of different moral beliefs and commitments. The market, its apologists say, does not favour one set of moral beliefs over another, but offers a mechanism by which a variety of different beliefs and commitments can be honoured, as far as possible. As such, it is preferable either to violent conflict between those with different commitments or a situation in which one group imposes its moral beliefs and commitments by force. In other words, supporters of the market not only argue that it is the most *efficient* mechanism for satisfying people's preferences but also that it is *morally* preferable to the alternatives. However, the fact–value distinction, on which this moral argument for the market depends, has not gone unchallenged, as we saw in Chapter 5, and shall see again later in this chapter.

Christian theologians whose theological principles lead them to agree in general with this view of the market nonetheless disagree vigorously about other economic and political questions. In particular, they differ as to how much the market can do by itself. Some, such as Michael Novak, while acknowledging that the State is needed for certain functions, want the market kept as free as possible from interference by the State. They hold that if the market functions freely, it will bring the greatest benefits to all. Others, such as the late Ronald Preston, place greater stress on the needs that the free market, left to itself, cannot meet. They therefore support a bigger role for the State, redistributing wealth and promoting social goods. Thus, what Long calls the dominant tradition includes those on both the 'right' and 'left' of contemporary Western politics.[12]

These different positions suggest different conclusions about the recommendations of the Trade Justice campaign. Christians who believe that the market should be kept as free as possible would presumably be sceptical as they would hold that economic growth and development are most effectively brought about by free trade and the operation of a free market. Interventions designed to favour poorer countries would 'distort' the market and might do more harm than good, for example by encouraging further inefficiency and corruption in developing countries.

Others might reply that developing economies need help and support to become established and internationally competitive. They might therefore support the Trade Justice recommendations, which basically operate within a market framework. Preston wrote relatively little about global economics, but his views would have accorded with some of the Trade Justice recommendations, though he opposed debt cancellation. Others sympathetic to Preston, such as Michael Taylor, have argued a case very much in line with the Trade Justice campaign.[13]

Those who take these different positions would presumably agree that the world's poorest countries need to develop their economies and become wealthier. They might underpin this agreement with basic theological and ethical principles, such as the value of human life, but would disagree about the most effective means to achieve this aim.

Thus, within the 'dominant tradition', the question as to whether or not the Trade Justice recommendations ought to be adopted is essentially a technical question for economists, not a theological or ethical one. Theology and ethics can dictate the ends, but we need to turn to economics to learn about the best means to those ends.

This, in turn, draws attention to some basic assumptions about the relationship between theology and economics that are widely shared within Long's dominant tradition. Christian writers on economics often argue that certain theological and ethical assumptions are needed to underpin capitalism and make it work. For example, economics could not work if the world were not basically reliable and predictable and the notion that it *is* reliable and predictable has its roots in the Christian doctrine of creation. Christians also understand the created world to be *finite* and the finitude of this world is what gives rise to relative scarcity and opportunity costs. Economist Denys Munby put the point neatly: 'In heaven no problem of scarcity arises, and in hell no possibility of choice exists; economics is a science dealing with the conditions of life in *this* world.'[14]

The self-interest that underpins the working of the market is linked to the Christian doctrine of sin and the insight that, in this world, selfishness is a ubiquitous part of human nature. More positively, Christian writers also comment that, in order to function properly, the market relies on some basic ethical assumptions, such as the notion that people can usually be trusted. Yet, they say, a capitalist economic framework cannot provide the foundation for these assumptions itself and may even erode the trust and other moral values that it relies on. So, there may be an important role for faith and morality in underpinning the market economy and supplying the basic moral values that it depends on and, as we saw earlier, apologists for the market tend to say that there are *moral* reasons, not just pragmatic ones, for its being preferable to other economic systems.

However, thinkers in this tradition tend to be suspicious of more specific Christian arguments about economic policy and practice based on biblical and theological premises. They tend to regard such arguments as naive attempts by Churches and theologians to pronounce on matters that they do not understand. For example, the early and medieval Church prohibited 'usury', which is the lending of money at interest – a practice that is central to the modern economy. The usury prohibition is rooted in both the Hebrew Bible and Aristotelian philosophy. Typically for thinkers in the 'dominant tradition', Preston regards this prohibition as archaic, unsustainable and based on fundamental misunderstandings about economic life. He uses its history as a cautionary tale about the dangers of theologians interfering in technical economic matters. He himself favours what is sometimes called the *middle axiom* method in Christian ethics. This approach (which is discussed further in Chapter 9) relies on an interaction between theology, relevant expertise (for example, from economists) and the experience of ordinary people, especially those on the margins of society. Out of this three-way conversation, broad policy guidelines will emerge that can then be translated into more detailed policies.

A more radical view comes from liberation theologians such as those surveyed earlier in this chapter. These are the theologians whom Stephen Long places in the *emergent tradition*. By giving it this name, he means to indicate that this tradition has emerged from the modern economic situation as a protest against the dominant tradition.

Whereas those in the dominant tradition agree that the market is the most efficient mechanism for allocating scarce resources, liberation theologians are sceptical about it. Starting from the experience of the poor has led them to choose different economic and sociological approaches in order to understand the causes of poverty and oppression. In particular, as we saw in section 3, they have often chosen approaches inspired in various ways by Karl Marx. For example, they have adopted Marxist notions that there is a fundamental economic and social conflict between the owners of capital and the working class. Marx held that the economic value added when a commodity is manufactured or a service performed comes from the labour that goes into it. If owners make a profit from selling a product over and above the pay that their workers are given to produce it, then the workers have, in effect, been robbed of part of the value of their labour.

Such an analysis offers an explanation for the inequalities in wealth within one society. To understand the disparities in wealth between nations, liberation theologians have drawn on so-called *dependency theory*, which holds that wealthy nations with economic and political power will tend to set up the conditions for international economic exchange in such a way as to keep poorer nations economically dependent on them. For example, they might supply markets for raw materials produced in poor countries, but at such a low price that the poorer countries' economic development is held back.

These forms of economic analysis are now widely reckoned to be in poor shape, both because many (though not all) economists believe Marxist theory to be seriously flawed and because almost all formerly communist countries have abandoned communism and adopted market economies since the end of the 1980s.[15] Accordingly, many liberation theologians and those sympathetic to them have distanced themselves from Marxist economic theory, but have remained highly suspicious of market economics and global capitalism, which, they hold, overwhelmingly favour the wealthy and powerful.

Christians who take such a theological stance might support the Trade Justice recommendations as a first step, but would probably wish to go much further. For example, a declaration from a forum of Reformed Protestant churches in developing countries calls for churches to 'press for the democratic redesign of the international financial and economic system, *replacing* the present institutions (IMF, [World Bank], WTO) which are mainly owned by and serve the interests of the rich countries'.[16]

Christians influenced by liberation theology would be likely to oppose any economic order based on a global free market, but their preferred alternative would not be an old-style communist 'command' system where the economy is controlled by central government planning. After the fall of the Berlin Wall in 1989 and the break-up of the Soviet Union, there is widespread agreement that this system does not work and requires totalitarian government to prop it up. They would be more likely to advocate more small-scale, locally based forms of economic organization. For example, Tim Gorringe argued in 1994 for a new form of economic order in which the local, rather than national or multinational, economy would be the 'central focus of interest'. Production, for example, might be centred on small-scale cooperatives and local communities. Work would be thought of differently, without a hierarchical structure of management and workforce. Taxation would be shifted away from personal income and towards land, environmentally damaging activities, imports and exports and international currency exchanges. In line with the teaching of the early and medieval Church, interest should no longer be charged on loans. Finally, economic activity should no longer be focused on unlimited growth, but instead on a sustainable equilibrium.[17]

Critics from within Long's dominant tradition would presumably think these proposals deeply flawed. They might be considered utopian, in the sense that they are unrealistic about human sin and selfishness and would therefore be likely to do more harm than good if they were implemented. They might also seem unrealistic in another sense – namely, that Gorringe offers a set of moral imperatives, but not an account of how to achieve those imperatives starting from where we are. Gorringe, though, insists that his proposals are neither utopian nor unrealistic and argues that, even within a global market system that is deeply unfavourable to them, aspects of them have been successfully practised.

According to Stephen Long, the real strength of liberation theology does not lie in its use of an alternative 'scientific' (that is, Marxist) form of social and economic analysis. That is its weakness, not its strength. The really important thing about it is that it challenges the *theological* assumptions underpinning capitalism. In particular, it questions the notion that relative scarcity – humans having limited resources and unlimited wants – is fundamental to human nature as created by God. According to Long, the dominant tradition makes relative scarcity into a fundamental and universal principle, whereas liberation theologians acknowledge that of course it exists, but deny that it has the importance the dominant tradition gives to it. They give more weight to *plenitude* – God's inexhaustible generosity and care for creation (I shall return to this point later in this section). However, Long argues that these two groups – the theological supporters of capitalism and the liberation theologians – though they look very different, share certain problematic assumptions. In particular, they follow the sociologist Max Weber in assuming a sharp distinction between *facts* (which can be determined scientifically and rationally argued about) and *values* (which are a matter of non-rational personal choice). Among other things, this distinction allows a separation of ends from means. Your faith commitment or moral values might tell you the ends you ought to seek (for example, greater prosperity for the poor), but how to achieve those ends is largely a technical matter, the preserve of economists rather than theologians or ethicists. That is partly why a writer like Preston is so reluctant to let the Bible or theology influence the details of economic practice in any direct way, as we saw in his treatment of the question of usury.

Furthermore, if values are separated from facts, they are no longer rooted in the way the world is or in the way that human beings are created. The choice of moral values and personal goals becomes a matter of irrational, arbitrary decision – that is, there is no way in which I can persuade you to adopt my values or in which you can show me that my values are wrong. This is essentially the problem with modern ethics that Alasdair MacIntyre identified, as we saw in Chapter 6. Within this framework, it is very difficult to speak of either natural law or the virtues in the way that, for example, Thomas Aquinas did (see Chapters 3 and 6). Both natural law and virtue theory, as Thomas develops them, depend on the claim that human beings have certain proper *ends* or *goals*; right actions and virtuous character traits are those that are consistent with our proper ends and help us to move towards them. Most importantly, our actions and characters should be directed towards our ultimate end of eternal life with God.

Long argues that both the dominant and emergent traditions of Christian economic thought are unsatisfactory because they separate economic thinking and practice from any vision of our ultimate end, though he thinks that the emergent tradition is a big improvement on the dominant. Instead of choosing either, he attempts to recover what he calls the *residual tradition*. By this he means an older way of thinking about economics found in the work of thinkers such as Thomas Aquinas, which places economic activity in the context of the virtues and ends of human life. Like some liberation theologians, Long challenges the notion that relative scarcity is the fundamental reality that economists have to deal with. A more basic feature of the creation is *plenitude* – the result of God's inexhaustible love and generosity seen most directly in the Eucharist, in which God gives God's self to us.

Critics sympathetic to mainstream economics might ask at this point if Long is setting up a false opposition between plenitude and relative scarcity. If relative scarcity reflects the fact that humans and the created world are finite, then it might be truer to say that *both* plenitude *and* finitude are fundamental features of God's creation. Now Long does not need to deny that humans, and the created world, are finite, nor that some goods are scarce. He accuses capitalism and its theological supporters, however, of saying much more than this – of giving an account of human nature in which scarcity is *the* fundamental feature of human life and constrains all our decisions. This, he says, theologians have to deny. Just because *some* goods are scarce does not mean that *all* human goods are scarce. My love for others, for example, is not a scarce resource that has to be carefully distributed, but has its source in God's inexhaustible love and goodness. Nor does it mean that scarcity is intended by God. God has created a *finite* world, but not a world of *scarcity*. Scarcity arises not just because resources are finite but also because humans have an inordinate desire to consume those resources. In other words, scarcity (as distinct from finitude) is a result of human sin; it exists because human desires are *disordered*. This brings us to another basic reality that, according to Long, a theological economics must deal with, namely, the *ends* or goals of human life.

As we have seen, in the theological tradition that Long wants to recover, any aspect of human life – including economic life – must be morally evaluated in the light of our ends and, supremely, our ultimate end, which is life with God. Human desires are *rightly ordered* if they are directed towards our ends and *disordered* if they are directed away from our proper ends.

Thinking about economics in terms of our ends means that economic life must be evaluated in the light of the *virtues* as these are the qualities that direct human beings towards their ends. In particular, the 'theological' virtues instilled in us by God, especially the virtue of love, direct our lives towards our ultimate end of life with God. The shape of the 'natural' virtues (including justice – the heading under which Thomas discusses economic matters) is determined by the theological virtues. Put another way, our economic life and practices, if they are to be theologically and morally acceptable, must enable us to practise the virtue of love.

Seen in this light, Long argues, capitalist economics will not do. It claims to be value-neutral, simply describing the facts of economic life without expressing an opinion about how people *ought* to order their lives. However, he believes that this is a false claim, for the following reason. Capitalist economic theory depends on the basic assumption that human beings act so as to maximize their preferences and, in marginalist theory, the measure of a product's value is the extent to which it satisfies the preferences of those in the marketplace. In other words, capitalist economics assumes a theory of human action in which value is measured by the satisfaction of preferences. Now this, of course, is a moral theory – as we saw in Chapter 4, it is a form of utilitarianism. According to MacIntyre and others, this is incompatible with a Christian account of moral being and action based on the virtues. As Long puts it, 'it gives us *values*, but it lacks virtue. In lacking virtue, it cannot help us to see God.'[18] This is part of the reason for his description, along with other theologians, including John Milbank and Ulrich Duchrow, of capitalism as a 'heresy' – it implicitly makes claims about the world, humankind and God that are distortions of the claims made by the Christian Church in its creeds and confessions. According to these thinkers, we cannot consistently accept a capitalist vision of the world and at the same time believe in the central claims of the Christian faith.

What practical conclusions would follow from the residual tradition? Long does not spell them out in detail as he is mainly concerned with the more foundational task of setting the terms on which theology and economics can engage with each other. However, a few examples of practical implications can be found in the sources that he uses. For instance, he supports the notion of the 'just wage' that was developed in the Middle Ages by Thomas Aquinas and others. The concept of the just wage suggests that workers' rates of pay should not be solely determined by market forces acting on the labour market, but, rather, workers should always be paid enough to sustain them and their dependants. Also, employers who offer rates of pay too low to sustain employees and their dependants are doing something intrinsically wrong.[19]

Another medieval teaching to which Long refers is the usury prohibition. He quotes with approval twentieth-century Catholic economist Bernard Dempsey, who argued that the way in which interest functions in the modern economy amounts to 'institutional usury' and this introduces a fundamental distortion and injustice into the economy.

More generally, Long follows John Milbank in arguing that a Christian analysis of economics calls for the abolition of capitalism and establishment of a socialist economy. However, this should not be the State socialism of the Soviet bloc before 1989, nor the 'scientific' socialism of Marx and Engels. Rather, Milbank and Long call for a return to an older form of Christian socialism in which economic exchanges are directed not solely towards profit but also towards justice and 'shared benefit'.[20]

It is not clear how this change is to be achieved, though Milbank seems to envisage working within the present economic system and, in effect, subverting it by changing its aims and direction from within. Like many Christian virtue ethicists, Long stresses the key role of the Church, which could act as an alternative kind of political economy, practising its economic life in a way that witnesses to God's generosity and embodies love and justice towards all. In this way it would point to the possibility of a different, and better, way in which humans might live their lives together. (There is some common ground between this proposal and my suggestion in Chapter 6 that the practices of the Christian community might shape Christian thinking about the allocation of healthcare resources.)

Those who follow Long's approach might support the Trade Justice recommendations as a first step in the right direction, as the Trade Justice campaign seeks ways to constrain the working of the global market so that the interests of the poor are protected. However, like liberation theologians, those who follow Long's 'residual tradition' would want to go much further. Their eventual aim would not be merely to strengthen the economies of developing countries so that they can compete effectively in a global free market, but to transform the whole basis on which international economic exchange takes place.

Questions

- Which of the three theological approaches to economics outlined in this section do you find most persuasive and why?
- In the light of your answer to the first question, how would you now modify or add to your initial response to the case study about the Trade Justice campaign?

Suggestions for Further Reading

Liberation Theologies

Daniel M. Bell, *Liberation Theology After the End of History: The Refusal to Cease Suffering*, London and New York: Routledge, 2001.

Andrew Bradstock and Christopher Rowland (eds), *Radical Christian Writings: A Reader*, Oxford: Blackwell, 2002.

Tim Gorringe, 'Liberation Ethics', in Robin Gill (ed.), *The Cambridge Companion to Christian Ethics*, Cambridge: Cambridge University Press, 2001, pp. 125–37.

John Parratt (ed.), *An Introduction to Third World Theologies*, Cambridge: Cambridge University Press, 2004.

Economics and Trade Justice

Wayne G. Boulton, Thomas D. Kennedy and Allen Verhey (eds), *From Christ to the World: Introductory Readings in Christian Ethics*, Grand Rapids, MI: Eerdmans, 1994, Chapter 12.

Elaine L. Graham and Esther D. Reed (eds), *The Future of Christian Social Ethics: Essays on the Work of Ronald H. Preston, 1913–2001*, special issue of *Studies in Christian Ethics*, 17 (2), 2004.

Max L. Stackhouse, 'Business, Economics and Christian Ethics', in Gill, *The Cambridge Companion to Christian Ethics*, pp. 228–42.

8

Critical Voices: Feminist Theologies and Christian Ethics

1 Case Study

Read the following case study and make notes on the questions. As before, you will be asked to refer back to your notes at the end of the chapter.

Abortion, Politics and the Churches[1]

Abortion has not traditionally been an election or party-political issue in Britain, but, during a brief period in the run-up to the general election of 2005, it hit the headlines in a big way.

It all started when the Catholic bishops published a letter to Catholics in England and Wales, as they do before each general election. The letter identified a number of issues, including abortion, about which Catholic voters might question their parliamentary candidates. Issuing the letter, the Archbishop of Westminster, Cardinal Cormac Murphy O'Connor, praised Conservative leader Michael Howard for supporting a reduction in the legal time limit for abortion to 20-weeks' gestation. Cardinal Murphy O'Connor said that Catholics would 'commend' this 'on the way to a full abandonment of abortion'. Some parts of the news media took this to mean that he was endorsing the Conservative Party even though he made it clear that he was not endorsing any one party, and went on to commend Prime Minister Tony Blair and Chancellor of the Exchequer Gordon Brown for their stance on global poverty.

The Conservative and Labour parties moved quickly to try and stop abortion becoming an election issue. A few days later, the Archbishop of Canterbury, Dr Rowan Williams, entered the fray with an article in *The Sunday Times*. He wrote that if it was generally agreed that abortion was not an election issue, this should not become 'an alibi for taking it seriously as a public issue'. A large majority of Christians, including him, found it 'impossible to regard abortion as anything other than the deliberate termination of a human life'. Although this view could not be taken for granted in British society, there was 'more and more of a shared unhappiness and bewilderment around our current law and its effects'. This, he said, made it a matter of some urgency to open up a serious public debate about it.

Reaction to the two archbishops' interventions and the ensuing public debate was, not surprisingly, mixed. The pro-choice campaigning group Abortion Rights strongly opposed making abortion an election issue. A press release the day after the issue of the Catholic bishops' election letter said, 'Opportunistic interventions to attempt to divide public opinion on the right to safe, legal abortion is both damaging to women and likely to be very unpopular. Politicians would do well to resist attempts to concede to the demands of anti-abortionists.' The group's director, Anne Quesney, was also quoted by BBC News as criticizing Dr Williams' intervention, saying, 'The anti-abortion lobby supported by the Church has the main intention of making abortion illegal.' Making abortion an election issue, she said, would show 'a lack of compassion to women who need access to those services'. However, a press release from the pro-life group LIFE welcomed the way in which the issue had 'moved centre-stage'. It praised 'the splendid way in which Cardinal Murphy O'Connor has helped to stir the media', and said that '[t]he crucial thing is that there is now a huge groundswell of public unease . . . The national conscience is deeply disturbed and we pro-lifers have the initiative as never before.'

Questions

- Is Rowan Williams right to regard abortion as 'the deliberate termination of a human life', in a morally weighty sense?
- If he is right, can Christians ever consider abortion morally justified? If so, under what circumstances and with what limits?
- What role(s) should Christians and the Churches seek to play in public and political debates on issues such as abortion?

We return to the first two of these questions in the last section of this chapter but consideration of the third is postponed until the next chapter (Chapter 9). Before returning to these questions, we shall explore an approach to Christian theology and ethics that has been very influential in modern discussions of abortion.

2 Feminist Theologies and Christian Ethics

Like the liberationist theologies introduced in Chapter 8, feminist theologies take as their starting point concrete experience and, in particular, the experience of oppression. The particular experience of oppression with which feminists are concerned is summed up in the concept of *patriarchy*.

Beverly Wildung Harrison defines patriarchy as 'patterned or institutionalized legitimations of male superiority'.[2] In other words, in many societies – including those Western societies in which Christianity has grown up and flourished – men have, for the most part, held most of the power. Women have had a subordinate place and often been regarded as being at men's disposal. This imbalance of power has had several implications. One is that these societies have tended to be organized for men's rather than women's benefit, so as to maintain the situation in which men hold the power. Second, such societies have developed understandings of the world, humanity and God that are distorted and incomplete; they understand the world from a male point of view and fail to pay attention to women's perspectives and experience. Furthermore, these distorted understandings of the world tend to 'legitimate' the imbalance of power – that is, they justify male superiority by, for example, portraying women as less rational than men, less able to hold power and naturally suited to private and domestic rather than public roles. They might even portray women as less fully human than men and they sometimes scapegoat women – particularly those who wish to assert their equality with men – blaming them for the conflicts and problems of society.

Feminist critics argue that the Church has been complicit in this oppression of women in many ways. For example, its power structures have tended to exclude women, particularly by restricting ordained ministry to men; it has taught that women should be subordinated to men; and its theological traditions have reflected male interests, by using mostly male language and imagery for God and articulating core Christian doctrines such as sin and redemption in ways that reflect male rather than female experience. The Church, like society at large, has tended to scapegoat women: in particular it has told the story of the 'fall' (see Genesis 3) in a way that suggests that Eve, and women in general, bear particular responsibility for the entry of sin into the world.

If feminist critics are right to say that patriarchy deeply influences the ways in which we understand and shape the world, then a theological response to it will have to go deeper than simply thinking up practical measures to improve the conditions of women's lives. What will be required is a fundamental shift in the mental maps we have of the world and the ways in which we live and act in it. Our 'symbolic world', as Richard Hays calls it (see Chapter 2) will need to be radically restructured.

There has been an enormous amount of writing in all the main areas of theology demonstrating various ways in which this feminist rethinking might be done. For example, in biblical studies, feminist interpreters have both challenged male-biased interpretations of biblical texts and critiqued the texts themselves for reflecting patriarchal perspectives. In systematic theology, feminists have offered many kinds of critical reappraisal of core Christian doctrines, such as the Trinity, Christology, creation and redemption. They have wanted to challenge, among other things, the dominance of male language and imagery in speaking of God, the notion that only men can represent Christ in certain ways (for example, as ordained priests) and theological arguments that justify the subordination of women. In practical and pastoral theology, feminists have sought to challenge patriarchal assumptions about the nature of ministry and pastoral care and the roles of women and men in the Church. They have also wished to give more wideranging critical analyses of Church structures and Christian practices.[3] (We return to feminist accounts of pastoral care in Chapter 9.)

Feminist theology is also a diverse global movement and, as we shall see later in this section, there is a rich variety of feminist theological reflection from different cultural contexts around the world.

Some feminist theologians have chosen to remain within Christianity and seek to transform the Church from within, despite regarding the Churches and their traditions as deeply sexist. Others, who sometimes identify themselves as 'post-Christian', have concluded that Christianity is irretrievably patriarchal and we need to develop new forms of spirituality and theology that are no longer bound to the Church or its traditions.[4]

How might feminists rethink Christian ethics? In her book *Feminism and Christian Ethics*, Susan Parsons offers three 'paradigms' for ethics that can be found in both secular and Christian feminism – in other words, three possible ways of going about this feminist reconstruction of Christian ethical thought.[5]

The Liberal Paradigm

Parsons' first paradigm, which she calls 'liberal', emphasizes the *similarity* between women and men. Both women and men are human beings and, as such, equally deserving of respect and have the same fundamental human rights. To use the Kantian language we encountered in Chapter 4, both women and men should be treated as ends in themselves, never merely as means. Christians who support this paradigm might appeal to Paul's bold affirmation that '[t]here is no longer Jew or Greek, there is no longer slave or free, there is no longer male and female; for all of you are one in Christ Jesus' (Galatians 3.28). They might also appeal to Jesus' friendships with women as well as men, which would have caused raised eyebrows, to say the least, in his context (see John 4.27), and evidence from the New Testament that women had greater equality of status and position in the earliest churches than in the surrounding societies.

As the Kantian language suggests, this paradigm has deep roots in the Enlightenment, with its emphasis on the dignity and rights of individual, autonomous human beings. It has undoubtedly had great effect in supporting women's claims for equal treatment in areas such as employment, pay, education and political power. Yet, increasingly, feminists have worried that this paradigm has too many male assumptions built into it. Humans are understood as autonomous individuals and competition is more basic than cooperation in their interactions with one another. Human relationships, communities and societies are a matter of negotiation between individuals, in which all parties are trying to achieve as much as possible of their own interests. Some feminists argue that this is a characteristically male rather than female way of understanding ourselves, that this paradigm may put women in the position of trying to gain equality with men by becoming more like men.

The Social Constructionist Paradigm

The second paradigm offers a more radical challenge to our assumptions about what it means to *be* a man or a woman. Parsons quotes Simone de Beauvoir's famous remark that '[o]ne is not born, but rather becomes, a woman'.[6] In other words, a lot of what it means for us to be men or women is a matter of social convention. Biologically, of course, we are born male or female (though even in biology there are occasional ambiguities). According to social constructionists, however, the behaviour, roles, attitudes and self-understanding of men and women are largely a product of our upbringing, environment, social pressures and expectations we experience and so forth. These things are not unchangeable laws of nature and they could be different. The problem is that the social structures, attitudes and assumptions that shape gender roles and identities are set up in ways that tend to benefit the powerful and maintain their power. So, for example, many people – including Church leaders and theologians – have claimed that men are better suited to public life and leadership and women to domestic and family life because men tend to be more rational and women to be more emotional.

The social constructionist paradigm invites women to be suspicious of what they have been brought up to believe about their nature and role in life. They might need to challenge (to 'deconstruct') prevailing expectations about the ways in which women are supposed to live and construct new forms of life and social roles. They might, for example, challenge the assumption that a woman should devote much of her time and energy to homemaking and childcare, arguing that if this role is socially imposed on women, it disadvantages them economically, politically and personally. Christians who adopt this paradigm might regard much of the Bible itself with suspicion as the writings of the Bible are largely the products of men in deeply patriarchal cultures. Feminists who approach the Bible with this kind of suspicion, however, might find subversive texts, stories and themes that tend to undermine the dominant patriarchal mindset. They might say, for example that Jesus was in the habit of treating the women around him as equals and this was a radical challenge to the prevailing social attitudes of his day. Again, stories such as the book of Esther, in which women take the initiatives and play the leading roles, unsettle the assumption that the 'movers and shakers' of history are most often men.

One danger with this paradigm is that, if taken to its conclusion, it could end up deconstructing *itself*. If every way of setting up human roles and relationships is merely a matter of social convention, it may be hard to find solid grounds for saying that one social convention is better than another. Thus, if every moral vision is simply a social construction, for example, what grounds are there for saying that equality is better than patriarchy and that those who prefer patriarchy are wrong? And, if everyone believes *that* to be the case, it may be that the social convention that wins out will simply be the one favoured by the strongest.

The Naturalist Paradigm

Whereas the liberal paradigm focuses on the essential similarities between men and women, Parsons' third paradigm emphasizes the *differences*. According to this paradigm, there are important differences between the ways that women and men think, act and see the world. For example, psychologist Carol Gilligan found that there were differences between boys and girls in the way that their moral awareness developed as they grew up.[7] Whereas boys and men tended to think in terms of rules and justice, girls and women tended to be more concerned about the relationships involved in a moral situation and were interested in seeing a moral dilemma from the perspectives of all concerned. Gilligan described these differences in terms of two different moral 'voices' – the 'justice voice' and the 'care voice'. The 'justice voice' is more characteristically male, while the 'care voice' more characteristically female, though Gilligan stressed that this is not a hard-and-fast distinction. Others have attempted to work out the implications of these gender differences by developing a feminist 'ethic of care'.[8] A 'care' approach to moral decision making will seek an empathetic understanding of the particular people involved in a situation, and will be concerned about the effect of a decision on those individuals and their relationships with one another. It will be less concerned about universal rules and more abstract notions of rights or justice.

According to this paradigm, the trouble with society is that it is set up to favour male rather than female ways of doing things. In education, employment, politics and other areas of public life, those who operate in characteristically 'male', individualistic, competitive and rule-based ways get on better than those who operate in more characteristically 'female', cooperative and relational ways. What is needed is a change in social attitudes, relationships and structures so that 'female' ways of living and working are not disadvantaged in the public domain.

The danger with the naturalist paradigm is that it could end up repeating the old stereotyped views of gender that have operated to women's disadvantage in the past – men are hard-headed and rational, women are emotional and caring, therefore men are better suited to roles that need hard heads and clear thinking and women to those that need warmth and caring. For example, the ethics of care approach has been quite influential in healthcare ethics, but critics worry that it will reinforce some old – and sexist – stereotypes about the division of labour in healthcare, with doctors (predominantly male) doing the thinking and decision making and nurses (predominantly female) doing the caring and obeying the doctors' orders.[9]

Parsons herself is reluctant to choose any one of these paradigms in preference to the other two. Instead, she attempts to draw out common threads from all of them that will help with the task of approaching ethical issues in a way that takes feminist concerns seriously. These include:

- an appropriate account of universal moral standards that will offer a basis for the right treatment of everyone
- a 'redemptive community' that will take us beyond the individualism that we have learned from the Enlightenment
- a new understanding of human nature in which both male and female are valued as made in the image of God.

I commented earlier that feminist theology should not be understood as merely a white, Western phenomenon, but, rather, as a diverse global and intercultural movement. This point is made strongly by Asian feminist theologian Kwok Pui-Lan, who argues that white, Western feminism should not be seen as a kind of prototype or pattern for feminist theologies from other parts of the world – this would be a new kind of colonialism. Instead, women from different places and cultural contexts need to find their own ways of reflecting on their contexts and challenge the oppression of women in those contexts.[10]

To give just one example of feminist Christian ethics emphatically not stemming from a white, Western perspective, black feminists in North America and Britain have been critical of white feminist thought for paying too little attention to racism and poverty. They are also critical of male-led liberation movements for ignoring sexism. Suffering a 'triple jeopardy' of racism, poverty and sexism, many black women have had to struggle, not only for equality or fulfilment, but also for sheer survival.

Katie Geneva Cannon reflected on the ethical significance of this experience in her pioneering book *Black Womanist Ethics*[11] ('womanist' is a term coined by some African-American women writers to describe a kind of black women's theology that is distinct and different from white, Western feminism). Cannon's starting point is the experiences of black women in the United States in the time of slavery and after its abolition. She argues that traditional ethics is of little help in giving an account of the moral experiences of these women, because moral rules and principles assume that people are *agents* – that they have the freedom and power to make decisions and determine the course of their own lives. However, this power was largely denied to black women, whose lives were under the power of others. Yet, even in such a radically oppressive situation, according to Cannon, a tradition of moral wisdom could be found that has provided black women with resources for survival, liberation and empowerment. She finds traces of this tradition in black women's literature. In the work of the writer Zora Hurston (1901?–60), for example, she finds the themes of 'invisible dignity', 'quiet grace' and 'unshouted courage' that help to map the moral character of lives lived under conditions of terrible injustice.

Others, such as Cheryl Sanders, build on Cannon's work, but argue that black women and men also need moral resources to empower them for new situations in which they are already experiencing liberation. For Sanders, many of these resources can and should be found within black-majority Christian churches. For example, churches can offer educational opportunities. They can be communities in which those who have achieved some advancement can help and encourage those who have not. They can be moral communities, developing and strengthening a sense of moral identity in those whom, as Cannon describes, society deprives of moral agency. Finally, they can be places where a kind of Christian ministry is practised that communicates the love of God to all.[12]

As I have noted, Kwok Pui-Lan argues strongly for the diversity of feminist theologies from different places and situations. However, she goes on to argue that feminist theologies in all parts of the world face a new, worldwide challenge from global capitalism, following the collapse of communism and the end of the Cold War. This brings us back to the issues raised by the case study in the previous chapter as many of the effects of globalization and free trade capitalism are felt in particular and distinctive ways by women.[13]

3 The Case Study Revisited

Abortion

Abortion means the premature ending of a pregnancy by the expulsion or removal of the products of conception (the embryo or foetus and the placenta) from the mother's womb, resulting in the death of the foetus. This can happen naturally for a variety of reasons – for example, because the foetus has died or has a severe developmental defect – but ethical debates are concerned with *induced abortion*, which is the use of a medical or surgical procedure to end a pregnancy artificially.

The reasons for performing an abortion are sometimes grouped into the following three categories, though it is fairly clear that they overlap and more than one reason may enter into a decision made about abortion.

- The mother does not wish the pregnancy to continue, for any of a variety of reasons. For example, she may believe that she lacks the resources or social support to care for the child, particularly if she already has other children, the pregnancy may have been unplanned and interrupt her educational or employment opportunities, or it may have resulted from rape or sexual abuse and she may not feel able to continue with it. It is also possible, of course, that she may be put under pressure to seek an abortion by others, such as her partner or family members, who do not wish the pregnancy to continue.
- The pregnancy endangers the mother's life or health.
- The foetus has an inherited disease or developmental disorder that may result in its being stillborn, having only a very short life after birth or having some kind of permanent disability or illness.

The first two of these reasons have been around for a long time – there are references to them, for example, in the writings of early Christian theologians such as Tertullian (*c*. 160–240 CE) and Augustine (354–430 CE)[14] – but the third has become important only in recent decades, thanks to modern medical techniques for detecting inherited diseases and foetal abnormalities during pregnancy.

As many Christians appeal to biblical texts to support a strong anti-abortion stance, it may come as a surprise that the Bible makes no direct explicit references to induced abortion, despite the fact that it was known and practised in parts of the ancient world. There are texts referring to accidental injuries resulting in miscarriage (Exodus 21.22–5), God's knowledge of us before our birth (Psalm 139.13–16, for example) and God's calling and inspiration of particular individuals even before they are born (such as Jeremiah 1.4–5; Luke 1.39–45), but none of these directly addresses the questions that are at issue in modern debates about abortion. This is not to say that they are irrelevant to the discussion for, as we shall see, these and other texts can be used extensively in Christian reflection about abortion.

Though the Bible makes no direct reference to abortion, references to it can be found in Christian writings from late New Testament times onwards. It is often said that, for most of Christian history, the Church's official teaching and theological traditions have been more or less uniformly opposed to abortion.[15] One ground for this opposition was that abortion, like contraception, interrupts the procreative purpose of sex (see Chapter 3). Another was that killing the foetus is a form of homicide. On this, there is some variation in the tradition. Early and medieval writers often held that the foetus was not 'ensouled' – it did not receive its human soul – until some time after conception.[16] In that case, it was only the killing of the 'ensouled' foetus that counted as homicide, though the killing of a foetus before it was 'ensouled' was still considered a serious moral wrong. In the eighteenth and nineteenth centuries, Catholic teaching shifted away from the idea that ensoulment happened some time after conception and towards the view that the embryo is entitled to the same respect as any human person from conception.

This account of the history has been challenged by some recent authors, including feminist theologian Beverly Wildung Harrison. She has argued that, during Christian history, Church leaders and theologians were less interested in abortion than modern anti-abortion writers sometimes assume and, when they did object to it, their objection was in large part about women's attempts to control their own fertility and procreation.[17]

Be that as it may, the second half of the twentieth century saw major shifts in both social attitudes and laws relating to abortion in many Western countries, including Britain. In the United Kingdom (apart from Northern Ireland), the legal turning point was in 1967. The current law is defined by the 1967 Abortion Act, as amended by the 1990 Human Fertilization and Embryology Act: abortion is lawful up to 24 weeks' gestation if the pregnancy poses a risk to the physical or mental health of the mother, and at any time before birth if it is 'necessary to prevent grave permanent injury' to the mother's physical or mental health, if the pregnancy poses a risk to the mother's life or if there is a 'substantial risk' that the child will be born 'seriously handicapped'.[18]

In many Western countries – most notoriously the United States – abortion has become a highly polarized political issue between those who want to maintain permissive abortion laws and those – often, but not always, members of faith communities – who oppose them. These political controversies are reflected by vigorous disputes within the Christian Churches about whether or not the traditional Christian prohibition of abortion should be maintained.

Two issues are at the heart of much of the public debate about abortion:

- the moral status, interests or rights of the foetus
- the moral status, interests or rights of the mother and, sometimes, also of any children she already has.

The debate is sometimes set up as a conflict between the foetus's right to life and the mother's right to choose an abortion, though, as we shall see below, the matter is more complex than that would suggest. (See the Appendix to Chapter 3 for a brief account of what might be meant by the 'rights' of the mother or the foetus. As I briefly suggested there and in Chapter 6, the language of rights has its problems from a Christian perspective. Nonetheless, it is extensively used by Christians and others in arguments about abortion.) Christian debates sometimes run along similar lines to secular arguments, though some Christian thinkers are highly critical of the terms in which secular debates are set up.

The Moral Status, Interests and Rights of the Foetus

The question about the moral status of the foetus, like that about the status of the embryo, tends to focus on *personhood*. In Chapter 2, I summarized five possible answers to the question, 'Is the embryo a person?' The same kinds of answer could be given to the corresponding question about the foetus:

- it is a person;
- it has a moral status no higher than that of human tissue
- it has a status somewhere between that of human tissue and that of a person

- we do not or cannot know if it is a person
- the question, 'Is the foetus a person?' is the wrong question to ask.

Indeed, some of the philosophical treatments of personhood that have been influential in these debates were initially developed with reference to abortion[19] and it was only later that the same arguments were applied to new issues such as in vitro fertilization and embryo research.

Not surprisingly, those who think that the foetus is nowhere near being a person are less likely to oppose abortion than those who do regard the foetus as a person. A number of secular philosophical defences of abortion have argued, in various ways, that the foetus does not meet the criteria by which we would normally identify others as persons, and so the normal moral prohibition on killing persons does not apply to foetuses.[20] One well-known exception among defenders of abortion is Judith Jarvis Thomson, who famously argued some years ago that, even if the foetus were a person, the mother would not be obliged to keep it alive by continuing with an unwanted pregnancy.[21]

Christian writers have generally been reluctant to deny that the foetus has anything like the status of a person, though some, such as Joseph Fletcher, have proposed similar criteria to those of Warren and Tooley for identifying personhood – or 'humanhood', as Fletcher put it.[22] Some have been reluctant to go so far as to say that the foetus is a person and have spoken instead of its being a *potential* person or gradually *becoming* a person. Others, though, have argued that, from conception, the foetus must be regarded as a person and shown the same care that we are accustomed to showing to people. This is the official position of the Catholic Church: 'The human being is to be respected and treated as a person from the moment of conception; and therefore from that same moment his rights as a person must be recognized, among which in the first place is the inviolable right of every innocent human being to life.'[23] This position is powerfully restated in Pope John Paul II's encyclical *Evangelium Vitae*. He argues that, while the Bible never mentions abortion directly, texts such as those I mentioned earlier (for example, Psalm 139.13–16; Jeremiah 1.4–5; and Luke 1.39–45) 'show such great respect for the human being in the mother's womb that they require as a logical consequence that God's commandment "You shall not kill" be extended to the unborn child as well'.[24] Furthermore, he says, Christian tradition, official Church teaching and canon law are unanimous in condemning abortion. He acknowledges that this position has been challenged by calling the personhood of the foetus into question, but responds that this issue is so serious that even if there is a mere *probability* that the foetus is a person this should justify an absolute prohibition on killing it. This takes us back to the argument, mentioned in Chapter 2, that if we do not know whether or not the embryo or foetus is a person, we should treat it as if it is: 'to be willing to kill what for all one knows is a person is to be willing to kill a person'.[25]

As we saw in Chapter 2, some authors, including Richard Hays, believe that the question about personhood is the wrong question to ask. Like the lawyer's question to Jesus, 'Who is my neighbour?' (Luke 10.29), the question 'Who is a person?' is an attempt to narrow down the category of those whom we are obliged to help. Jesus' reply to the lawyer's question was the parable of the good Samaritan (10.30–7), which shows that some very surprising people can turn out to be our neighbours and calls on us to *widen* – not narrow – our moral concern by *becoming* neighbours to those who are helpless and in need.[26]

It is worth noting a different way in which the interests of the foetus enter into the abortion debate. Where the foetus has a serious inherited disease or developmental defect that will result in major disability or suffering, it is sometimes said that it is in the foetus' (or future child's) interests for the pregnancy to be terminated. In effect, it is being said that the quality of the child's life would be so poor that it would be better for him or her not to be born in the first place, that the child's future life is reckoned not to be worth living.

A similar claim, of course, is also implied when people request euthanasia either for themselves or others. This claim is not without its problems, even in the context of euthanasia. A particular difficulty when it is made in relation to foetuses (or, of course, newborn infants) is that it is being made on behalf of another individual and, in the nature of the case, there is no possibility of knowing whether or not that individual's life would seem to be worth living when experienced 'from the inside'. This is not to say that it is impossible to make such judgements – indeed, it may be almost impossible to avoid making them when deciding on the appropriate treatment for infants who have been born with the most severe of inherited diseases, for example. However, it does mean that such claims should be treated with a great deal of caution.

The Moral Status, Interests and Rights of the Mother

In the past few decades, abortion has been something of a defining issue for feminism. Many feminists argue that if society is to treat women justly, giving them equal status, freedom and opportunity to those enjoyed by men, it must allow them the freedom to choose to have abortions. At one level, this is an argument about women's well-being in quite concrete ways. Pregnancy, childbirth and parenthood make large demands on any woman. If the pregnancy is unplanned, particularly if the mother is young, poor and lacking support from a partner, family or friends, then those demands may be too great to bear. Pregnancy and caring for a baby might severely disrupt her education or make it more difficult for her to earn a living. In addition, if she already has other children, she may judge that she will be unable to care adequately for them if she continues with the pregnancy. Arguments about well-being have particular force when the pregnancy is the result of sexual violence, such as rape or incest. Beverly Wildung Harrison insists that, in such cases, abortion is not merely justifiable, but:

> is a moral good because it is not rational to treat a newly fertilized ovum as though it had the same value as the existent, pregnant female person and because it is morally wrong to make the victim of sexual violence suffer the further agonies of unwanted pregnancy and childbearing against her will.[27]

However, the argument is not just that the option of abortion is necessary to safeguard some women's well-being. Feminists also argue that it is necessary in order for women to be treated as persons in their own right, with a moral status equal to that of men. For centuries, patriarchal societies have subjected women to the control of men and often more or less regarded them as men's possessions. Women have been seen as at men's disposal for sexual pleasure, to bear and rear children and to maintain homes. If women are to be liberated from these forms of oppression, say feminists, they will need to be able to take control of their own bodies, sexuality and procreation, so access to abortion (among other things) is essential for this. This is not to say that abortion is desirable – Harrison remarks that '[w]e need . . . to step back from the dilemma of abortion and treat it for what it is: a negative condition for stopping pregnancy when all else fails'[28] – but, from this viewpoint, it must be available.

How do 'pro-choice' feminists respond to 'pro-life' arguments that the foetus should be treated as a person with the same rights as other persons? As we have seen, some feminists deploy philosophical arguments that the foetus fails to meet the criteria to be counted as a person, so is not entitled to the same care that should be shown to children and adults. Theologians such as Harrison do not necessarily follow this line – she remarks that, on the status of the foetus, 'morally sensitive people's judgments diverge' – but they do argue that 'pro-lifers' are inconsistent in that they place more emphasis on the personhood and rights of foetuses than of women: 'Those who proclaim that a zygote at the moment of conception is a person worthy of citizenship continue to deny full social and political rights to women.'[29]

This critique is directed at the institutional Churches and their official teachings on abortion. Harrison and others regard traditional Christian teaching on abortion as oppressive of women, in part because it fails to pay proper attention to the concrete experience of women struggling to control their fertility and procreation. Accordingly, when the Churches speak out or campaign against abortion, this is often seen by feminists as an attack on women's well-being and a move that threatens to reverse the gains that women have made in Western societies in the last few decades. Some of this feeling seems to have been behind the criticisms levelled at the Archbishops of Canterbury and Westminster for their pre-election comments about abortion, as described in the case study. If so, the criticisms were perhaps wide of the mark in this case as the Archbishop of Canterbury, for one, stressed that the questions he was raising did not come primarily from 'patriarchal clerics', but from the experience of women themselves.[30]

As this might suggest, not all feminists share Harrison's view of abortion.

For example, Sidney Callahan, who identifies herself as a 'pro-life feminist', argues that, in many ways, pro-choice arguments about abortion are out of line with important aspects of feminism.[31] For example, she finds some similarity between the arguments used to deny foetuses the status of a person and those that have sometimes been used in the past to question the moral status of women, black people and others. There have been those who thought that women and black people were too 'biological', driven too much by instinct and emotion and insufficiently rational to be given the same legal, moral and political status as white males. Feminists would thus be unwise, Callahan argues, to deny personal status to foetuses on the grounds that they are immature and dependent. To do so would risk showing the kind of contempt for biological, embodied human life that has been detrimental to women in the past.

Pro-choice feminists sometimes emphasize that women need to achieve the same autonomy and opportunity for individual choice as men have historically enjoyed. Callahan cautions that to overemphasize autonomy distorts the picture of moral responsibility. Neither men nor women should be understood as isolated, autonomous individuals, but as people embedded in complex networks of relationships that display many kinds of dependence and interdependence. There are strong echoes here of the feminist 'ethics of care' that I mentioned in the last section.

Finally, Callahan argues that pro-choice feminists have made the mistake of accepting a male-orientated erotic model of sexuality that encourages people to enjoy a variety of sexual partners and experiences 'without long-term commitment or reproductive focus'. While this has been satisfactory for many men, she says, it is destructive for many women: 'Women can only play the erotic game successfully when . . . they are young, physically attractive, economically powerful, and fulfilled enough in a career to be willing to sacrifice family life.'[32] She argues that feminists would do better to promote a vision of sexual life in which both men and women are expected to show faithfulness and long-term commitment to one another and take responsibility for their children. Ironically, easy access to abortion can make it easier for men to avoid commitment and responsibility and the wider community to deny responsibility for mothers and children by saying, in effect, 'She could get rid of the baby, so if she chooses to keep it, that's her problem.'

I have suggested that much Christian discussion of abortion is set up in similar ways to that of the secular abortion debate. Some Christian authors, such as Richard Hays, argue that it is a great mistake for Christians to follow the pattern of secular arguments.[33] Instead, they should locate their discussion firmly in the context of a community formed by Scripture. Hays believes that this move would call into question certain lines of argument widely used by both pro-choice and pro-life camps, such as the competing claims about the personhood of the foetus and the view that abortion is a conflict between the foetus' right to life and the mother's right to autonomy. It would require churches to become communities where their members act sacrificially in welcoming and supporting unwanted children and mothers facing unplanned pregnancies. Within churches, fathers should also be expected and helped to take their share of responsibility for caring for their children. Hays holds that if churches truly lived in this way, 'many of the usual arguments for abortion would fall away'.[34] Furthermore, this would be a far more effective mode of engagement with the wider public debate than campaigning for restrictive abortion laws or demonstrating outside abortion clinics. The argument is that in this, as in other public ethical issues we have explored, the business of the Church is not so much to try and persuade politicians to change the law as to be a countercultural community that witnesses to the possibility of a different way of life.

These last remarks point towards the third question that I posed in relation to the case study: what role(s) should Christians and Churches seek to play in public and political debates on issues such as abortion? A fuller discussion of that question is to be found in the next chapter.

Question

- Review your answers to the first two case study questions at the beginning of the chapter. In the light of your work on this chapter, how would you now change or add to your answers?

Suggestions for Further Reading

Feminist Theologies

Ursula King (ed.), *Feminist Theology from the Third World: A Reader*, London: SPCK, and Maryknoll, NY: Orbis, 1994.

Ann Loades (ed.), *Feminist Theology: A Reader*, London: SPCK, and Louisville, KY: Westminster John Knox, 1990.

Susan Frank Parsons (ed.), *The Cambridge Companion to Feminist Theology*, Cambridge: Cambridge University Press, 2002.

Abortion

Michael Banner, 'The Practice of Abortion: A Critique', in his *Christian Ethics and Contemporary Moral Problems*, Cambridge: Cambridge University Press, 1999, pp. 86–135.

Beverly Wildung Harrison, *Our Right to Choose: Toward a New Ethic of Abortion*, Boston, MA: Beacon Press, 1983.

Richard B. Hays, *The Moral Vision of the New Testament*, Edinburgh: T & T Clark, 1997, Chapter 18.

Stephen E. Lammers and Allen Verhey (eds), *On Moral Medicine: Theological Perspective in Medical Ethics*, 2nd edn, Grand Rapids, MI: Eerdmans, 1998, Chapter 13.

John Noonan (ed.), *The Morality of Abortion: Historical and Legal Perspectives*, Cambridge, MA: Harvard University Press, 1970.

9

Christian Ethics: Pastoral and Public

1 Introduction

In this chapter, we explore the relationships between Christian ethics and other areas of thought and practice – two borders, as it were, that appear at the edges of the map of Christian ethics. The first is the relationship between Christian ethics and pastoral care. The second is between Christian thinking and wider public debates about ethical issues.

We explore each of these borderlands with reference to an issue that we first encountered in Chapter 4 – euthanasia. The first part of the chapter discusses Christian ethics and pastoral care. In order to think about this relationship, you will be invited to imagine that something like Lord Joffe's Bill, to legalize assisted suicide and euthanasia, has become law in the United Kingdom and think about a scenario that might arise if euthanasia were legal. The second part of the chapter returns to the public and political debate about the Joffe Bill. It looks at various ways in which Christians whose ethical convictions are shaped by their faith tradition might engage with such public and political debates.

In each main section of this chapter, I sketch a range of possible answers to the question posed in that section, which is about the relationship between Christian ethics and pastoral care in the first section and the role of Christian ethics in public debates in the second. The sketches are all based on real views found in the literature, though, in some cases, they give rather simplified accounts of complex positions. In each section, some of the views are mutually exclusive. For example, I doubt if you could hold a 'therapeutic' view of pastoral care together with the view argued by Hauerwas and Willimon, nor the 'common moral ground' view of Christian ethics in the public sphere with Banner's account of 'dogmatic Christian ethics'. However, some of the views given in each section *can* be held together and many ethicists' answers to these questions will include elements of several of the views outlined here. Nor have I given anything like a complete list of possible Christian answers to either question. I hope, though, that the range of answers I have sketched out will encourage you to think about other possibilities and develop your own answers to these questions.

2 Christian Ethics and Pastoral Care

Imagine that, some time in the near future, legislation like Lord Joffe's Assisted Dying for the Terminally Ill Bill (described at the beginning of Chapter 4) has become law in the United Kingdom. The following scenario takes place.

> Helen and Paul are a committed Christian couple with three school-age children – Becky, Jodie and James. The family is actively involved in a variety of ways in the local Anglican church. However, for some years, Helen has suffered from motor neurone disease – an incurable condition that causes progressive loss of muscle function, paralysis and, ultimately, death. Death is often caused by respiratory complications, as the muscles involved in breathing cease functioning. Mental awareness and ability, however, are unaffected by the condition.[1]
>
> Helen's condition has now advanced to the stage where she cannot feed herself or carry out any of her own personal care – it all has to be done for her.
>
> Helen is afraid of the suffering and indignity that the terminal stages of the disease will bring and is also worried about the effect that her dying in such a way will have on the children. She and Paul have considered requesting euthanasia. Indeed, they have taken medical and legal advice,

which has confirmed that Helen would meet the criteria for euthanasia under the recently passed Euthanasia and Assisted Suicide Act. However, they are uncertain whether or not euthanasia, even though legal, would be *right* from a Christian point of view. They turn to their vicar, Geraldine, and ask her for advice and help in making their decision.

Question

• How should Geraldine respond to Helen and Paul?

Geraldine's response to Helen and Paul will depend on her understanding of her role as an ordained Christian minister. In particular, there are many possible ways in which Geraldine might understand her *pastoral* responsibilities towards Helen, Paul and their children and this will influence the way in which she responds to their request for help with their ethical problem.

This section will outline four possible understandings of pastoral care, each of which will have different implications for the way in which pastoral care and Christian ethics interact.

Non-directive Pastoral Care

Some pastoral carers understand the care they offer to be more or less a form of *counselling* or, as Gordon Lynch puts it, 'providing a therapeutic relationship in which clients are able to think about their experience and take decisions about their lives'.[2]

This view has its roots particularly in the 'humanistic psychology' of Carl Rogers, who believed that if counsellors could offer their clients a relationship of understanding, genuineness and unconditional acceptance, this would enable them to understand their own lives and experiences better and live more constructive and fulfilling lives.

Counsellors whose understanding of their work is along these lines will be extremely reluctant to tell their clients what to do. Rather, they will try to help clients understand their own fundamental needs, aspirations and commitments and make their own decisions on that basis. If Geraldine's understanding of her pastoral role agrees with this view, she will probably try to avoid giving Paul and Helen direct moral advice or guidance or expressing an opinion about the rights and wrongs of euthanasia. Instead, she might try to help them clarify their own moral doubts about euthanasia. Do these doubts reflect a deep and genuine moral conviction on their part or a more superficially held opinion that they have received from others which is not rooted in their own authentic experience and self-understanding? She might try to enable them to understand their own needs, desires, hopes and fears more fully, working out in the light of that understanding whether or not euthanasia for Helen would be the best thing for them.

Those who understand pastoral care in this way often find *situation ethics* (see Chapter 4) an attractive approach and it is not difficult to understand why. Counsellors are often suspicious of absolute moral rules, partly because they see clients for whom absolute rules have been painful and destructive. Situation ethics says that there are no absolutes, except the command to love your neighbour as yourself, and that love means acting in the way that will result in the greatest good for the greatest number. If Geraldine were a situationist, she would not have to consider the possibility that euthanasia was always and absolutely wrong: it might or might not be the right thing for these people in this situation, and she would be free to help them discover whether or not it was in fact the right thing for them to do.

In fact, the points of contact between situationism and a Rogerian understanding of counselling go deeper than this. Both seem to rely on some similar philosophical assumptions. In particular, both assume some version of *personalism* – roughly, the notion that persons and personal experience are the key to understanding reality and value – and some form of *pragmatism* – the view that 'an idea is right and true if it has fruitful consequences'.[3]

I suggested in Chapter 4 that situationism has serious weaknesses as a theological theory of ethics. If that is so, it might also call non-directive counselling models of pastoral care into question. However, it might be possible to understand pastoral care in this sort of way without being an ethical situationist. Geraldine, for example, might have a very clear conviction that euthanasia is always inconsistent with Christian faith and practice, but she might also think that it is inappropriate for her to 'impose' this moral conviction on Paul and Helen. She might, for example, have a strong view of human *autonomy*, believing that all individuals should be free to live their lives as they choose, even if that means that they choose wrongly. She might, therefore, think that it is appropriate for her to help Helen and Paul clarify their own moral thinking, but it would undermine their autonomy if she were to take advantage of the caring relationship in an attempt to persuade them that her view was right. It is not clear how consistent with Christian convictions such a view of autonomy is. It seems to be in some tension, for example, with the notion that human beings are created with particular 'ends' or 'purposes' – a notion that underpins both natural law theory (see Chapter 3) and virtue ethics (see Chapter 6). As we shall see later in this section, 'therapeutic' models of pastoral care are frequently criticized for other reasons as well. In particular, they are often said to be too individualistic, neglecting both the place of the Christian community in pastoral care and the social, political and economic factors that influence human well-being. Defenders of therapeutic models, however, might argue that care of this kind is an important aspect of pastoral work, even if it is not the whole picture. The unconditional acceptance and understanding offered to the client by the carer might be seen as an expression of God's unconditional love for humankind, which we see supremely in Jesus Christ.

Pastoral Care as Practical Moral Thinking

By contrast with those who understand pastoral care in therapeutic ways and bracket ethical judgements out of the pastoral encounter, practical theologian Don Browning is well known for insisting that pastoral theology should be understood as 'a dimension of theological or religious ethics'. In an article originally published some years ago, he argued that it should express a vision of the human lifecycle (the experience of birth, growth, maturity, sexuality and relationships, ageing and death) that combines theological ethics with psychological and other social-scientific perspectives. It must also give an account of 'those pastoral acts through which this . . . vision . . . is appropriately mediated to individuals and groups' and it must do all this in a pluralistic society in which people have very diverse religious, cultural and ethical stances. Pastoral care must take account of 'both the religious dimension of common [human] experience as well as the explicit faith themes of the historic Judeo-Christian tradition'.[4]

In more recent writings, Browning has developed a complex ethical scheme, drawing on many of the theoretical perspectives outlined in previous chapters of this book, including deontological and consequentialist ethics, aspects of virtue theory and the evolutionary perspective of sociobiology. His scheme describes five 'dimensions' of practical moral thinking, from the *visional* (an overarching moral and theological understanding of the world, somewhat akin to what Richard Hays calls a 'symbolic world' – see Chapter 2) right down to the *rule–role* dimension that describes our concrete decisions, actions and ways of living from day to day.[5]

If Geraldine were to understand her pastoral responsibility in this way, she would seek to be aware of the psychological needs, pressures and influences affecting Helen's and Paul's thinking, such as Helen's attitude to her approaching death, her concerns for Paul and their children, Paul's and the children's responses to the prospect of their bereavement, their reactions to Helen's suffering and disability and so on. However, she would also want to help them grow and develop morally in ways that were consistent with their Christian faith. While she would certainly not wish to force a particular moral decision on Paul and Helen, she might well think it appropriate to state her own moral views about euthanasia and engage in serious moral conversation with them.

Furthermore, Browning emphasizes that pastoral care is not (or should not be) just a matter of encounters between individuals, but, rather, is set in the context of the community of faith. Helen and Paul's pastoral care and their moral deliberations about euthanasia may be focused on meetings and conversations between them and Geraldine; and what is said and done in those meetings will almost certainly be confidential to the individuals involved. However, when Geraldine offers love and care to Helen, Paul and their children, she does so on behalf of a wider community of faith. They have particular roles in that community; their moral vision is (or should be) shaped by it; and the community as a whole will (or should) care for them in a variety of ways. Thus, the encounter between Geraldine, Helen and Paul is one important focus – but not necessarily the only one – of this care offered by the community as a whole.

Pastoral Care as Building Communities of Character

Stanley Hauerwas was introduced earlier in this book, particularly in Chapter 6 on virtue ethics. He has argued powerfully over many years that Christian ethics must be fundamentally located in the life and worship of the Church. The Church is called to be a distinctive, countercultural community, its identity and character formed by the Christian story and its life lived in a fundamentally different way from the secular society around it. The character and virtues of Christians should be shaped by participating in this community, hearing the Christian story and 'inhabiting' that story in the Church's worship.

Given that view of Christian ethics, Hauerwas might be expected to be unsympathetic to therapeutic models of pastoral care with a theoretical base in humanistic psychology. Indeed, in their book *Resident Aliens*, he and his co-author, William Willimon, are sharply critical of the notion that ministry is one of the 'helping professions'.[6] They resist therapeutic models of pastoral care, the aim of which is to help people become better adjusted to modern society. Instead, the role of ministers and the purpose of pastoral care are to build up the Christian community with its distinctive character, to enable the community to be what it is called to be and to help individual Christians play their parts in the community's life.

Pastoral care, understood in these terms, could mean a variety of things. It could include enabling a church's members to grow in Christian character by providing them with 'significant examples' – the 'saints' of local congregations – to observe, imitate and be inspired by. It could involve giving such 'saints' the opportunity to challenge, question and inspire the church to live in ways that are faithful to its story. It could mean that the church supports its members and enables them to be better people than they could be left to their own devices. It could also mean practising a radically different scale of values to those of secular society, so that those regarded by society as insignificant or problematic – those with learning disabilities, to use just one of Hauerwas and Willimon's examples – may be important and honoured members of the church.[7] It is also clear from this account that pastoral care is not only, or even primarily, the responsibility of individual ministers and pastors. Rather, it is the community as a whole that is the primary agent of pastoral care. The role of ministers and pastors is not to do all the caring themselves and certainly not to try and imitate counsellors or psychotherapists, but, instead, enable and encourage the church to be the kind of community that cares for its members in the ways that Hauerwas and Willimon describe.

This understanding of ministry has much in common with Browning's account of pastoral care, but there are important differences. Hauerwas and Willimon would probably argue that Christian pastoral care should be concerned with the distinctive and peculiar story that Christians are called to shape their lives to match and should not address itself to the 'religious dimension of common experience', as Browning puts it. Also, while it is clear that they acknowledge the value of helping professions such as therapy and counselling, Hauerwas and Willimon would probably give less weight than Browning to psychological theory and counselling skills in informing the practice of Christian pastoral care.

How might this model inform Geraldine's response to Paul, Helen and their family? Hauerwas has frequently argued against suicide and euthanasia, essentially on the grounds that they are inconsistent with the Christian conviction that life is God's gift and they undermine the relationships of trust that bind a community such as the Church together.[8] Geraldine, if she understood the relationship between ethics and pastoral care in this way and held these convictions about euthanasia, certainly need not be reluctant to share her convictions with Helen and Paul – though presumably she would not do so in an overbearing or coercive manner. However, the most important pastoral and ethical task would not be hers alone, but the church's, and it would not be to *give* Helen and Paul moral advice, but to *be* a certain kind of community. The church would be called to be the kind of community – and give the necessary support to Helen, Paul and their children – that would enable them to face Helen's suffering, indignity and death and understand even these things as part of the totality of a life lived in response to Christ.

Pastoral Care as Liberation

In Chapters 7 and 8, we encountered liberationist and feminist theologies and explored some of their significance for Christian ethics. As we saw, these approaches are attempts to do theology from the perspectives of those who are marginalized and oppressed. They involve an analysis and critique of the causes of oppression and factors that maintain it, including aspects of Christian tradition and practice. They have a strong focus on practice, seeking to transform attitudes and social structures so that powerless and oppressed people may be empowered and liberated. In various ways, they seek to recover from the Christian tradition resources that can promote liberation.

Feminist and (to a lesser extent) liberation theologies have had an important influence on modern pastoral theology.[9] For example, feminist pastoral theologians draw attention to patriarchy as a factor that blights women's lives and criticize the Church's thought and practice for supporting it. They argue that commonly accepted notions of human maturity and wholeness – including those that inform Christian pastoral care – tend to be male biased and represent women's experience as immature or pathological. If this is so, then pastoral care needs to pay more attention to women's experience and develop new, more inclusive notions of the human good.

Feminists also question the male dominance of Church structures and ministry, and approaches to pastoral care that focus mainly on the practices of ordained ministers. Like the previous two models I have outlined (though for somewhat different reasons), they might therefore want to shift the focus of pastoral theology away from the work of individual pastors and ministers and towards the Church community as a whole and a variety of its members.

Feminist and liberationist pastoral theologians would also want to shift the focus away from the Church community and out towards the wider community and society. They would argue that pastoral care should mean not only the Church looking after its members but also working for the transformation of the wider community and society in which it is set, so that all people have the opportunity to flourish as human beings.

This also means that feminists and liberationists would challenge common assumptions about the aims of pastoral care. A standard definition is that it has to do with 'healing, sustaining, guiding and reconciling'. Bonnie Miller-McLemore argues that, instead, from a feminist and liberationist perspective, it must be centrally concerned with 'resisting, empowering, nurturing and liberating'.[10]

One theologian who has written extensively about medical ethics from a feminist–liberationist perspective is Karen Lebacqz. In a brief essay on euthanasia, Lebacqz has argued that caring – an important theme in feminist ethics, as we saw in Chapter 8 – surely means that we will want to prevent the suffering of those we care for. From a Christian perspective, death is not the greatest possible evil, but can sometimes 'serve the values of life'. Accordingly, 'As a way of bringing about death, active euthanasia can serve evil or it can serve the values of life. When it serves the values of life, it can be morally justified.'[11]

If Geraldine understood pastoral care from a feminist–liberationist perspective, this might motivate her to pay close and empathetic attention to the particular circumstances, experiences and relationships that structure the lives of Helen, Paul and their children, as a feminist 'ethic of care' would recommend. She would also wish to be sensitive to the ways in which Helen might be marginalized or disempowered. The fact that Helen is a woman might make her particularly susceptible to certain moral and social pressures. Some feminists argue that women have been taught for so long to be unselfish and put others' needs before their own that they risk neglecting their own needs and failing to fulfil their God-given potential. The fact that Helen is a very sick patient also makes her vulnerable. She has relatively little power and control over her own life – to a large extent, she is in the hands of the healthcare system and the professionals who are caring for her. The pastoral care of people like Helen may include advocacy to ensure that they are treated justly by the system and, as far as possible, empowered rather than disempowered.

From a feminist–liberationist standpoint, Geraldine would be suspicious of moral judgements that served to increase the suffering and vulnerability of people who are already vulnerable and powerless. She might, therefore, agree with Lebacqz that, in cases like Helen's, voluntary euthanasia could 'serve the values of life' and be morally acceptable. Like Lebacqz, though, she would be alert to the dangers of abuse. Though Lebacqz believes that euthanasia can in some cases 'serve the values of life', she is cautious about legislating for it, because of the risk that legislation would result in vulnerable people being pressured to accept euthanasia against their will.[12]

Questions

- Write a few sentences to summarize your understanding of Christian pastoral care.
- What part should moral reasoning and moral judgement play in pastoral care as you understand it?
- What would this imply for Geraldine and the church community in their pastoral response to Helen, Paul and their children?

3 Christian Ethics and Public Policy

For this section, you are invited to travel back from the near future to the not too distant past – to the parliamentary debates and discussions about Lord Joffe's Assisted Dying for the Terminally Ill Bill that began in March 2004.

We saw in Chapter 4 that the Anglican and Catholic bishops opposed the Bill, at least partly on the basis of fundamental Christian convictions about the value of human life. We saw that many Christians would agree with this stance, though some have developed theological arguments that voluntary euthanasia and assisted suicide *could* be legitimate from a Christian perspective. However, the debate over the Joffe Bill not only raised the question of whether or not euthanasia and assisted suicide could be morally acceptable from a Christian point of view. It also raised the question what part that Christian perspective should play in shaping public policy in a society such as the UK, in which only a minority are active Christians. Is it the business of Christians and the Churches to engage in these debates? If so, what can they bring to them and how can they most helpfully and effectively make their particular contributions? Writers on Christian ethics have suggested, and practised, many possible answers to this question and some possibilities follow.[13]

Seeking the Moral Common Ground

According to the first possible view, if Christians go into public debates arguing explicitly on the basis of their theological convictions, they are unlikely to persuade anyone who does not share those convictions. Therefore, they should instead seek the moral common ground – instead of appealing to specifically Christian sources or assumptions, they should base their public moral arguments on premises that are shared by everyone, Christian or not. There may be a place for specifically Christian arguments within the Christian community, but not outside it.

Something like this position is held by the 'Autonomy' school of thought within Roman Catholic moral theology, which I introduced briefly in Chapter 1. This school of thought holds that Christian faith teaches nothing about the *content* of moral obligation that could not, in principle, be known by any person of good will, regardless of his or her religious commitments. In other words, ethics is autonomous.

This means that Christians entering into public ethical debates should be arguing in favour of conclusions that hold good for all the participants in those debates and ones that any of the participants should, in principle, be able to work out for themselves. If that is so, there is no need for Christians to back up their public arguments by appealing to specifically Christian articles of faith as they can say what they need to say by starting from the basic assumptions of those they are arguing with.

In medical ethics, one approach of this kind has been enormously influential. It is the so-called *four principles approach* devised by the philosophers Tom Beauchamp and James Childress.[14] Beauchamp and Childress argue that medical ethics should be guided by four key moral principles:

- *autonomy*
- *non-maleficence* – the principle that we should avoid doing harm
- *beneficence* – we should do good
- *justice*.

They believe that these principles are part of a 'common morality' that can be agreed on by a wide variety of people, whatever their specific religious or moral commitments. When we face any issue in medical ethics – such as the question of legalizing euthanasia and assisted suicide – one or more of these principles may apply. If two or more of the principles suggest conflicting answers, we shall have to balance them against one another and decide which takes precedence in this instance. For example, in the euthanasia debate, the principle of autonomy might suggest that everyone should have the right to end their lives at the time and in the manner that they choose.

The principles of non-maleficence and beneficence might suggest that health professionals have an obligation to help patients who wish to end their suffering by hastening their death. However, this argument would also need to be balanced against the risk of the harm that would be done if legalization led to involuntary euthanasia or pressure on patients to ask for euthanasia.

The principle of justice has also entered the euthanasia debate. Diane Pretty, whose case led to calls for a change in the law (see Chapter 4), argued (unsuccessfully) that, because her disability made her unable to commit suicide, she was unjustly deprived of the right that an able-bodied person would have to end his or her own life.

On the other side of the argument, opponents might argue that legalization would result in pressure on the sick and elderly to end their lives and, in that respect, have an *unjust* effect on some of the most powerless and vulnerable members of society.

Seeking Wisdom

A second approach that has something in common with the first is based on the theological notion of *wisdom*.[15] God is the source of all wisdom and the created order reflects the wisdom of God. Human wisdom, originating in the wisdom of God, may be found in many places and people – it is not the sole preserve of any one community or tradition. However, human wisdom can never encompass the totality of divine wisdom and, for the Christian, human understanding is radically challenged by the surprising wisdom of Christ's cross.

In contrast to the fragmented nature of much modern knowledge, particularly modern science, wisdom has the capacity to integrate different areas of knowledge and different kinds of understanding, such as the kind based on factual evidence and that based on intuition. Wisdom also has a moral quality. In some biblical sources, such as the book of Proverbs, folly is not merely stupidity but a kind of moral deficiency and may be seen as a choice to ignore 'God's whisper' to the world.[16] Because of its moral quality, wisdom can not only reintegrate different kinds of knowledge but also reconcile knowledge and goodness, which have become split off from one another in our modern scientific age.

This approach encourages Christians to listen for expressions of wisdom from all the participants in public debates, but to be ready to challenge those debates when wisdom is forgotten or ignored. An illustration of this approach is found in the work of Celia Deane-Drummond and her colleagues on public perceptions of GM crops. Analysing transcripts of focus group interviews that were conducted without any theological questions in view, they find a highly sophisticated and nuanced range of responses in which some participants appear to be articulating religious or theological questions, perhaps without even realizing it. Yet, these questions have tended to be excluded from 'official' public debates about GM foods. They conclude that '[t]he conversation that we as a society need to have – and that the public seems to be demanding – is a theological one', which requires an equally nuanced and sensitive response from theologians.[17] A similar approach to public debates about euthanasia and assisted suicide would require a willingness to seek common ground that could be shared by many of the participants and an openness to moral insights from many sources. It would also require Christians to listen carefully for theological insights and questions about fundamental issues, such as the value of life and the meaning of suffering and death, and be ready to express Christian convictions about such matters.

Turning the World Upside Down

The third approach contrasts sharply with the first two. Michael Banner, in his essay 'Turning the World Upside Down', calls it a 'dogmatic Christian ethics'.[18] 'Dogmatic' here does not mean doctrinaire or authoritarian, but that this account of ethics is firmly rooted in the self-revelation of God in Jesus Christ. One of the most important exponents of this approach was the great Protestant theologian Karl Barth. Following Barth, Banner is highly critical of what he calls 'apologetic Christian ethics'. By this he means any account of Christian ethics that seeks to justify itself and its conclusions in terms of any other system, such as the approach that I called 'seeking the common moral ground'. For Banner, the only accountability that Christian ethics should acknowledge is to 'the kingdom of Jesus Christ', as Barth put it. This does not mean, however, that Christian ethics cannot engage with other ethics in the public arena. It can do so in a variety of ways, such as by asserting 'what it knows to be good and right' (pp. 36–7), denouncing what it knows to be wrong and exposing the weaknesses and inconsistencies of other systems and approaches. Whenever dogmatic Christian ethics enters the public arena, however, 'it does so on the basis of its own distinctive premise . . . of faith in the life, death and resurrection of Jesus Christ' (p. 39).

Another of Banner's essays, 'Christian Anthropology at the Beginning and End of Life' (pp. 47–85), shows how some of these modes of engagement might work in debates about euthanasia. Thus, he examines the case for voluntary euthanasia on its own terms and argues that, even in terms of its own 'self-understanding', the case is seriously flawed. However, he also challenges that self-understanding, arguing that it 'expresses more regard for death than for life and . . . is determined by a doubtfulness about life's beginning and, above all, a fear of its end' (pp. 68–9). He contrasts this with the way in which the Church has traditionally understood *martyrdom*. He argues that a Christian view of martyrdom implies an understanding of humanity that 'expresses a respect for life and not death' (p. 68) and is shaped, not by fear, but by the hope expressed in Jesus Christ's words in Revelation: 'Fear not, I am the first and the last, and the living one' (Revelation 1.17–18, quoted on p. 48). This Christian hope and respect for life are inconsistent with the practice of euthanasia. Instead, they demand practices such as hospice care which imply that our ultimate hope does not depend on prolonging our earthly life by technological means.

A City Set on a Hill

The fourth approach is the one developed by Stanley Hauerwas. It is similar in some ways to Banner's, though Banner takes pains to distinguish his approach from that of Hauerwas. For Hauerwas, as we have seen before, Christian ethics is highly distinctive and specific – it is shaped by the life and worship of the Christian community, the character of which is formed by the story of Jesus Christ. Hauerwas, therefore, has little time for Christian strategies of public debate that seek common moral ground, but this does not mean that the Church has nothing to offer to public ethics. The contribution that Christians are called to make is of a very different kind. As Hauerwas puts it, 'the first social ethical task of the Church is to be the Church'.[19] In other words, it is called to be an alternative *polis* or political community, displaying a different way of living together in faithfulness to its distinctive story. This acted-out witness to the possibility of a different way of life is the most important and helpful thing that the Church can offer to the world.

This means that Hauerwas' primary concern is not to supply answers to questions about public policy or legislation – indeed, when commenting on such issues he is apt to change the question. For example, his essay 'Religious Concepts of Brain Death and Associated Problems' was written in response to medical and legal debates about the right way to define and identify death, but he begins by observing that 'there is nothing in Christian convictions that would entail preference for one definition of death over another'. He goes on to articulate some central Christian convictions about life, death and our responsibility to die well and claims that '[t]he necessity we feel to define the "moment of death" is partly the result of our attempt to avoid preparing for death and thus making the moment of our death unexpected'. In other words, from a Christian perspective, we are asking the wrong question (or, at any rate, not the most important question) if we are preoccupied with criteria for defining *when* a person has died, rather than asking what it might mean to fulfil our responsibility to die *well*.[20]

The most important things that the Church has to say about euthanasia are only likely to make sense in the context of its life and worship. As we saw in the last section, Hauerwas believes that euthanasia should be prohibited, but his most important reasons for this are not pragmatic ones, such as the danger of the slippery slope or other harmful consequences. Rather, they have to do with the Church's basic theological convictions, such as that life is God's gift and our life together depends on trust to sustain it:

> Our unwillingness to kill ourselves even under pain is an affirmation that the trust that has sustained us in health is also the trust that sustains us in illness and distress; that our existence is a gift ultimately bounded by a hope that gives us a way to go on; that the full, present memory of our Christian story is a source of strength and consolation for ourselves and our community.[21]

However, Christians cannot expect these convictions to make sense in public debate detached from the corporate life and worship of the Christian community, which makes them intelligible. So, while the Churches are called to bear public witness to their basic theological convictions and the implications of those convictions, the most important way that they do this may not be by lobbying for or against changes in the law, but by being the kind of communities in which dying people can find the resources to endure pain, suffering and indignity.

This insistence on the centrality of the Church for Christian ethics has led many of Hauerwas' critics to describe his thought as 'sectarian' and unhelpful for public debate. According to Nigel Biggar, this charge of sectarianism is undeserved because Hauerwas does not advocate *retreating* from the political world into the Church, but argues that the life of the Church is the necessary *condition* for Christian engagement with politics.[22] However, others sympathetic to Hauerwas' concerns nonetheless seem to feel the need for a middle way between his resolutely Church-centred ethic and the 'common ground' approaches outlined earlier. This perceived need for a middle way leads us to the next approach.

Theological Fragments

This approach is drawn from Duncan Forrester, who is sympathetic to thinkers such as Hauerwas, but hesitant to draw such sharp lines as Hauerwas does between the Church and the public arena.

In his book *Christian Justice and Public Policy*, Forrester examines the problem of justice in a pluralist society – the twin difficulties of saying what justice *is* and *practising* it. He finds secular theories wanting, but is also aware that Christianity has a mixed record where justice is concerned and does not think that the Church of today either can or should try to produce a comprehensive theological theory of justice. What it *can* do, however, is offer *theological fragments*. By 'fragments' he means ideas, insights and practices that come from a 'quarry' of coherent Christian thought, which, when introduced into the public arena, can act as irritants, challenges and insights that move debate and practice in new directions.[23] Forrester's examples are wide-ranging and include *statements*, such as the Barmen Declaration (produced in 1934 by the German 'Confessing Church' in opposition to the ideology of the Nazi regime), *insights*, such as the need for a concept of forgiveness in a criminal justice system, and *examples of practice*, such as the South African Truth and Reconciliation Commission. Fragments in isolation from their quarry can be misunderstood or misused, so Christians have a twofold task of contributing fragments to the public arena, while at the same time continuing to do the basic theological work to maintain and develop the theological 'quarry'.[24]

Forrester's own examples make clear that 'theological fragments' need not only be fragments of speech or text but also of practice. In the agonizing human situations that give rise to calls for euthanasia, fragments of practice may well be more powerful and appropriate contributions than speech or text alone. The hospice movement, in its origins and at least some of its present expressions, can be seen as a hugely important and influential 'theological fragment' in response to the questions raised by illness, pain and dying.[25]

Middle Axioms

A different kind of middle way uses what are rather misleadingly known as *middle axioms*.[26] This approach was very influential in Anglican social thought during the twentieth century. One of its main advocates was Ronald Preston, whom we met in Chapter 7 and who favoured this approach as a way of making connections between Christian ethics and economic policy. The approach is outlined briefly in Preston's book *Religion and the Ambiguities of Capitalism*, in which he argues that the gap between general theological affirmations and detailed policy prescriptions must be taken very seriously. Theology, of itself, is not able to bridge this gap – and so attempts to read policy decisions directly from theological principles are apt to be naive, ridiculous or even dangerously misleading. In order to find our way through the middle ground between general theological statements and detailed policies, says Preston, we must bring together people with various kinds of relevant expertise, including theologians, but also, for example, economists, scientists and so on. He insists that we must also attend to the experience of those affected by the issues being discussed and particularly to 'those marginalized in society, who frequently fail to get a hearing'.[27]

A number of Church of England publications on social ethics show signs of the middle axiom approach, including its report on euthanasia, *On Dying Well*, originally produced in 1975. This report has been very influential and demonstrates many of the important features of this approach. It begins with case studies and incorporates more at a later stage of the report, which draw attention to the experiences of terminal illness, pain and suffering that have led to calls for legalized euthanasia. Moral, theological, medical and legal considerations are each given a separate chapter, after which the authors state their conclusions:

- if standards of patient care were raised, there would be few situations where there was a good case for euthanasia
- there might still be exceptional cases where it could be morally justified
- nonetheless, a change in the law is not justified, because it cannot be shown that 'such a change would remove greater evils than it would cause'.[28]

Despite the great influence of this approach, even its sympathetic critics suggest that it needs a major overhaul.[29] One frequent criticism is that it is elitist, tending to rely on experts and working parties of the great and the good. This charge may not be entirely justified because, as we have seen, Preston insisted that those doing Christian social ethics must also pay attention to the experiences of the marginalized and the voiceless. However, it is still probably fair to say that the middle axiom method, as it was practised in the twentieth century, had a tendency to be somewhat top-down in its approach. In that respect, it contrasts sharply with our last approach.

The View from Below

The liberationist and feminist perspectives introduced in earlier chapters would suggest a sharply contrasting way of setting up the relationship between Christian reflection and public debate. These are theologies done 'from below', by the poor and oppressed and those who stand in solidarity with them, not by the privileged on their behalf. Liberationists and feminists would probably therefore be suspicious of policy discussions dominated by elites, experts and the powerful.

On this view, reflection on public policy must begin with the concrete experience of the oppressed, marginalized and vulnerable and it must be directed towards positive change. It should ask hard questions about why some people are oppressed in various ways and would be willing to use tools from outside theology to understand the causes of oppression. However, it would not simply baptize secular theories – biblical and theological reflection are also essential to guide understanding and practice. In an essay originally published in 1980, Karen Lebacqz argued that bioethical thinking paying attention to feminist and liberation theologies would be less preoccupied with particular dilemmas and decisions and more concerned with structural questions, such as 'Who holds the power to make decisions about medical ethics?' and 'What effect do developments in medicine have on vulnerable and marginalized groups in society?' It would be less individualistic and less dominated by scientific forms of rationality. It would pay more attention to the stories of people's lives, embedded in networks of relationships and communities, and would attend to concrete experience, particularly the experiences of the oppressed, as well as scientific data, in order to understand the issues about which decisions must be made.[30]

In the argument about legalizing euthanasia and assisted suicide, for example, such an approach would certainly require us to listen carefully to the stories and experiences of the people most closely concerned, such as Diane Pretty and Brian Blackburn (see Chapter 4). However, it would also require us to ask about the social, political and economic context that shaped these experiences. We might ask, for example, if the organization and economics of healthcare mean that some people (particularly the poor) do not have access to good palliative care and other kinds of support. We might also ask if the structures of our communities and society mean that some people face their deaths largely alone and unsupported. Asking questions like these might lead us to seek public policies that, as far as possible, do away with the need for euthanasia and assisted suicide.

That said, such solutions would not completely solve the problems that lead some people to argue for legalizing euthanasia and assisted suicide. Accordingly, paying attention to the concrete experience of terminally ill people leads some liberationist thinkers to support voluntary euthanasia. As we saw earlier, Lebacqz argues that, in some cases, active euthanasia could 'serve the values of life' and therefore be morally justified. However, the same concern for vulnerable people leads her to be very cautious about legislating for euthanasia as this could lead to situations where these people are put under pressure to request euthanasia or are euthanized without their consent.

Questions

- Assess the strengths and weaknesses of the various approaches described in this section.
- In the light of your assessment of these approaches, how, if at all, should Christians and the Churches attempt to influence legislation such as the Joffe Bill?

Suggestions for Further Reading

Christian Ethics and Pastoral Care

David J. Atkinson and David H. Field (eds), *New Dictionary of Christian Ethics and Pastoral Theology*, Leicester: IVP, 1995.

Paul Ballard and John Pritchard, *Practical Theology in Action: Christian Thinking in the Service of Church and Society*, London: SPCK, 1996.

Rodney J. Hunter (ed.), *Dictionary of Pastoral Care and Counseling*, Nashville, IN: Abingdon, 1990.

James Woodward and Stephen Pattison (eds), *The Blackwell Reader in Pastoral and Practical Theology*, Oxford: Blackwell, 2000.

Christian Ethics and Public Policy

Michael Banner, *Christian Ethics and Contemporary Moral Problems*, Cambridge: Cambridge University Press, 1999.

Duncan Forrester, *Truthful Action: Explorations in Practical Theology*, Edinburgh: T & T Clark, 2000.

Robert Gascoine, *The Public Forum and Christian Ethics*, Cambridge: Cambridge University Press, 2000.

Robin Gill, *Moral Leadership in a Postmodern Age*, Edinburgh: T & T Clark, 1997.

10

Conclusion

In the Introduction I said that Christian ethics asks questions on a number of different levels. There are the 'What to decide' questions about divorce and remarriage, homosexuality, abortion, euthanasia, war, economic practice and many others. Then there are the 'How to decide' questions about the use of the Bible, the validity of natural law theory, the place of duty and consequentialist reasoning in Christian moral decision making, how Christian ethics should take account of experiences of oppression and so forth. Finally, there are questions about what sorts of people, and communities, we ought to be – questions about virtue and character.

As we have seen in this book, different Christian ethicists give different weight to these three kinds of question. Some focus mostly on the 'What' and 'How' questions, while others (such as Stanley Hauerwas) give a higher priority to questions of virtue and character.

In the course of this book, we have explored a number of specific 'What to decide' questions – 'practical' ethical issues, for want of a better term – and a number of 'theoretical' approaches (again, for want of a better term) that address the 'How to decide' and 'What sort of people to be' questions.

In the Introduction, I suggested that practical and theoretical questions are linked in close and complex ways. Christian ethics is not as simple as developing a moral decision-making formula into which you can feed any problem and get the answer out at the end. To be sure, the decisions we make about ethical theory or method will affect our conclusions about practical questions. If we reject Thomas Aquinas' account of the natural ends of human beings (Chapter 3), we are unlikely to agree with his view that homosexual intercourse is sinful by virtue of being 'a breakdown in a proper reasonable order in exercising the sex act' because it 'rules out reproduction by nature'.[1] However, this example also shows how complex the relationship is: it would be possible to accept at least the broad outlines of Thomas' teleological view of human nature *without* sharing his view about same-sex intercourse. Conversely, many Christians who do not accept Thomas' natural law theory do agree with him that same-sex intercourse is morally wrong, taking their cue from the biblical texts about homosexuality that we surveyed in Chapter 3.

However, if our decisions about ethical theory influence our practical conclusions, it works the other way around as well – that is, thinking about practical issues raises questions about ethical theories and methods. As we saw in Chapter 4, Kant's ethical theory has long been criticized on account of some of the alarming practical conclusions to which it seems to lead – for example, that it would be wrong to tell a lie even to protect someone from a homicidal maniac. Again, in Chapter 2, practical moral issues, such as remarriage after divorce, human cloning and stem cell research raised methodological questions about how the Bible should be used in Christian ethics.

It seems, then, that there is a complex interplay between Christian ethical 'theory' and 'practical' ethics, in which each informs and questions the other. That is why the terms 'ethical theory' and 'practical ethics' are less than fully satisfactory – we cannot really talk of a neat separation between theory and practice in Christian ethics, as we might be able to, for example, in physics.

Accordingly, I hope that your study of various practical moral questions in the course of this book has informed and clarified your understanding of those issues and others like them. I also hope that the work you have done on both practical moral questions and aspects of ethical theory has informed and clarified your understanding of the 'How to decide' and 'What sort of people to be' questions. The following exercise should help you to test whether or not it has done so.

Exercise

Look back at the section in Chapter 1 describing the sources of Christian ethics – Scripture, tradition, reason and experience. Write an account, in two or three paragraphs, of the role that you think each source should play in Christian moral deliberation and action, the weight that should be given to each and their relationship to one another.

In the Introduction I likened this book to a map of the territory known as 'Christian ethics' and remarked that, if you want to get to know a place, merely looking at a map is no substitute for actually visiting the place yourself. What I meant was this. Ethics, Christian or otherwise, is fundamentally a practical discipline in the sense that it is concerned, in various ways, with how we live our lives. It is concerned with what it is right for us to do, as individuals and as communities, how we make coherent and defensible decisions about what to do and what sort of people and communities we ought to be – in other words, our vision of what a good human life and a good human community or society look like.

No doubt it is possible, to some extent, to discuss questions like these as an abstract academic exercise, simply for the purpose of passing an exam or earning a living by teaching the subject. However, it would be odd, to say the least, if our thinking about these questions had no connection with the choices we make in our own lives and the moral visions that shape those lives. Suppose I were a scientist with a well-established career in human embryo research and then I began to study Christian ethics in my spare time. If, in my studies, I encountered highly persuasive arguments that human embryos should be treated as persons from the very beginning of their existence, I might expect to feel some kind of tension (to say the least) between my ethical thinking and the way in which I was living my life. There are various ways in which I might resolve this tension. For example, there might be aspects of my scientific experience that prompted me to question the arguments for treating early embryos as persons, or, alternatively, I might find those arguments so convincing that I decided to move out of human embryo research at the earliest opportunity. The point is that it seems odd to imagine my ethical thinking as being totally unconnected with the way I live my life.

If that is the case, then the study of Christian ethics is an opportunity not only to become acquainted with a body of knowledge and learn how to think about certain kinds of question, but also to reflect on, and clarify, the moral commitments according to which we live our own lives.

Whether you consider yourself a member of some Christian tradition, some other faith community or none, I hope that working through this book has stimulated you to reflect critically on the basic moral commitments by which you live your own life. It may be, for example, that, on reading about one or more of the ethical traditions outlined here, you have experienced what Alasdair MacIntyre calls a 'shock of recognition',[2] finding that it resonates with some of your own basic convictions and commitments, and helps you to understand those convictions and commitments more fully. Equally, you may find yourself reading about one of these ethical traditions and thinking, 'Yes, but . . .', bringing the account of that tradition into critical dialogue with your own moral commitments and experience. Alternatively, you may have found yourself fundamentally opposed to every ethical stance presented here, in which case your opposition might prompt you to think further about what ethical stance *would* resonate with your own convictions and commitments.

The concluding exercise may help you to chart any ways in which your understanding of your own moral convictions and commitments has changed or developed in the process of studying this subject.

Exercise

- Refer back to the story of a moral experience that you wrote down and reflected upon for the second exercise in Chapter 1. Answer the following questions in the light of your study of Christian ethics.

  - Would you now understand and describe the experience differently in any respect from the way in which you described it in Chapter 1? If so, in what ways would your understanding and description be different and why?
  - Would you adopt a different approach to any moral dilemmas or decisions that were part of the experience? How would your approach now be different and why?

— If you were faced with a similar situation again, would you now act any differently? If so, how and why?

You might conclude that, if you were faced with a similar situation again, you would think and act in much the same way, but you now understand better why you would do so. Alternatively, you might conclude that you would think differently in certain ways and, possibly, that there are things you would do differently. Equally, you might discover that your experience seems less clear and more confusing than it did before you started studying Christian ethics. It has been said that confusion can be a sign of progress in philosophy, and the same is sometimes true in Christian ethics.

In any event, the opportunity for growth in our understanding of ourselves, others and the ways in which we live and act in the world is one of the things that makes Christian ethics, in my thoroughly biased opinion, one of the most interesting and rewarding of theological disciplines to study. If this book has stimulated your interest in this subject and whetted your appetite to learn more about it, it will have done at least part of what it was intended to do.

Notes

Chapter 1 Introduction: Deciding How to Decide

1 The chapter title and headings of sections 2 and 3 are borrowed from Wayne G. Boulton, Thomas D. Kennedy and Allen Verhey (eds), *From Christ to the World: Introductory Readings in Christian Ethics*, Grand Rapids, MI: Eerdmans, 1994, p. 8.

2 Richard B. Hays, *The Moral Vision of the New Testament: Community, Cross, New Creation*, Edinburgh: T & T Clark, 1997, pp. 209–11, 296–8. See also Alister McGrath, *Christian Theology: An Introduction*, 3rd edn, Oxford: Blackwell, 2001, Chapter 6.

3 Hays, *Moral Vision*, p. 210.

4 Alasdair MacIntyre, *After Virtue: A Study in Moral Theory*, 2nd edn, London: Duckworth, 1985, pp. 221–2.

5 MacIntyre, *After Virtue*, especially pp. 36–78.

6 McGrath discusses the relationship between Scripture and tradition in *Christian Theology*, pp. 186–8, and *Reformation Thought: An Introduction*, 2nd edn, Oxford: Blackwell, 1993, Chapter 7. The quotation from Sebastian Franck is on p. 187 of *Christian Theology*. For Hays' discussion, see note 2 above.

7 Stanley Hauerwas' virtue ethics can be found in many books, including *The Peaceable Kingdom: A Primer in Christian Ethics*, 2nd edn, London: SCM Press, 2003.

8 Vincent MacNamara, 'The Distinctiveness of Christian Morality', in Bernard Hoose (ed.), *Christian Ethics: An Introduction*, London: Cassell, 1998, pp. 149–60. See also MacNamara, *Faith and Ethics*, Dublin: Gill and Macmillan, 1985.

9 Gustafson and Hauerwas' comments in this paragraph are quoted in the editors' introduction to Gerald P. McKenny and Jonathan R. Sande (eds), *Theological Analyses of the Clinical Encounter*, Dordrecht: Kluwer Academic, 1994, p. vii.

10 Emil Brunner and Karl Barth, *Natural Theology*, English transl., London: Geoffrey Bles, 1946. The possibility, or otherwise, of natural theology, is a massive issue in Christian theology, which cannot be directly explored in any depth in this book, but is helpfully introduced by Daniel L. Migliore, *Faith Seeking Understanding: An Introduction to Christian Theology*, Grand Rapids, MI: Eerdmans, 1991, pp. 252–67.

11 For an indication of what is meant by a non-conformist church in the Reformed tradition, visit: www.urc.org.uk/about_the_urc/what_is_the_urc/index.htm (accessed 9 September 2005).

Chapter 2 The Bible in Christian Ethics

1 This case study is based on Tim Radford and David Adam, 'Koreans Succeed in Stem Cell First', *The Guardian*, 13 February 2004.

2 Allen Verhey, *Remembering Jesus: Christian Community, Scripture, and the Moral Life*, Grand Rapids, MI: Eerdmans, 2002, p. 10.

3 Verhey, *Remembering Jesus*, p. 10.

4 Alister McGrath, *Christian Theology: An Introduction*, 2nd edn, Oxford: Blackwell, 1997, pp. 193–5.

5 Daniel L. Migliore, *Faith Seeking Understanding: An Introduction to Christian Theology*, Grand Rapids, MI: Eerdmans, 1991, pp. 40–55.

6 Vincent MacNamara, 'The Distinctiveness of Christian Morality', in Hoose, *Christian Ethics: An Introduction*, pp. 149–60, at p. 154.

7 Allen Verhey, 'Bible in Christian Ethics', in John Macquarrie and James Childress (eds), *A New Dictionary of Christian Ethics*, London: SCM Press, 1986, pp. 57–61.

8 Karl Barth, *Church Dogmatics*, vol. 1.2, English trans., Edinburgh: T & T Clark, 1956, pp. 457–537. See Migliore, *Faith Seeking Understanding*, pp. 46–8, for a helpful summary and discussion of Barth's view.

9 Richard B. Hays, *The Moral Vision of the New Testament*, Edinburgh: T & T Clark, 1997, pp. 208–9.

10 Leslie Houlden, *Ethics and the New Testament*, London and Oxford: Mowbray, 1975, pp. 119–20.

11 Houlden, *Ethics and the New Testament*, pp. 117–18.

12 Hays, *Moral Vision*, pp. 294–5.

13 Hays, *Moral Vision*, pp. 3–7.

14 Hays, *Moral Vision*, pp. 298–306.

15 Tom Deidun, 'The Bible and Christian Ethics', in Hoose, *Christian Ethics*, pp. 3–46.

16 For detailed discussions, see Hays, *Moral Vision*, Chapter 15, and Adrian Thatcher, *Liberating Sex: A Christian Sexual Theology*, London: SPCK, 1993, pp. 118–25.

17 Helen Oppenheimer, 'Marriage', in Macquarrie and Childress (eds), *A New Dictionary of Christian Ethics*, pp. 366–8.

18 See, for example, Emil Brunner, *The Divine Imperative: A Study in Christian Ethics*, English trans., London and Redhill: Lutterworth, 1947, pp. 340–83. This view, among others, is briefly discussed by Don Browning, 'World Family Trends', in Robin Gill (ed.), *The Cambridge Companion to Christian Ethics*, Cambridge: Cambridge University Press, 2001, pp. 243–60.

19 The language of 'the goods of marriage' goes back at least as far as Augustine: see *Of the Good of Marriage*, available online at: www.newadvent.org/fathers/1309. htm (accessed 9 September 2005). For a more recent discussion of the purposes of marriage, see Stanley Grenz, *Sexual Ethics: An Evangelical Perspective*, 2nd edn, Louisville, KY: Westminster John Knox, 1997, pp. 66–71.

20 'The Form of Solemnization of Matrimony', Book of Common Prayer (1662). Online versions are available at: www.eskimo.com/~lhowell/bcp1662/index. html and www.vulcanhammer.org/anglican/bcp-1662.pdf (both accessed 9 September 2005).

21 For example, Thomas Aquinas, *Summa Theologiae*, 3a, q. 65 (for some hints on how to find your way around the *Summa*, see Chapter 3). A convenient abridged version is Timothy McDermott (ed.), *Summa Theologiae: A Concise Translation*, Allen, TX: Christian Classics, 1989, pp. 560–1.

22 For discussions of marriage as a sacrament, see Helen Oppenheimer, *Marriage*, London: Mowbray, 1990, pp. 57–64, and Thatcher, *Liberating Sex*, pp. 87–90.

23 See Lesley Macdonald, 'Nightmares in the Garden: Christianity and Sexual Violence', in Kathy Galloway (ed.), *Dreaming of Eden: Reflections on Christianity and Sexuality*, Glasgow: Wild Goose Publications, 1997, pp. 47–56.

24 John Harris, *On Cloning*, London and New York: Routledge, 2004, pp. 34–66.

25 'Genotype' is a technical term for the sum total of an individual's genetic characteristics.

26 Oliver O'Donovan, *Begotten or Made?*, Oxford: Oxford University Press, 1984.

27 Arguments about control are spelled out more fully in Neil G. Messer, *The Ethics of Human Cloning*, Grove Ethical Studies no. 122, Cambridge: Grove, 2001. For a debate about these arguments, see also D. Gareth Jones, 'Human Cloning: Unwarranted Control or Legitimate Stewardship?', *Science and Christian Belief*, 14, 2002, pp. 159–80, and Neil Messer, 'Cloning, Creation and Control', *Science and Christian Belief*, 16, 2004, pp. 45–63.

28 For example, see Karl Barth, *Church Dogmatics*, vol. III.4, English trans., Edinburgh: T & T Clark, 1961, pp. 356–74.

29 For more information about the embryo, see the entry on 'Fetal Development' in the *Medline Plus Medical Encyclopedia*, at: www.nlm.nih.gov/medlineplus/ency/article/002398.htm (accessed 9 September 2005).

30 For more detailed Christian discussion of human embryos, see Brent Waters and Ronald Cole-Turner (eds), *God and the Embryo: Religious Voices on Stem Cells and Cloning*, Washington, DC: Georgetown University Press, 2003, and David Albert Jones, *The Soul of the Embryo: An Enquiry into the Status of the Human Embryo in the Christian Tradition*, London: Continuum, 2004.

31 For a helpful account of the history of the concept of 'person', see John Habgood, *Being a Person: Where Faith and Science Meet*, London: Hodder & Stoughton, 1998.

32 Mary Warnock (Chairman), *Report of the Committee of Inquiry into Human Fertilisation and Embryology*, London: Her Majesty's Stationery Office, 1984, pp. 58–69. Also available online at: www.bopcris.ac.uk/imgall/ref21165_1_1.html (accessed 9 September 2005).

33 Robert Song, 'To Be Willing to Kill What for All One Knows Is a Person Is to Be Willing to Kill a Person', in Waters and Cole-Turner, *God and the Embryo*, pp. 98–107, quoting Germain Grisez, *The Way of the Lord Jesus*, vol. 2, Quincy, IL: Franciscan Press, 1993, p. 497.

34 Hays, *Moral Vision*, p. 451.

Chapter 3 Natural Law

1 This case study is based on the following sources:
Government News Network, 'Landmark Civil Partnership Bill Receives Royal Assent', press release, Friday 19 November 2004, at: www.dti.gov.uk (accessed 9 September 2005)
'Church Says Government Proposals Would Amount to Gay Marriage (1/10/03)', 'Blessings for Same Sex Relationships Increasing in C of E (22/11/04)' and 'Senior Anglican Sanctions Liturgy for Gay Couples (09/01/05)', all at: www.ekklesia.co.uk (accessed 9 September 2005).

2 This section draws on the helpful summary in Ian C. M. Fairweather and James I. H. McDonald, *The Quest for Christian Ethics: An Inquiry into Ethics and Christian Ethics*, Edinburgh: Handsel Press, 1984, Chapter 7.

3 Thomas Aquinas, *Summa Theologiae*, 60 volumes, English trans., London: Blackfriars, 1964–76.

4 Thomas Aquinas, *Summa Theologiae: A Concise Translation*, ed. Timothy McDermott, Allen, TX: Christian Classics, 1989.

5 This section draws on Stephen J. Pope, 'Natural Law and Christian Ethics', in Gill, *The Cambridge Companion to Christian Ethics*, pp. 77–95.

6 Fairweather and McDonald, *The Quest for Christian Ethics*, pp. 152–3.

7 Richard Hooker, *Of the Laws of Ecclesiastical Politie,* 1594. Available online at: http://justus.anglican.org/resources/pc/hooker (accessed 9 September 2005).

8 The official Catholic prohibition of artificial contraception was set out in the papal encyclical letter *Humanae Vitae* (1968). Catholic social teaching is found in a series of encyclicals, including *Rerum Novarum* (1891), *Quadragesimo Anno* (1931), *Populorum Progressio* (1967) and *Centesimus Annus* (1991). All of these are available online at the Vatican's website at: www.vatican.va/holy_father (accessed 9 September 2005).

9 See John Finnis, *Natural Law and Natural Rights*, Oxford: Oxford University Press, 1980, pp. 81–99.

10 Thomas Aquinas, *ST*, 1a2ae, q. 94, art. 3 (p. 287 in McDermott's translation).

11 Joseph Ratzinger, 'Letter to the Bishops of the Catholic Church on the Pastoral Care of Homosexual Persons (1986)', reprinted in Jeffrey S. Siker (ed.), *Homosexuality in the Church: Both Sides of the Debate*, Louisville, KY: Westminster John Knox, 1994, pp. 39–47.

12 See, for example, Elizabeth Stuart and Adrian Thatcher, *People of Passion: What the Churches Teach about Sex*, London: Mowbray, 1997, Chapter 7, and Gareth Moore, *The Body in Context: Sex and Catholicism*, London: SCM Press, 1992.

13 Pope, 'Natural Law and Christian Ethics', pp. 90–3.

14 For a detailed treatment, arguing in a compassionate tone of voice for a conservative position, see Richard B. Hays, *The Moral Vision of the New Testament*, Edinburgh: T & T Clark, 1997, Chapter 16.

15 Karl Barth, *Church Dogmatics*, vol. III/1, English trans., Edinburgh: T & T Clark, 1958, p. 290.

16 Barth, *Church Dogmatics*, vol. III/4, English trans., Edinburgh: T & T Clark, 1961, p. 166.

17 For example, Michael Vasey, *Strangers and Friends: A New Exploration of Homosexuality and the Bible*, London: Hodder & Stoughton, 1995, pp. 118–24.

18 For the range of Church views described in this paragraph and the next, see Ratzinger, 'Letter to the Bishops of the Catholic Church'; The House of Bishops of the General Synod of the Church of England, *Issues in Human Sexuality*, London: Church House Publishing, 1991; and Stuart and Thatcher, *People of Passion*, p. 192.

19 For general discussions, see R. John Elford, 'Christianity and War', and Robin Gill, 'The Arms Trade and Christian Ethics', both in Gill, *The Cambridge Companion to Christian Ethics*, pp. 171–82 and 183–94 respectively.

20 Bainton's typology is in Roland H. Bainton, *Christian Attitudes Toward War and Peace*, London: Hodder & Stoughton, 1961, p. 14.

21 Thomas Aquinas, *ST*, 2a2ae, q. 40 (p. 367 in McDermott's translation).

22 For Bishop Bell's stance on the bombing of German cities, see Adrian Hastings, *A History of English Christianity 1920–2000*, 4th edn, London: SCM Press, 2001. For a natural law critique of nuclear weapons, see John Finnis, Joseph M. Boyle Jr and Germain Grisez, *Nuclear Deterrence, Morality and Realism*, Oxford: Clarendon Press, 1987.

23 For just war arguments about Kosovo, see Hugh Beach, 'Interventions and Just Wars', *Studies in Christian Ethics*, 13, 2000, pp. 15–31. For the Bishop of Oxford's speech on war in Iraq, see Richard Harries, 'Iraq', House of Lords Speeches: 26 February 2003, at www.oxford.anglican.org/page/312 (accessed 9 September 2005).

24 For a vigorous argument in favour of the 'war on terror' on just war grounds, see Jean Bethke Elshtain, *Just War against Terror: The Burden of American Power in a Violent World*, New York: Basic Books, 2003.

25 Ramsey's position is set out briefly in *Basic Christian Ethics*, new edn, Louisville, KY: Westminster John Knox, 1993 (originally published 1950), pp. 166–84.

26 Hays, *Moral Vision*, Chapter 14.

27 John Howard Yoder's position can be found in *The Politics of Jesus*, 2nd edn, Grand Rapids, MI: Eerdmans/Carlisle: Paternoster, 1994. Stanley Hauerwas' pacifism is defended in many of his books, including *The Peaceable Kingdom: A Primer in Christian Ethics*, London: SCM Press, 1984.

28 Glen Stassen (ed.), *Just Peacemaking: Ten Practices for Abolishing War*, Cleveland, OH: Pilgrim Press, 1999.

29 John Rawls, *A Theory of Justice*, Cambridge, MA: The Belknap Press of Harvard University Press, 1971, p. 303.

30 Alasdair MacIntyre, *After Virtue*, pp. 66–70.

Chapter 4 Duty, Consequences and Christian Ethics

1 The case study is taken from the following sources:
Owen Dyer, 'Parliament to Look Again at Issue of "Assisted Dying" for Terminally Ill Patients', *British Medical Journal*, 327, 2003, p. 1186. Available online at http: bmj.bmjjournals.com/cgi/content/full/327/7425/1186-c; *Hansard* House of Lords, 10 March 2004, columns 1316–17. Available online at: www.publications. parliament.uk/pa/ld200304/ldhansrd/vo040310/text/40310-06.ntm#40310-06-head0 Anonymous, 'Helping the Terminally Ill to Die', BBC News Online, 30 November 2004, at: http://news.bbc.co.uk/go/pr/fr/-/1/hi/health/4054619.stm Anonymous, 'Right-to-die Law "Must Change"', BBC News Online, 14 January

2005, at: http://news.bbc.co.uk/go/pr/fr/-/1/hi/uk/4175043.stm

Anglican Communion News Service, 'Bishops Oppose "Misguided and Unnecessary" Euthanasia Bill', press release, 7 September 2004. Available online at: www.anglicancommunion.org/acns/articles/38/75/acns3880.cfm (this and all above websites accessed 9 September 2005).

The quotation from Lord Joffe is from *Hansard*.

2 Some of the general discussion of deontological theories in this section is based on Nancy (Ann) Davis, 'Contemporary Deontology', in Peter Singer (ed.), *A Companion to Ethics*, Oxford: Blackwell, 1991, pp. 205–18, and Fairweather and McDonald, *The Quest for Christian Ethics*, pp. 3–21.

3 Fans of the BBC television drama *Spooks* may recognize this scenario from an episode first screened on 6 December 2004.

4 For more on Ross and prima facie duties, see Jonathan Dancy, 'An Ethic of Prima Facie Duties', in Singer, *A Companion to Ethics*, pp. 219–29.

5 For a helpful introduction to Kant's ethics, see Onora O'Neill, 'Kantian Ethics', in Singer, *A Companion to Ethics*, pp. 175–85.

6 Kant's *Groundwork* is available in a number of English translations; one that is frequently used is H. J. Paton, *The Moral Law: Kant's Groundwork of the Metaphysic of Morals*, London: Hutchinson, 1948. (Note that this translation has been republished as Kant, *Groundwork of the Metaphysic of Morals*, London and New York: Routledge, 2005.)

7 Immanuel Kant, *Critique of Pure Reason*, English trans. Norman Kemp Smith, London: Macmillan, 1929.

8 Paton, *The Moral Law*, p. 85.

9 The three formulations of the categorical imperative quoted here are taken from Paton, *The Moral Law*, pp. 84, 91, 100.

10 O'Neill, 'Kantian Ethics', pp. 178–9.

11 Kant, *Religion Within the Limits of Reason Alone*, English trans. Theodore M. Greene and Hoyt H. Hudson, New York: Harper & Row, 1960.

12 Paul Ramsey, *Basic Christian Ethics*, p. 116.

13 Many editions are available, but I have used Jeremy Bentham, *An Introduction to the Principles of Morals and Legislation*, ed. J. H. Burns and H. L. A. Hart, London: The Athlone Press, 1970.

14 Bentham, *Introduction to the Principles*, p. 11.

15 Bentham, *Introduction to the Principles*, pp. 38–41.

16 David Hume, *A Treatise of Human Nature*, ed. L. A. Selby-Bigge, rev. P. H. Nidditch, Oxford: Oxford University Press, 1978 (originally published 1739–40), pp. 469–70.

17 Again, many editions of Mill's work are available, but I have used the Every-

man edition: John Stuart Mill, *Utilitarianism, On Liberty, Considerations on Representative Government and Remarks on Bentham's Philosophy*, 3rd edn., ed. Geraint Williams, London: J. M. Dent, 1993, pp. 1–67. Further page references to this work are given in brackets in the text.

18 The different versions of contemporary utilitarianism are discussed by Robert E. Goodin, 'Utility and the Good', in Singer, *A Companion to Ethics*, pp. 241–8. One of the best-known preference utilitarians is Peter Singer himself, who has applied this theory to many practical issues, particularly in medical ethics, sometimes with controversial results. See Peter Singer, *Practical Ethics*, 2nd edn, Cambridge: Cambridge University Press, 1993.

19 Thomas Aquinas, *ST*, 1a2ae, qq. 1–5. For an abridged modern translation, see McDermott, *Summa Theologiae*, pp. 171–81.

20 Joseph Fletcher, *Situation Ethics*, London: SCM Press, 1966.

21 Fletcher, *Situation Ethics*, p. 134.

22 Thomas Aquinas, *ST*, 2a2ae, q. 64, art. 5; p. 389 in McDermott's translation.

23 John Paul II, *Evangelium Vitae*, paragraph 66. Available online at: www.vatican.va/holy_father (accessed 9 September 2005).

24 Barth, *Church Dogmatics*, vol. III/4, pp. 401–13.

25 Paton, *The Moral Law*, pp. 85, 91–2.

26 John Paul II, *Evangelium Vitae*, para. 65.

27 Barth, *Church Dogmatics*, vol. III/4, pp. 423–7.

28 Joseph Boyle, 'Limiting Access to Health Care: A Traditional Roman Catholic Analysis', in H. Tristram Engelhardt and Mark J. Cherry (eds), *Allocating Scarce Medical Resources: Roman Catholic Perspectives*, Washington, DC: Georgetown University Press, 2002, pp. 77–95, at pp. 79–81.

29 Stanley Hauerwas, *Suffering Presence: Theological Reflections on Medicine, the Mentally Handicapped, and the Church*, Edinburgh: T & T Clark, 1988, p. 92.

30 David Hume, 'Of Suicide', in *Philosophical Works*, vol. 4, Thomas H. Green and Thomas H. Grose (eds), London: Longman Green, 1882, reprinted Aalen: Scientia Verlag, 1964, pp. 406–14.

31 For example, Singer, *Practical Ethics*, pp. 88–9.

32 John Stuart Mill, *On Liberty*, in *Utilitarianism*, etc., pp. 69–185.

33 Paul Badham, 'Should Christians Accept the Validity of Voluntary Euthanasia?', in Robin Gill (ed.), *Euthanasia and the Churches*, London: Cassell, 1998, pp. 41–59.

34 House of Lords Select Committee on the Assisted Dying for the Terminally Ill Bill, *Assisted Dying for the Terminally Ill Bill (HL), Volume II: Evidence*, London: The Stationery Office, 2005, pp. 492–509. Also available online at: www.publications.parliament.uk/pa/ld200405/ldselect/ldasdy/86/86ii.pdf (accessed 9 September 2005).

35 Michael Banner, *Christian Ethics and Contemporary Moral Problems*, Cambridge: Cambridge University Press, 1999, pp. 47–85.

Chapter 5 Critical Voices: Science, Technology and Christian Ethics

1 International Human Genome Sequencing Consortium, 'Initial Sequencing and Analysis of the Human Genome', *Nature*, 409, 2001, pp. 860–921.

2 Erik Parens, 'Genetic Differences and Human Identities: On Why Talking about Behavioral Genetics Is Important and Difficult', *Hastings Center Report Special Supplement*, 34 (1), 2004, pp. S1–S36.

3 John Bryant and Peter Turnpenny, 'Genetics and Genetic Modification of Humans: Principles, Practice and Possibilities', in Celia Deane-Drummond (ed.), *Brave New World?: Theology, Ethics and the Human Genome*, Edinburgh: T & T Clark, 2003, pp. 5–26.

4 For concerns about gene doping, see 'Tests to Find Gene Cheats', *New Scientist*, 11 December 2004, p. 4. For a sceptical view of the prospects for genetic enhancement, see Mary J. Sellar, 'Genes, Genetics and the Human Genome: Some Personal Reflections', in Deane-Drummond, *Brave New World?*, pp. 27–43.

5 For a readable introduction to evolutionary psychology, see Robert Wright, *The Moral Animal: Why We Are the Way We Are*, London: Abacus, 1996. For a critique, see Hilary Rose and Steven Rose (eds), *Alas, Poor Darwin: Arguments Against Evolutionary Psychology*, London: Jonathan Cape, 2000.

6 'Parents "could pick babies' sex"', BBC News Online, 24 March 2005, available at: news.bbc.co.uk/1/hi/health/4376041.stm (accessed 9 September 2005).

7 This case study was compiled from reports on BBC News Online, at: http://news.bbc.co.uk/ (accessed 9 September 2005).

8 For example, Richard Dawkins, *Climbing Mount Improbable*, London: Penguin, 1997, and Daniel C. Dennett, *Darwin's Dangerous Idea: Evolution and the Meanings of Life*, London: Penguin, 1996.

9 For example, John F. Haught, *God after Darwin: A Theology of Evolution*, Boulder, CO, and Oxford: Westview, 2000; Alister McGrath, *Dawkins' God: Genes, Memes and the Meaning of Life*, Malden, MA, and Oxford: Blackwell, 2005; Kenneth R. Miller, *Finding Darwin's God: A Scientist's Search for Common Ground Between God and Evolution*, New York: Perennial (HarperCollins), 2002; Arthur Peacocke, *Paths from Science Towards God: The End of All Our Exploring*, Oxford: Oneworld, 2001.

10 On the relationship between science and theology generally, see further Jean Dorricott, *SCM Studyguide: Science and Religion*, London: SCM Press, 2005.

11 William D. Hamilton, 'The Evolution of Altruistic Behavior', *American Naturalist*, 97, 1963, pp. 354–6; Robert L. Trivers, 'The Evolution of Reciprocal Altruism', *Quarterly Review of Biology*, 46, 1971, pp. 35–56.

12 For an explanation of the modular (or 'Swiss army knife') model of the mind, see Steven Pinker, *How the Mind Works*, London: Penguin, 1998, pp. 3–58. For a critique, see Annette Karmiloff-Smith, 'Why Babies' Brains Are Not Swiss Army Knives', in Rose and Rose, *Alas Poor Darwin*, pp. 144–56.

13 Herbert Spencer, *The Data of Ethics*, London and Edinburgh: Williams and Norgate, 1879, pp. 8–46.

14 G. E. Moore, *Principia Ethica*, Cambridge: Cambridge University Press, 1903.

15 David Hume, *A Treatise of Human Nature*, ed. L. A. Selby-Bigge, rev. P. H. Nidditch, Oxford: Clarendon Press, 1978 (originally published 1739–40), p. 469.

16 MacIntyre, *After Virtue*, pp. 56–9.

17 See, for example, Oliver O'Donovan, *Resurrection and Moral Order: An Outline for Evangelical Ethics*, 2nd edn, Leicester: Apollos, 1994, pp. 85–91.

18 British legislation is based on the recommendations of the Clothier Committee in Sir Cecil Clothier (Chairman), *Report of the Committee on the Ethics of Human Genetic Manipulation*, London: Her Majesty's Stationery Office, 1992.

19 Joseph Fletcher, *The Ethics of Genetic Control: Ending Reproductive Roulette*, Garden City, NY: Doubleday, 1974, p. 200, quoted in Ronald Cole-Turner (ed.), *Human Cloning: Religious Responses*, Louisville, KY: Westminster John Knox, 1997, p. xii.

20 Paul Ramsey, *Fabricated Man: The Ethics of Genetic Control*, New Haven, CT: Yale University Press, 1970, p. 138.

21 This term was coined by Philip Hefner in *The Human Factor: Evolution, Culture and Religion*, Minneapolis, MN: Fortress, 1993, pp. 35–42.

22 For an argument in favour of somatic cell gene therapy but against other forms of genetic intervention, see Robert Song, *Human Genetics: Fabricating the Future*, London: Darton, Longman & Todd, 2002. For an account that draws a line between therapy and enhancement, see Neil Messer, 'Human Cloning and Genetic Manipulation: Some Theological and Ethical Issues', *Studies in Christian Ethics*, 12, 1999, pp. 1–16. For a more positive view of genetic enhancement, see Ted Peters, *Playing God?: Genetic Determinism and Human Freedom*, New York and London: Routledge, 1997, pp. 143–56.

23 Lynn White Jr, 'The Historical Roots of our Ecologic Crisis', *Science*, 155, 1967, pp. 1203–7, reprinted in Robin Gill (ed.), *A Textbook of Christian Ethics*, 2nd edn, Edinburgh: T & T Clark, 1995, pp. 408–17.

24 Celia E. Deane-Drummond, *The Ethics of Nature*, Oxford: Blackwell, 2004, pp. 29–53.

25 For Ruth Page's cautiously positive view of 'stewardship', see her book *God and the Web of Creation*, London: SCM Press, 1996, pp. 158–68. For Stephen Clark's critique, see his *How to Think about the Earth: Philosophical and Theological Models for Ecology*, London: Mowbray, 1993, pp. 53, 106–16.

26 Sallie McFague, *Models of God: Theology for an Ecological, Nuclear Age*, London: SCM Press, 1987, quotations from pp. 62 and 78.

27 Michael S. Northcott, *The Environment and Christian Ethics*, Cambridge: Cambridge University Press, 1996, pp. 226–56, quotation from p. 255; Deane-Drummond, *The Ethics of Nature*, pp. 9–22.

28 Michael S. Northcott, '"Behold I have set the land before you" (Deut. 1.8): Christian Ethics, GM Foods and the Culture of Modern Farming', in Celia Deane-Drummond and Bronislaw Szerszynski with Robin Grove-White (eds), *Re-ordering Nature: Theology, Society and the New Genetics*, Edinburgh: T & T Clark, 2003, pp. 85–106; Donald Bruce and Don Horrocks (eds), *Modifying Creation?: GM Crops and Foods: A Christian Perspective*, Carlisle: Paternoster, 2001.

Chapter 6 Critical Voices: The 'Recovery of Virtue'

1 The phrase 'the recovery of virtue' is borrowed from Jean Porter's book of that title – *The Recovery of Virtue: The Relevance of Aquinas for Christian Ethics*, London: SPCK, 1994.

2 The cases of 'Child B' and 'Baby Ryan' are based on the accounts in Michael Parker and Donna Dickenson (eds), *The Cambridge Medical Ethics Workbook*, Cambridge: Cambridge University Press, 2001, pp. 236–8.

3 This case study is based on information and reports from the website of the Médecins Sans Frontières Campaign for Access to Essential Medicines at: www.accessmed-msf.org (accessed 9 September 2005).

4 More on the approaches to healthcare resource allocation described in this section can be found in Neil Messer, 'Health Care Resource Allocation and the "Recovery of Virtue"', *Studies in Christian Ethics*, 18, 2005, pp. 89–108 and the references in that paper. See also Michael Banner, 'Economic Devices and Ethical Pitfalls: Quality of Life, the Distribution of Resources and the Needs of the Elderly', in *Christian Ethics and Contemporary Moral Problems*, Cambridge: Cambridge University Press, 1999, pp. 136–62.

5 Norman Daniels's approach is set out in his *Just Health Care*, Cambridge:

Cambridge University Press, 1985. John Rawls' theory is very fully spelled out in his *A Theory of Justice*, Cambridge, MA: Harvard University Press, 1971. It is helpfully summarized and discussed by Duncan Forrester, *Christian Justice and Public Policy*, Cambridge: Cambridge University Press, 1997, pp. 113–39.

6 Alasdair MacIntyre, *After Virtue: A Study in Moral Theory*, 2nd edn, London: Duckworth, 1985.

7 This section draws on MacIntyre, *After Virtue*, Chapters 10–18, and Jean Porter, 'Virtue Ethics', in Gill, *The Cambridge Companion to Christian Ethics*, pp. 96–111.

8 Thomas Aquinas, *ST*, 1a2ae, q. 58, art. 4 (p. 238 in McDermott's concise translation – see Chapter 3 for details).

9 Thomas Aquinas, *ST*, 1a2ae, qq. 55–67 (pp. 231–47 in McDermott's translation).

10 MacIntyre, *After Virtue*, p. 263.

11 For example, see Deane-Drummond, *The Ethics of Nature*.

12 Stanley Hauerwas, *The Peaceable Kingdom: A Primer in Christian Ethics*, London, SCM Press, 1984, p. 76.

13 Stanley Hauerwas and William H. Willimon, *Resident Aliens*, Nashville, TN: Abingdon, 1989, p. 95 (emphasis in original).

14 See, for example, Frank G. Kirkpatrick, *The Ethics of Community*, Oxford: Blackwell, 2001, pp. 106–12.

15 Stanley Hauerwas, *A Community of Character: Towards a Constructive Christian Social Ethic*, Notre Dame, IN: University of Notre Dame Press, 1981, p. 6.

16 For example, see Samuel Wells, 'How Common Worship Forms Local Character', *Studies in Christian Ethics*, vol. 15.1, 2002, pp. 66–74.

17 Hauerwas and Willimon, *Resident Aliens*, pp. 93–7; quotation at pp. 96–7.

18 These arguments are spelled out more fully in Messer, 'Health Care Resource Allocation and the "Recovery of Virtue"'.

19 This point is made by Jean Porter, *The Recovery of Virtue*, pp. 152–4.

20 Allen Verhey, *Reading the Bible in the Strange World of Medicine*, Grand Rapids, MI, and Cambridge: Eerdmans, 2003, pp. 359–93.

Chapter 7 Critical Voices: Liberation Theologies and Christian Ethics

1 Christian Aid, *Taking Liberties: Poor People, Free Trade and Trade Justice*, 23.09.04, available online at: www.christianaid.org.uk/indepth/409trade/index.htm (accessed 9 September 2005).

2 Quoted, for example, by Gustavo Gutiérrez, *A Theology of Liberation*, revised edn, English trans., London: SCM Press, 1988, p. 123.

3 Tim Gorringe, 'Liberation Ethics', in Gill, *The Cambridge Companion to Christian Ethics*, pp. 125–37, at pp. 128–9.

4 Thomas L. Schubeck, *Liberation Ethics: Sources, Models and Norms*, Minneapolis, MN: Fortress, 1993.

5 Gutiérrez, *A Theology of Liberation*, p. 11.

6 Gorringe, 'Liberation Ethics', p. 134.

7 On anti-apartheid theology in South Africa, see *The Kairos Document: A Theological Comment on the Political Crisis in South Africa*, 2nd edn, London: Catholic Institute for International Relations, 1986. On North American black theology, see James H. Cone, *A Black Theology of Liberation: Twentieth Anniversary Edition*, Maryknoll, NY: Orbis, 1990, and *God of the Oppressed*, Maryknoll, NY: Orbis, 1997. On British black theology, see Robert Beckford, *Jesus Is Dread: Black Theology and Black Culture in Britain*, London: Darton, Longman & Todd, 1998, and his *Dread and Pentecostal: A Political Theology for the Black Church in Britain*, London: SPCK, 2000.

8 On African theologies, see Kwame Bediako, *Jesus and the Gospel in Africa: History and Experience*, Maryknoll, NY: Orbis, 2004, and Ernest Munachi Ezeogu, 'Bible and Culture in African Theology, Part 1', available online at: www.munachi.com/t/bibleculture1.htm (accessed 6 July 2005). On Dalit theology, see George Oommen, 'The Emerging Dalit Theology: A Historical Appraisal', available online at: www.religion-online.org/showarticle.asp?title=1121 (accessed 9 September 2005). On theologies of disability, see Nancy L. Eisland, *The Disabled God: Towards a Liberatory Theology of Disability*, Nashville, TN: Abingdon, 1994, and John Hull, *In the Beginning There was Darkness: A Blind Person's Conversations with the Bible*, London: SCM Press, 2001. On queer theologies, see Elizabeth Stuart with Andy Brannston, Malcolm Edwards, John McMahon and Tim Morrison, *Religion Is a Queer Thing: A Guide to the Christian Faith for Lesbian, Gay, Bisexual and Transgendered People*, London: Continuum, 1998.

9 D. Stephen Long, *Divine Economy: Theology and the Market*, London and New York: Routledge, 2000.

10 The two quotations are from Adam Smith, *An Inquiry into the Nature and Causes of the Wealth of Nations*, book 1, chapter 2, and book 2, chapter 2, respectively, quoted by Timothy J. Gorringe, *Capital and the Kingdom: Theological Ethics and Economic Order*, Maryknoll, NY: Orbis/London: SPCK, 1994, p. 34.

11 For a brief discussion of these points, see Ronald H. Preston, *Religion and the Ambiguities of Capitalism*, London: SCM Press, 1991, pp. 17–24. For a helpful

introduction to the concept of diminishing marginal utility, visit: www.
theeconomicconversation.com/book/ch5.5.php (accessed 15 July 2008), a pre-
publication version of Arjo Klamer, Deirdre McCloskey and Stephen Ziliak, *The
Economic Conversation*, Palgrave Macmillan, forthcoming (2009).

12 For example, Michael Novak, 'The Lay Task of Co-Creation', in Max L. Stackhouse, Dennis P. McCann, Shirley J. Roels and Preston N. Williams (eds), *On
Moral Business: Classical and Contemporary Resources for Ethics in Economic Life*,
Grand Rapids, MI: Eerdmans, 1995, pp. 903–8; Preston, *Religion and the Ambiguities of Capitalism*, pp. 24–30.

13 See, for example, Preston, *Religion and the Ambiguities of Capitalism*, pp. 111–25;
Michael H. Taylor, 'Faith in the Global Economic System', *Studies in Christian
Ethics*, 17.2, 2004, pp. 197–215.

14 Quoted by Preston, *Religion and the Ambiguities of Capitalism*, p. 21, emphasis
added.

15 For example, both these views are expressed by Preston, *Religion and the Ambiguities of Capitalism*, pp. 49–62.

16 World Alliance of Reformed Churches, *Faith Stance on the Global Crisis of
Life*, available online at: www.urc.org.uk/faith_stance/faith_stance_full.htm
(accessed 9 September 2005), emphasis added.

17 Gorringe, *Capital and the Kingdom*, pp. 164–8.

18 Long, *Divine Economy*, p. 240, emphasis in original.

19 John F. Sleeman, 'Just Price and Just Wage', in Macquarrie and Childress, *A New
Dictionary of Christian Ethics*, pp. 327–8.

20 Long, *Divine Economy*, p. 260.

Chapter 8 Critical Voices: Feminist Theologies and Christian Ethics

1 This case study was compiled from:
'The General Election: A Letter from the Bishops' Conference to Catholics in
England and Wales', March 2005, available online at: www.catholic-ew.org.uk/
election/documents/GeneralElectionLetter.pdf
'Cardinal Spells Out his Position', press release from the Catholic Communi-
cations Service, 15 March 2005, available online at: www.catholic-ew.org.uk/
cn/05/050315a.htm
Rowan Williams, 'Why Abortion Challenges us All', *The Sunday Times*, 20
March 2005, available online at: www.archbishopofcanterbury.org/sermons_
speeches/050320.htm
'US-style Election Furore on Abortion Unpopular and Bad News for Women', press

release from Abortion Rights, 16 March 2005, available online at: www.abortion rights.org.uk/index.php?option=com_content&task=view&id=75&Itemid=46 'The Prolife Cause Has Moved Centre-stage – We Have the Initiative, Says LIFE', press release, 22 March 2005, available online at: www.lifeuk.org/news/news. php?subaction=showfull&id=1111501463&archive=&start_from=&ucat=& news reports and comments dated between 15 and 22 March 2005, available online at: www.guardian.co.uk; www.telegraph.co.uk; http://news.bbc.co.uk (all accessed 9 September 2005).

2 Beverly Wildung Harrison with Shirley Cloyes, 'Theology and Morality of Procreative Choice', in Beverly Wildung Harrison, *Making the Connections: Essays in Feminist Social Ethics*, ed. Carol S. Robb, Boston, MA: Beacon Press, 1985, pp. 115–34, at p. 117.

3 For these and other aspects of feminist theology, see Ann Loades (ed.), *Feminist Theology: A Reader*, London: SPCK, 1990; Bonnie J. Miller-McLemore and B. Gill-Austern (eds), *Feminist and Womanist Pastoral Theology*, Nashville, TN: Abingdon, 1999; Susan Frank Parsons (ed.), *The Cambridge Companion to Feminist Theology*, Cambridge: Cambridge University Press, 2002.

4 See Daphne Hampson, *After Christianity*, 2nd edn, London: SCM Press, 2002; Daphne Hampson (ed.), *Swallowing a Fishbone?: Feminist Theologians Debate Christianity*, London: SPCK, 1996.

5 Susan Frank Parsons, *Feminism and Christian Ethics*, Cambridge: Cambridge University Press, 1996.

6 Simone de Beauvoir, *The Second Sex*, quoted by Parsons, *Feminism and Christian Ethics*, p. 66.

7 Carol Gilligan, *In a Different Voice: Psychological Theory and Women's Development*, Cambridge, MA: Harvard University Press, 1982.

8 Nel Noddings, *Caring: A Feminine Approach to Ethics and Education*, Berkeley, CA: University of California Press, 1984.

9 For a helpful introduction to the 'ethics of care' with particular reference to healthcare, see Rita C. Manning, 'A Care Approach', in Helga Kuhse and Peter Singer (eds), *A Companion to Bioethics*, Oxford: Blackwell, 1998, pp. 98–105. For a critique, see Helga Kuhse, *Caring: Nurses, Women and Ethics*, Oxford: Blackwell, 1996.

10 Kwok Pui-Lan, 'Feminist Theology as Intercultural Discourse', in Parsons, *The Cambridge Companion to Feminist Theology*, pp. 23–39. For many examples of feminist theology coming from diverse geographical and cultural contexts, see Ursula King (ed.), *Feminist Theology from the Third World: A Reader*, London: SPCK, and Maryknoll, NY: Orbis, 1994.

11 Katie Geneva Cannon, *Black Womanist Ethics*, Atlanta, GA: Scholars Press,

1988. For more general works of womanist theology, see, for example, Emilie Townes (ed.), *A Troubling in My Soul: Womanist Perspectives on Evil and Suffering*, Maryknoll, NY: Orbis, 1993, and Delores S. Williams, *Sisters in the Wilderness: The Challenge of Womanist God-Talk*, Maryknoll, NY: Orbis, 1993.

12 Cheryl J. Sanders, *Empowerment Ethics for a Liberated People: A Path to African American Social Transformation*, Minneapolis, MN: Fortress, 1995.

13 Kwok Pui-Lan, 'Feminist Theology as Intercultural Discourse', pp. 33–7.

14 See Lisa Sowle Cahill, 'Abortion', in Macquarrie and Childress, *New Dictionary of Christian Ethics*, pp. 1–5, for more details.

15 See, for example, Cahill, 'Abortion', and John T. Noonan, 'An Almost Absolute Value in History', in John T. Noonan (ed.), *The Morality of Abortion: Historical and Legal Perspectives*, Cambridge, MA: Harvard University Press, 1970, pp. 51–9.

16 For example, Thomas Aquinas, *ST*, 1a, q. 76 art. 1, q. 118 art. 2.

17 Harrison, 'Theology and Morality of Procreative Choice'. See also her *Our Right to Choose: Toward a New Ethic of Abortion*, Boston, MA: Beacon Press, 1983.

18 See the summary of abortion law on the British Medical Association website at: www.bma.org.uk/ap.nsf/Content/abortion#Legalconsiderations (accessed 9 September 2005).

19 See, for example, Mary Anne Warren, 'On the Moral and Legal Status of Abortion', *The Monist*, 57, 1973, pp. 43–61, available online at: http://people.cohums.ohio-state.edu/cole253/Abor.pdf (accessed 9 September 2005).

20 See, for example, Warren, 'On the Moral and Legal Status of Abortion', and Michael Tooley, *Abortion and Infanticide*, Oxford: Oxford University Press, 1983.

21 Judith Jarvis Thomson, 'A Defense of Abortion', *Philosophy and Public Affairs*, 1, 1971, pp. 47–66, reprinted in John Harris (ed.), *Bioethics*, Oxford and New York: Oxford University Press, 2001, pp. 25–41. For a critique, see Gilbert Meilaender, 'The Fetus as Parasite and Mushroom', in Stephen E. Lammers and Allen Verhey (eds), *On Moral Medicine: Theological Voices in Medical Ethics*, 2nd edn, Grand Rapids, MI: Eerdmans, 1998, pp. 612–16.

22 Joseph F. Fletcher, 'Four Indicators of Humanhood – The Enquiry Matures', in Lammers and Verhey, *On Moral Medicine*, pp. 376–80.

23 Congregation for the Doctrine of the Faith, *Donum Vitae*, 1987, I, no. 1, available online at: www.vatican.va/roman_curia/congregations/cfaith/documents/rc_con_cfaith_doc_19870222_respect-for-human-life_en.html (accessed 9 September 2005).

24 John Paul II, *Evangelium Vitae*, 1995, paragraph 61; available online at: www.vatican.va/edocs/ENG0141/_PQ.htm (accessed 9 September 2005).

25 Germain Grisez, *The Way of the Lord Jesus*, vol. 2, Quincy, IL: Franciscan Press, 1993, p. 497.

26 Richard B. Hays, *The Moral Vision of the New Testament*, Edinburgh: T & T Clark, 1997, p. 451.

27 Harrison, 'Theology and Morality of Procreative Choice', p. 124.

28 Harrison, 'A Feminist–Liberationist View of Abortion', in Lammers and Verhey, *On Moral Medicine*, pp. 617–23, at p. 622.

29 Both quotations in this paragraph are from Harrison, 'Theology and Morality of Procreative Choice', p. 127.

30 Williams, 'Why Abortion Challenges us All'.

31 Sidney Callahan, 'Abortion and the Sexual Agenda: A Case for Pro-Life Feminism', in Lammers and Verhey, *On Moral Medicine*, pp. 623–32.

32 Callahan, 'Abortion and the Sexual Agenda', p. 631.

33 Hays, *Moral Vision*, pp. 444–61.

34 Hays, *Moral Vision*, p. 452.

Chapter 9 Christian Ethics: Pastoral and Public

1 The information about motor neurone disease is taken from 'Facts About Amyotrophic Lateral Sclerosis (ALS)', available online at: www.mdausa.org/publications/fa-als.html (accessed 9 September 2005). Amyotrophic lateral sclerosis (ALS) is the usual American name for motor neurone disease.

2 Gordon Lynch, 'Pastoral Counselling and Pastoral Theology', in James Woodward and Stephen Pattison (eds), *The Blackwell Reader in Practical and Pastoral Theology*, Oxford: Blackwell, 2000, pp. 221–32, at p. 227.

3 Antony Flew (ed.), *A Dictionary of Philosophy*, 2nd edn, London: Pan, 1984, p. 184.

4 Don Browning, 'Pastoral Theology in a Pluralistic Age', in Woodward and Pattison, *The Blackwell Reader in Pastoral and Practical Theology*, pp. 89–103. The quotations in this paragraph are from pp. 90, 91 and 94, in that order.

5 Don S. Browning, *A Fundamental Practical Theology: Descriptive and Strategic Proposals*, Minneapolis, MN: Fortress, 1996, pp.105–9.

6 Hauerwas and Willimon, *Resident Aliens*, pp. 112–43.

7 Hauerwas and Willimon, *Resident Aliens*, pp. 93–111.

8 For example, see Stanley Hauerwas and Richard Bondi, 'Memory, Community and Reasons for Living: Reflections on Suicide and Euthanasia', in Stanley Hauerwas with Richard Bondi and David B. Burrell, *Truthfulness and Tragedy: Further Investigations into Christian Ethics*, Notre Dame, IN: University of Notre Dame Press, 1977, pp. 101–15.

9 For example, Bonnie J. Miller-McLemore and B. Gill-Austern (eds), *Feminist and Womanist Pastoral Theology*, Nashville, IN Abingdon, 1999, and Stephen Pattison, *Pastoral Care and Liberation Theology*, London: SPCK, 1997.

10 Bonnie J. Miller-McLemore, 'How Sexuality and Relationships Have Revolutionized Pastoral Theology', in Woodward and Pattison, *Pastoral and Practical Theology*, pp. 233–47, at p. 242.

11 Karen Lebacqz, 'Reflection', in Lammers and Verhey, *On Moral Medicine*, pp. 666–7.

12 Lebacqz, 'Reflection', p. 667.

13 This section is adapted from Neil Messer (ed.), *Theological Issues in Bioethics: An Introduction with Readings*, London: Darton, Longman & Todd, 2002, pp. 263–9.

14 Tom L. Beauchamp and James F. Childress, *Principles of Biomedical Ethics,* 5th edn, New York: Oxford University Press, 2001.

15 See, for example, Celia Deane-Drummond, *Creation Through Wisdom: Theology and the New Biology*, Edinburgh: T & T Clark, 2001.

16 See Deane-Drummond, *Creation Through Wisdom*, pp. 148–9.

17 Celia Deane-Drummond, Robin Grove-White and Bronislaw Szerszynski, 'Genetically Modified Theology: The Religious Dimensions of Public Concerns about Agricultural Biotechnology', *Studies in Christian Ethics*, 14.2, 2001, pp. 23–41, at p. 41.

18 Michael Banner, *Christian Ethics and Contemporary Moral Problems*, Cambridge: Cambridge University Press, 1999, pp. 1–46. Further references to this work are given as page numbers in the text.

19 Stanley Hauerwas, *The Peaceable Kingdom: A Primer in Christian Ethics*, London: SCM Press, 1984, p. 99.

20 Stanley Hauerwas, 'Religious Concepts of Brain Death and Associated Problems', in *Suffering Presence: Theological Reflections on Medicine, the Mentally Handicapped and the Church*, Edinburgh: T & T Clark, 1988, pp. 87–99, quotations from pp. 87 and 96–7.

21 Hauerwas and Bondi, 'Memory, Community and Reasons for Living', p. 111.

22 Nigel Biggar, 'Is Stanley Hauerwas Sectarian?', in Mark Thiessen Nation and Samuel Wells (eds), *Faithfulness and Fortitude: In Conversation with the Theological Ethics of Stanley Hauerwas*, Edinburgh: T & T Clark, 2000, pp. 141–60.

23 Duncan Forrester, *Christian Justice and Public Policy*, Cambridge: Cambridge University Press, 1997, pp. 195–204.

24 Duncan Forrester, *Truthful Action: Explorations in Practical Theology*, Edinburgh: T & T Clark, 2000, pp. 143–57.

25 See Shirley du Boulay, *Cicely Saunders: The Founder of the Modern Hospice Movement*, London: Hodder & Stoughton, 1984, pp. 155–71.

26 Ronald Preston, 'Middle Axioms', in Macquarrie and Childress, *A New Dictionary of Christian Ethics*, p. 382.

27 Ronald Preston, *Religion and the Ambiguities of Capitalism*, London: SCM Press, 1991, p. 108.

28 Church of England Board for Social Responsibility, *On Dying Well: A Contribution to the Euthanasia Debate*, 2nd edn, London: Church House Publishing, 2000, p. 68.

29 See, for example, Malcolm Brown, 'Some Thoughts on Theological Method', in Council of Churches for Britain and Ireland, *Unemployment and the Future of Work: An Enquiry for the Churches*, London: Council of Churches for Britain and Ireland, 1997, pp. 293–8.

30 Karen Lebacqz, 'Bio-Ethics: Some Challenges from a Liberationist Perspective', in Lammers and Verhey, *On Moral Medicine*, pp. 83–9.

Chapter 10 Conclusion

1 Thomas Aquinas, *ST*, 2a2ae, q. 153, art. 3 and q. 154, art. 1 (p. 431 in McDermott's concise translation).

2 Alasdair MacIntyre, *Whose Justice? Which Rationality?*, London: Duckworth, 1988, p. 394.

Index of Names and Subjects